Global Production, National Institutions, and Skill Formation

Global Production, National Institutions, and Skill Formation

The Political Economy of Training and Employment in Auto Parts Suppliers from Mexico And Turkey

Merve Sancak

OXFORD

UNIVERSITY PRESS

OXFORD
UNIVERSITY PRESS

Great Clarendon Street, Oxford, OX2 6DP,
United Kingdom

Oxford University Press is a department of the University of Oxford.
It furthers the University's objective of excellence in research, scholarship,
and education by publishing worldwide. Oxford is a registered trade mark of
Oxford University Press in the UK and in certain other countries

First Edition published in 2022
Impression: 1

Published in the United States of America by Oxford University Press
198 Madison Avenue, New York, NY 10016, United States of America

British Library Cataloguing in Publication Data
Data available

Library of Congress Control Number: 2021941322

ISBN 978-0-19-886065-5

DOI: 10.1093/oso/9780198860655.001.0001

Printed and bound by
CPI Group (UK) Ltd, Croydon, CR0 4YY

Münevver Hanım & Yunus Bey

my parents

Acknowledgements

This book is based on the research I conducted as part of my PhD in Economic Sociology at the University of Cambridge. Both the PhD process and the book afterwards have been a challenging but at the same time a rewarding and an enriching experience. I am very pleased to be at this point today and to have the opportunity to thank all of those who supported me in this journey.

I would like to thank my PhD supervisor Professor Christel Lane, and the Sociology Department and Darwin College at Cambridge. I am very grateful to Christel not only for her excellent supervision, which contributed to my work through critical and to-the-point comments, and helped me to substantially enrich my research, but also for her time and commitment. In addition to her professional help with my work, she has supported me through engaging me with the social life in Cambridge and has always shown great interest in any concerns I may have had. Without a doubt, she has made the PhD experience much more pleasant, and I am very grateful that we have become lifelong colleagues. I also would like to thank the examiners of my PhD thesis, Marius Busemeyer and Geoffrey Wood, who have played an important role in the current shape of this book through their comments on my thesis. I want to particularly thank to who has provided me important support and critical comments in the making of this book. The academic and administrative staff, as well as my PhD fellows in the Department of Sociology, provided an academic environment that allowed this research to be carried out in the best way and fed this research process with critical thinking. Darwin College supported me in the process not only with the academic community that includes academics from different disciplines, but also the social environment and the friendships a PhD student needs the most.

I would like to thank to the Sheffield Political Economy Research Institute (SPERI) for hosting me and providing me the stimulating academic environment and all the support necessary for completing such a challenging book. I would particularly thank to my mentors Colin Hay and Michael Jacobs, and my colleagues at SPERI for our inspiring discussions and their critical comments on my work, which has influenced my thinking for this book. I also want to thank the institutions that financially supported this research and the making of this book, including the University of Cambridge, Cambridge Political Economy Society, Mexican Agency for International Development, and Global Development Network. Special thanks to the GDN also for providing me the links with Miguel Székely, and thanks to Miguel for his critical contribution to the discussion about Mexico in this book.

El Colegio de Mexico deserves special thanks for hosting me during my fieldwork in Mexico. I would like to say a wholehearted thank you to Ilán Bizberg, who helped me to get involved in critical discussion groups that enriched my learning about the political economy of Mexico. Special thanks to Ken Dubin, who supported me in my desire to conduct a comparative study, convinced me to study Mexico, and greatly contributed to developing my research design. I also would like to thank the academics in Mexico who supported my project with their engagement in the fieldwork and discussions in this book, including Ívico Ahumada and Carlos Alba. Special thanks to the ITIAM and Alex Covarrubias for involving me in the Network, and providing me the necessary contacts for enhancing my knowledge about the Mexican automotive industry.

Ziya Öniş deserves very special thanks for supporting my academic work and for igniting my interest in academic research. He made time to discuss my research and provided me crucial comments, which have allowed me to improve my work. I also would like to thank Işık Özel, who shared my enthusiasm for comparing Mexico with Turkey and contributed to my work through our critical discussions in the making of this book. I also would like to thank Ben Schneider for his encouragement to research skill systems, his constructive and critical feedback on my work, and his support for my academic life.

I would like to thank all the people who generously gave their time for interviews and were willing to share their experiences with me. Special thanks to IECA, Luis Rossano, and Federico Garza from Mexico, and the TOBB, Çağlayan Dündar, and Saygın Baban from Turkey, for helping me to develop contacts with the interviewees in Mexico and Turkey, respectively.

Throughout the journey of this book, I was extremely lucky to be surrounded by a great family and friends, who have always made me feel wonderfully supported. To Ben, thanks for being next to me and showing your support in this challenging journey and always being there with your love and great encouragement, with which I have felt stronger. To Zehra and Mehmet, thank you for being my eternal best friends and for your unwavering belief in me. Lastly, I would like to thank my parents, Yunus and Münevver, who have committed their life to social justice, education, and fair work, and have given me the inspiration and strength and support necessary to embark on and complete this work. I would like to dedicate this book to them.

Table of Contents

List of Figures and Tables

Figures

Tables

Abbreviations

AAC	Auto parts-automotive value chain
AAI	Auto parts-automotive industry
AKP	*Adalet ve Kalkınma Partisi* (Justice and Development Party, Turkey)
AMIA	*Asociación Mexicana de la Industria Automotriz* (Mexican Automotive Industry Association)
BÉCATE	*Programa Becas para la Capacitación para el Trabajo* (Scholarships Programme for Job Training, Mexico)
BIBB	*Bundesinstitut für Berufsbildung in der Bundesstadt* (German Federal Institute for Vocational Education and Training)
BRIC	Brazil, Russia, India, China
CAINTRA	*Cámara de la Industria de Transformación de Nuevo León* (Industrial Chamber of Nuevo León)
CAMEXA	*Cámara Mexicano-Alemana de Comercio e Industria* (German-Mexican Chamber of Commerce)
CANACINTRA	*Cámara Nacional de la Industria de la Transformación* (National Chamber of the Industry of Transformation, Mexico)
CBTIS	Centre of Industrial Technology and Services High School
CC	Comparative capitalism
CECATI	*Centros de Capacitación para el Trabajo* (Training for Work Centres, Mexico)
CETIS	*Centros de Estudios Tecnológicos Industrial y de Servicios* (Centres of Industrial Technology and Services Studies, Mexico)
CHMN	*Consejo Mexicano de Hombres de Negocios* (Mexican Businessmen Council)
CLAUT	*Cluster Automotriz de Nuevo León* (Automotive Cluster of Nuevo León, Mexico)
CME	Coordinated market economy
CONALEP	*Colegio Nacional de Educación Profesional Técnica* (National College of Technical Professional Education, Mexico)
CONCAMIN	*Confederación de Cámaras Industriales de los Estados Unidos Mexicanos* (Confederation of Industrial Chambers of the United States of Mexico)
CONOCER	*Consejo Nacional de Normalización y Certificación de Competencias Laborales* (National Skill Standards Board, Mexico)
COPARMEX	*Confederación Patronal de la República Mexicana* (Employers' Confederation of Mexico)
CROC	*Confederación Revolucionaria de Obreros y Campesinos* (Revolutionary Confederation of Workers and Peasants, Mexico)

CTM	*Confederación de Trabajadores de México* (Mexican Confederation of Workers)
ÇSGB	*Çalışma Ve Sosyal Güvenlik Bakanlığı* (Ministry of Labour and Social Security, Turkey)
CVET	Continuing vocational education and training
DGETI	*Dirección General de Educación Tecnológica Industrial* (Directorate General for Industrial Technological Education, Mexico)
ERG	Education Reform Initiative
FDI	Foreign direct investment
GDP	Gross domestic product
GVC	Global value chain
HMEs	Hierarchical market economies
HPWS	High-performance work system
HRM	Human resource management
IATF	International Automotive Task Force
ICAT	*Institutos de Capacitación para el Trabajo* (Work and Training Institute, Mexico)
IADB	Inter-American Development Bank
IECA	*Instituto Estatal de Capacitación* (State Institute of Training, Mexico)
IICPSD	Istanbul International Centre for Private Sector in Development
IKOSB	*Ikitelli Organize Sanayi Bolgesi* (Ikitelli Organised Industrial Zone, Turkey)
ILO	International Labour Organisation
INA	*Industría Nacional de Autopartes A.C.* (National Auto parts Industry)
ISI	Import substituting industrialisation
İŞKUR	*Türkiye İş Kurumu* (Turkish Employment Agency)
ISO	International Organization for Standardization
IVET	Initial vocational education and training
LME	Liberal market economy
MEB	*Milli Eğitim Bakanlığı* (Ministry of Education Turkey)
MBA	Master of business administration
MEKSA	Foundation for Supporting Vocational Education and the Small Enterprises
MEM	*Mesleki Egitim Merkezi* (Vocational Training Centre, Turkey)
MESS	*Türkiye Metal Sanayicileri Sendikası* (Turkish Employers' Association of Metal Industries)
MIC	Middle-income country
MIKTA	Mexico, Indonesia, Korea, Turkey, Australia
MINT	Mexico, Indonesia, Nigeria, Turkey
MIST	Mexico, Indonesia, South Africa, Turkey
MMDT	*Modelo Mexicano de Formación Dual* (Mexican Model of Dual Training)
MNC	Multinational corporation
MÜSİAD	*Müstakil Sanayici ve İşadamları Derneği* (Independent Industrialists and Businessmen Association, Turkey)

MYK	*Mesleki Yeterlilikler Kurumu* (Vocational Qualifications Authority, Turkey)
MYO	*Meslek Yüksek Okulu* (Postsecondary Vocational Education Institute, Turkey)
NAFTA	North American Free Trade Agreement
NEET	Not in education, employment, or training
NGO	Non-governmental organisation
OEM	Original equipment manufacturer
OIB	*Uludağ Otomotiv Endüstrisi İhracatçıları Birliği* (Automotive Industry Exporters' Association)
OIZ	Organised industrial zone
PPP	Purchasing power parity
RCA	Revealed comparative advantage
SEP	*Secretaría de Educación Publica* (Secretary of Public Education, Mexico)
SIEM	*Sistema de Información Empresarial* (Mexican Business Information System)
SME	Small and medium-sized enterprise
SNC	*Sistema Nacional de Competencias* (National System of Competences, Mexico)
STPS	*Secretaría del Trabajo y Previsión Social* (Secretary of Work and Social Policy, Mexico)
TAYSAD	*Taşıt Araçları Tedarik Sanayicileri Derneği* (Association of Automotive Parts and Components Manufacturers, Turkey)
TESK	Turkish Tradesmen's and Artisans' Confederation
THS	Technological High School (Mexico)
TOBB	*Türkiye Odalar ve Borsalar Birliği* (Union of Chambers and Commodity Exchanges of Turkey)
TPHS	Technical Professional High School (Mexico)
TU	Technological University
TÜSİAD	*Türkiye Sanayicileri ve İşadamları Derneği* (Turkish Industry and Business Association)
UMEM	*Uzmanlaşmış Meslek Edindirme Merkezleri* (Specialised Occupation Centres Programme, Turkey)
UMYS	*Ulusal Mesleki Yeterlilik Sistemi* (National Qualifications Framework)
VET	Vocational education and training
VHS	Vocational High School
VoC	Varieties of capitalism

PART 1

STUDYING SKILL FORMATION SYSTEMS

1
Introduction

This book examines the political economy of skill systems and discusses the implications of these systems for the development of middle-income countries (MICs). More specifically, it studies how dynamics in the global economic system and national institutional structures affect skill formation in MICs, and it analyses the implications of skill systems for high- or low-road development.

Many MICs grew fast in the 1990s and early 2000s,[1] which helped them to shift from low-income to middle-income status. The vast availability of low-cost workers in these countries and the focus on labour-intensive sectors played a major role in this economic growth. However, such focus on labour-intensive sectors has led to a predominantly 'low-road' development, and many MICs have been facing challenges to attain 'high-road' development. By this is meant, first, economic growth has rarely been *inclusive* in many MICs, where the benefits of economic growth have not been distributed evenly while high levels of income inequality have persisted, and even increased in some. Second, the economic growth of MICs has not always been *continuous*: despite their fast growth in the 1990s and early 2000s—although challenged by economic crises—the economic growth rate slowed down by the 2010s in many MICs. As a result, several MICs have been facing the danger of remaining in the 'middle-income trap' unless they shift from labour-intensive, low value-added production to higher value-added activities that require better skills (Doner and Scheider, 2016).

Intermediate skills and vocational education and training (VET) systems that generate these skills are critical for addressing the challenges of MICs in achieving high-road development. On the one hand, VET can facilitate an *inclusive* development, as these systems provide the intermediate skills that can help to improve the job prospects of individuals from low-income groups (Acemoglu, 1996; Rueda and Pontusson, 2000; Estevez-Abe, Iversen, and Soskice, 2001; Thelen, 2004; Busemeyer, 2015a). On the other hand, VET systems are likely to facilitate the *continuity of* economic growth, as they can help to generate intermediate skills that are necessary for producing medium technology-intensive products with higher value-added, and hence help them to upgrade from low value-added labour-intensive sectors to higher value-added ones (Jürgens and Krzywdzinski, 2009, 2013, 2015, 2016; Krzywdzinski, 2017). In fact, VET has been increasingly suggested as a key strategy for promoting development in many MICs, both by national governments and international

---

[1] 2000s corresponds to 2000–2010 throughout this chapter.

Global Production, National Institutions, and Skill Formation: The Political Economy of Training and Employment in Auto Parts Suppliers from Mexico And Turkey. Merve Sancak, Oxford University Press. © Merve Sancak 2022.
DOI: 10.1093/oso/9780198860655.003.0001

organisations including the World Bank, United Nations Development Programme (UNDP), and Organisation for Economic Co-operation and Development (OECD) (OECD/CERI, 2009; World Bank, 2013; Valiente, 2014; Ricart, Morán, and Kappaz, 2014; UNDP IICPSD, 2018; OECD, 2018).

Despite the importance of intermediate skills and the skill systems to develop them, the academic research in this regard has remained scarce. The studies on the comparative political economy of skill formation (CPEoSF) have not included MICs in their analysis, while the research on the political economy development in MICs has not considered skill systems as a key area of study. Skill formation therefore has remained 'policy in need of a theory' for MICs (McGrath, 2012), and still little is known about how the skill systems in MICs function or about the political and economic dynamics that affect the skill systems and the outcomes of these systems for workers, firms, and the development prospects of MICs.

This book addresses this gap. It provides a comprehensive discussion on the skill systems of Mexico and Turkey, two key countries that have been in the 'upper-middle-income' group in the classification of the World Bank.[2] It investigates how the global and national political economic dynamics and the interactions between these dynamics affect skill systems, and how these skill systems influence the high- or low-road development prospects of these countries. The book focuses the empirical analysis on the generation of intermediate skills in the local auto parts- automotive industry (AAI), which is a key industry for moving to high-income group for both Mexico and Turkey, and many MICs. Bringing together the research on global value chains (GVCs), comparative capitalisms (CCs), and employment systems (ESs) and human resource management (HRM), the book scrutinises how the interactions between the governance structures in global auto parts-automotive value chains (AACs) (Peters, 2012) and the national institutions in Mexico and Turkey affect the hiring, training, and employee development practices of local auto parts suppliers from the two countries. Furthermore, the book investigates the outcomes of these practices for workers and smaller firms, which then helps to make inferences about the development implications of skill systems.

The book argues that state involvement in national institutions is key for skill systems that will promote high-road development. Although competition in the global economy creates pressures on firms and influences their skilling[3] practices, these pressures are *mediated by national institutions*, and these institutions are shaped by the *state*. In countries where the state's commitment to VET, involvement in regulating the economy, and implementing the regulations are *high*, like in Turkey, there is less room for GVC governance structures to influence suppliers' activities. Suppliers in these countries link their skilling practices with the public VET system,

---

[2]   In March 2021, these were the countries with GNI per capita level of $4,046–$12,535, and comprised 56 countries (World Bank, 2021a).

[3]   The book uses the term 'skilling' as an overarching term for 'firms' strategies to have workers with the necessary skills for their shop floor posts, and for firms' recruitment, training and employee development practices.

which leads to generation of more general skills that are also accessible to smaller firms and give important opportunities to workers for career development and income progression. In contrast, in countries where the state's involvement is *low*, like in Mexico, the institutional environment is looser, and, thus, there is more room for the GVCs to affect suppliers' skilling practices. This results in several types of skilling practices in supplier firms that are shaped by a variety of factors including the governance structures in GVCs and firms' size and region, which leads to segmentation between different firms and workers. Therefore, this book suggests that even in a globalised economy, state involvement is crucial for skill systems that will promote more inclusive and more continuous development.

This book is innovative in two main ways. The first innovation concerns the book's **conceptual framework** that stems from its *multilevel understanding of skill systems*, which helps to realise the 'impact of varied coordination mechanisms prevalent in the multi-level worlds of capitalist economies' (Bohle and Greskovits, 2009, p. 365). Informed by the Regulation School, the term 'skill system' in this book refers to (i) firm-level hiring, training, and employee development practices; (ii) national institutions that affect the firm-level skilling practices; and (iii) governance structures in GVCs that influence the activities and thus the skilling practices of firms in these chains. This contrasts with most of the studies in the literature on the CPEoSF, which focus on VET systems only and do not consider the pressures in the global economy or the 'other' institutions that complement VET systems and which focus on macro-level institutions and do not (empirically) link the national VET systems with the firm-level skilling practices. In order to study the multilevel skill systems, the book seeks to *cross-fertilise* three main fields of study that have previously remained separate but have important potential to contribute to one another. For studying firm-level hiring, training, and employee development practices, namely skilling practices, and the outcomes of these practices for workers and firms, the book benefits from the research in the literature on ESs, and particularly research on HRM. For understanding the national institutions and global dynamics that influence the firm-level skilling practices, the book links firm-level analysis with studies on CCs—and particularly those on the CPEoSF—and GVCs, and it investigates how national institutions and governance structures in GVCs influence firm-level skilling practices.

The second innovation of this book is its **empirical richness** drawn from in-depth research on two key MICs. Despite the importance of skill systems for high-road development in MICs, the studies in the fields of CCs, GVCs, and HRM do not provide a comprehensive discussion on skill systems in these countries. While the literature on the CPEoSF focuses on advanced industrialised countries only, the studies in the CCs literature on emerging economies or MICs do not consider the skill systems of these countries as important institutions, and centre their discussion on other institutions, such as business associations and the relations of these with the state. Similarly, the research on GVCs focuses on understanding the governance structures in these chains and, sometimes, the implications of the governance structures for the upgrading of supplier firms or the working conditions in supplier firms.

Nevertheless, the GVC literature has rarely studied the influence of governance structures on supplier firms' skilling practices. Lastly, although the literature on international HRM has made important contributions to our understanding about how national institutions in some developing countries influence the HRM practices applied by the subsidiaries of multinational corporations (MNCs), this literature has been less concerned about the HRM activities of local firms from these countries. This book provides important contribution to each of these fields based on substantial evidence from Mexico and Turkey, which includes *macro-level research* on national institutions of the two countries and the governance structures in global AACs, as well as a *micro-level research* on firms from the two countries. The macro-level research is based on the thematic analysis of 42 interviews with various stakeholders of the skill system and the AAI, as well as primary and secondary documents, such as the reports of national and international organisations on the VET systems and AAIs of the two countries. The micro-level inquiry on the Mexican and Turkish auto parts producers comprises the thematic analysis of semi-structured, in-depth interviews with 86 representatives from 39 firms producing metal or plastic parts for global AACs (20 Turkish and 19 Mexican).

1.1 Comparing Mexico and Turkey

To examine the influence of global dynamics and national institutions on skill systems and these systems' implications for development, this book carries out a 'most similar case' comparison, which allows one to make generalisable statements by analysing variation between similar cases (George and Bennett, 2005). It compares Mexico and Turkey, which are *crucial cases* for such study due to the similarities and differences with respect to their links with the global economy, institutional and economic structures, and development experiences.

1.1.1 Similarities and differences regarding the political economy of Mexico and Turkey

Turkey and Mexico have a number of similarities in their economic, political, and institutional structures that stem from their 'nearly simultaneous' development trajectories (Özel, 2014, p. 8). Both countries initially applied **import substituting industrialisation** (ISI) with high state involvement as their development strategy until the late 1970s, and the state played a key role through the ownership of key industries and the development strategies executed thorough 5-year development plans. Large family conglomerates benefited from their privileged economic status and gained access to policymaking through clientelist links with governing parties and direct participation in politics in both Mexico and Turkey (Heper, 1991; Schneider, 2009a; Özel, 2014). The state also had substantial control on collective labour organisation in both countries and formed clientelist relations with the main labour union confederations, namely the Confederation of Mexican Workers (*Confederación de Trabajadores de México*—CTM) in Mexico and the Confederation of Turkish Trade Unions (*Türkiye İşçi Sendikaları Konfederasyonu*—Türk-İş) in Turkey (Kuş and Özel, 2010).

After experiencing major economic and political crises, both countries have been adopting **neoliberal policies** since the 1980s, which have involved rapid economic liberalisation, mass privatisation, and financialisaton in both countries (Marois, 2012). Despite the recurrent crises in the neoliberal era, Mexico and Turkey displayed **significant economic growth** from their economic liberalisation up to the 2010s, which led to the consideration of both Mexico and Turkey as the new BRICS (Brazil, Russia, India, China, and South Africa) (O'Neill, 2001). The two countries have been frequently grouped together within various economic groupings such as the MIST (Mexico, Indonesia, South Korea, and Turkey), MINT (Mexico, Indonesia, Nigeria, and Turkey), and MIKTA (Mexico, Indonesia, South Korea, Turkey, and Australia). The two countries have been the only members of the OECD with low per capita GDP, and have been in the middle-income trap for a while (Kharas and Kohli, 2011; Alonso and Ocampo, 2020).

With their economic liberalisation and opening of their markets to the global economy, both Mexico and Turkey have been developing **deeper links with the world economy** since the 1980s. Both have been considered as a bridge for economic and political exchanges between the Global North and South. Foreign MNCs have played an important role in the economies of Mexico and Turkey not only through direct investments in these locations, but also through importing goods and services from these countries in global production networks (Figures 1.1 and 1.2).

The **structure of the economy** has also been very similar in Mexico and Turkey, with manufacturing being a significant industry for development. Low- and medium-technology-intensive manufacturing has constituted the main share of exports, resulting in the very similar comparative advantage of Mexico and Turkey in the global economy (Figure 1.3). As a result of their linkages with the global

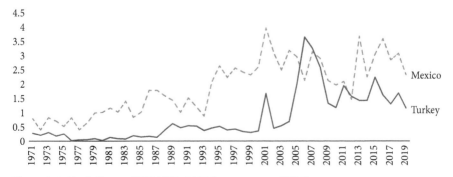

Figure 1.1 Net inflows of FDI 1971–2019 (percentage of GDP)
Source: World Bank (2021b)

Figure 1.2 Exports of goods and services 1960–2018 (as percentage of GDP)
Source: World Bank (2021c)

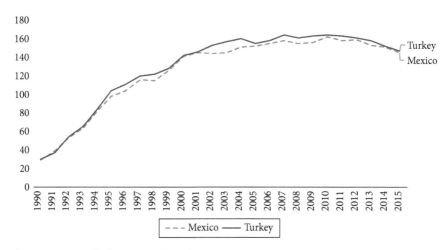

Figure 1.3 Revealed comparative advantage 1990–2015
Source: World Bank (2020a)

economy and the structure of local economy, both Mexico and Turkey became 'the poster children of international financial institutions' (Özel, 2014, p. 7), both having substantial relations with the International Monetary Fund (IMF) and joining regional economic organisations dominated by the advanced capitalist economies, namely the North American Free Trade Agreement (NAFTA) in 1994 for Mexico, and the European Customs Union in 1995 for Turkey.

The economic liberalisation and integration to the global economy have had similar influence on **labour organisation and labour markets** in Mexico and Turkey. Although labour unions in both countries were influential actors prior to the 1980s, union power was substantially curtailed after the economic liberalisation, with unions today being characterised by low unionisation rates, weak collective bargaining, and marginal influence on public policy (Kohli, 2004; Kuş and Özel, 2010; Çelik, 2013; Bensusán, 2015; Bizberg, 2015a; Bozkurt-Güngen, 2018; Özkiziltan, 2019).

The weakening of collective labour organisations has been followed by labour market flexibilisation in both Mexico and Turkey. Even though the labour regulations may seem 'strict' in the two countries at first instance (OECD, 2020a), employment protection has been *de facto* very weak due to additional regulations that provide important flexibilities to employers, such as the possibility of subcontracting, and the gaps between *de jure* labour regulations and their *de facto* implementation. In fact, informal employment has been prominent in both Mexico and Turkey, in which workers have not had access to employment or social protection (ILO, 2014; Karaca and Kaleli, 2019). The labour regulations that lead to flexibilisation, and the gap between labour regulations and their implementation have led to 'segmentation' in the labour markets of both countries between the workers of large companies and the public sector, employees in smaller companies, and those working in the informal economy (Schneider, 2009a; Schneider and Karcher, 2010; Sancak, 2011).

Despite the similarities with regards to their development paths, integration into the global economy, and labour dynamics, there has been important divergence in the neoliberal era between Mexico and Turkey concerning **the role of the state** (Özel, 2014; Sancak and Özel, 2018; Witt et al., 2018; Bizberg, 2019). Although the state's involvement in several spheres of the economy has decreased in the neoliberal era, the state has assumed very different roles regarding *its relations with businesses* and the *welfare policies* it has followed, which may result in different skill formation systems in the two countries.

In the neoliberal era 'both the patrons and clients [of these political alliances] have been shuffled [in Turkey] whereas in Mexico clients have more or less persisted' (Özel, 2014, p. 5). State–business relations in Mexico took the shape of 'an Anglo-Saxon style of lobbying', where the Mexican state has maintained its links with business associations representing the interests of large businesses including the Coordination of Corporate Bodies of External Trade (*Coordinación de Organismos Empresariales de Comercio Exterior*—COECE) and Mexican Businessmen's Council (*Consejo Mexicano de Hombres de Negocios*—CHMN) (Vega, 2005; Schneider, 2013b; Özel, 2021). In addition to the dominance of domestic conglomerates' interests, foreign multinational enterprises have held substantial power in Mexico as both the federal and state governments have focused on attracting foreign direct investment (FDI) and integrating the Mexican economy with global production networks (Robertson, 2003; Bizberg and Théret, 2015; Bizberg, 2019). In contrast, small and medium-sized enterprises (SMEs) in Mexico have lost significant power and representation in the neoliberal era, especially with the abolition of compulsory membership to business chambers in 1994 (Shadlen, 2002, 2004).

The National Chamber of the Industry of Transformation (*Cámara Nacional de la Industria de Transformación*—CANACINTRA) and the Confederation of Industrial Chambers (*Confederación de Cámaras Industriales*—CONCAMIN) predominantly represent the interests of the SMEs and were influential actors during the ISI period through the corporatist structure that was introduced in 1941, and the links of these organisations with the state (Shadlen, 2004). Nonetheless, the abandoning of the corporatist structure and the state's increasing alliance with large businesses—and associations representing these businesses—have led to the marginalisation of the SME associations and, thus, the interests of SMEs in policymaking during the neoliberal era (Shadlen, 2004). The political marginalisation of SMEs has played a role in their economic marginalisation, and vice versa, and the acquisition of many Mexican SMEs by large, and foreign, enterprises. Consequently, even though SMEs today constitute a large segment of the employment in Mexico, their share in the economic value-added and exports has remained very small, and much smaller when compared to the SMEs in Turkey (Figure 1.4).

In contrast to Mexico, SMEs have gained important economic and political power in Turkey in the neoliberal era, while the power of big businesses has been challenged, especially in the early 2000s. Membership to local chambers of commerce and industry has been mandatory in Turkey since 1925, and the local chambers from 82 cities of Turkey are organised under the umbrella organisation, The Union of Chambers and Commodity Exchanges of Turkey (*Türkiye Odalar ve Borsalar Birliği*—TOBB). The TOBB has been a key institution for organising and representing the SMEs' interests since the establishment of the Turkish Industry and Business Association (*Türkiye Sanayicileri ve İşadamları Derneği*—TÜSİAD) in 1971, which is an exclusive business association also known as 'the club of the rich', and with its establishment, large domestic corporations have focused organising their interests through TÜSİAD, which has left more room to SMEs in the TOBB. Unlike Mexico, the corporatist structure has been maintained in the neoliberal era in Turkey, which has given important representational and financial power to the TOBB. The TOBB comprises 365 local chambers in every city throughout Turkey, with about 1.3 million

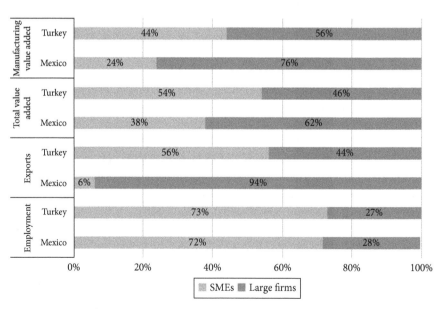

Figure 1.4 Role of SMEs in Mexico and Turkey in 2014
Source: OECD (2017)

member firms (Özel, 2021). Based on this power, as well as its relations with the governing Justice and Development Party (*Adalet ve Kalkınma Partisi*—AKP), the TOBB has been the default representative of business' interests in tripartite policymaking platforms in the early 2000s, which has been a key mechanism for vocalising the interests of the SMEs (ETF, 2004; Sancak, 2020). In addition to the TOBB, SMEs' interests have been organised and represented through voluntary business associations including the Independent Industrialists' and Businessmen's Association (*Müstakil Sanayici ve İşadamları Derneği*—MÜSİAD) and the Turkish Confederation of Businessmen and Industrialists (*Türkiye Sanayiciler ve İşadamları Konfederasyonu*—TUSKON).[4] These associations developed close links with the governing AKP in the early 2000s, which has prioritised the interests and requests of firms belonging to these associations (Buğra and Savaşkan, 2014; Özel, 2014). The increased collective organisation of SMEs through the TOBB and voluntary associations has played a key role in the economic growth of these firms. Currently, the SMEs have an important share in the Turkish economy regarding several aspects including employment, exports, and economic-value added (Figure 1.4).

Another divergence between the Mexican state and the Turkish state concerns the policies followed regarding the workers (Sancak and Özel, 2018; Özel, 2021; Sancak, 2020). Although unions have been oppressed and labour markets have been 'flexibilised' in both countries, the state strategies regarding social benefits and workers' wages have been different in Mexico and Turkey. In order to address the interests of domestic large firms and foreign MNCs, which have focused on maintaining low labour costs, the state in Mexico has followed an 'international outsourcing capitalism' that is subordinate to external markets (Bizberg, 2019). In this regard, the wages have been suppressed; the implementation of labour regulations have been relaxed; the welfare system has been contracted out; and public investment in VET and innovation has been restricted (Bizberg, 2004, 2019; Bensusán, 2015, 2016). While attracting FDI and integrating into world markets have also been major strategies for the Turkish state in the neoliberal era, it has followed a 'social' and 'regulatory' neoliberalism in these years, which has affected wages and social spending in very different ways (Öniş, 2012; Dorlach, 2015). This distinction has resulted in divergence between Mexico and Turkey in three main aspects.

Firstly, even though social spending has been increasing in both countries, this increase has been much higher in Turkey (Figure 1.5). Secondly, the social policies in Mexico have continued focusing on the traditional 'protective' policies such as old age pensions and conditional cash transfers, while 'productive' policies, including active labour market policies and healthcare policy, have remained weak (Bizberg, 2015b). In contrast, the welfare policies in Turkey have focused on more 'productive' rather than protective social policies, where active labour market policies, healthcare, and education and training have constituted an important part in the welfare system (Figures 1.6–1.8) (Dorlach, 2015).

---

[4] The relations worsened later because of the group's links with the Gülen movement.

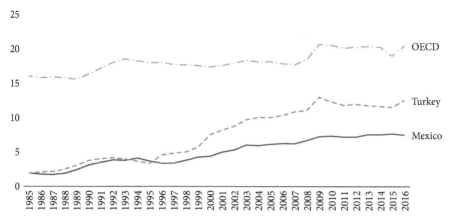

Figure 1.5 Public social spending in 1985–2015 (percentage GDP)
Source: OECD (2020b)

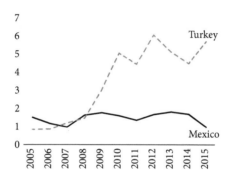

Figure 1.6 Public spending for active labour market policies (USD per person, at current prices and PPPs)
Source: OECD (2020b)

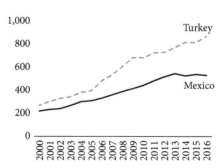

Figure 1.7 Public spending for healthcare (USD per person, at current prices and PPPs)
Source: OECD (2020b)

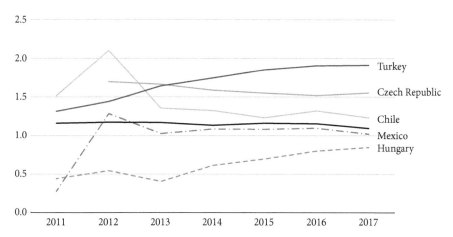

Figure 1.8 Public spending for VET at upper-secondary level (percentage, total government spending)
Source: OECD (2020c)

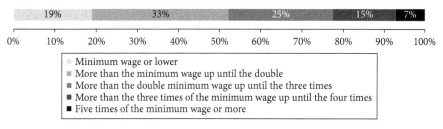

Figure 1.9 Share of formal employees based on their earnings in 2016 (Mexico)
Source: INEGI (2020)

Thirdly, the wages have differed significantly between the two countries in the neoliberal era. In the absence of collective bargaining structure, the minimum wage has been a key institution to define wages in both countries. Figure 1.9 shows the distribution of the wages in Mexico. According to this, about more than half of the *formally* employed receive twice the minimum wage or below, while approximately 45 per cent of the workforce in Turkey receive the minimum wage (Eurostat, 2020a). The state has played a role in deciding the minimum wage in both countries through the so-called tripartite commissions that include the representatives of the state, businesses, and workers, which are the National Minimum Wage Commission (*Comisión Nacional de los Salarios Mínimos*—CONASAMI) in Mexico and the Minimum Wage Commission in Turkey (*Asgari Ücret Tespit Komisyonu*). Focusing on minimising labour costs, the Mexican state has kept the minimum wage extremely low. In contrast, the minimum wage, which has been used as a way of welfare provision in Turkey (Korkmaz, 2004), has been much higher not only compared to Mexico but also to other MICs and emerging economies (Figure 1.10).

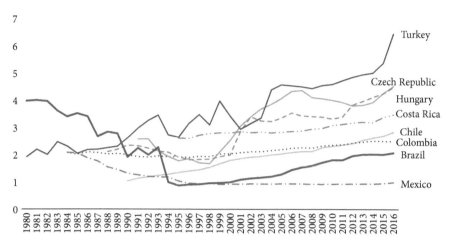

Figure 1.10 Hourly minimum wage 1980–2016 (USD, 2019 constant prices at PPPs)
Source: OECD (2021a)

The similarities regarding their development paths, economic structures, integration to the world economy and flexible labour markets with weak unionisation, and the differences *vis-à-vis* the state's relations with different businesses and welfare policies during the neoliberal era make Mexico and Turkey crucial cases for understanding the impact of global dynamics and national institutions on skill systems. On the one hand, if the arguments on globalisation and convergence are true, the similar economic structures and integration into the world market will result in similar skill systems in Mexico and Turkey. On the other hand, if the arguments on divergence due to national institutions are true, the different role of the state in the neoliberal era will result in different skill systems in the two countries.

1.1.2 Diverging development experiences

In addition to their significance for studying the influence of global dynamics and national institutions on skill formation, the distinct development experiences in the early 2000s make Mexico and Turkey important cases to analyse the implications of skill systems for high-road development. One divergence between Mexico and Turkey concerns the *continuity* of their economic growth. Although both countries have been growing fast and have been part of the upper-middle-income group in World Bank's classification, the GDP growth rate and GDP per capita have been much higher in Turkey than Mexico since the early 2000s (Figure 1.11). Furthermore, productivity in Turkey has been increasing fast, while productivity in Mexico has not changed much since the 1990s, which can jeopardise the continuity of growth in Mexico (Figure 1.12).

Another important divergence between the development experiences of Mexico and Turkey is about the *inclusivity* of development. The economic growth in Turkey

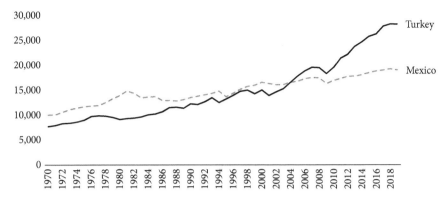

Figure 1.11 GDP per capita (USD, constant prices, 2015 PPPs)
Source: OECD (2019)

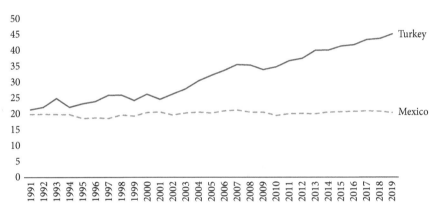

Figure 1.12 Labour productivity (GDP per hour worked, USD, constant prices, 2015 PPPs)
Source: OECD (2021b)

has been accompanied by improved socioeconomic development in the early 2000s, which has made Turkey a good example of 'inclusive growth' according to the World Bank (Raiser and Azevedo, 2013). Income inequality between different regions and occupational groups has fallen in Turkey, while the incomes of the poorest households have increased (Azevedo and Atamanov, 2014; OECD, 2015). The middle-class has expanded due to the upward mobility of people from formerly lower income classes (Azevedo and Atamanov, 2014; Buğra and Savaşkan, 2014). In contrast to Turkey, high rates of poverty and inequality have persisted in Mexico, where the size of the middle-class has shrunk significantly (Bizberg and Théret, 2015; OECD, 2015) (Figure 1.13).

The skill systems of Mexico and Turkey will have an important influence on their different development experiences of regarding the continuity and inclusivity of development, although there will be also other elements affecting this divergence.

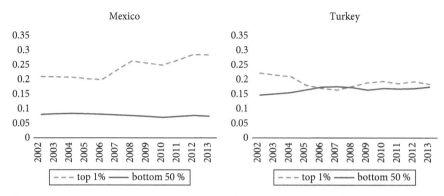

Figure 1.13 Inequality 2002–2013 (pretax national income, share of top 1 per cent and bottom 50 per cent)
Source: World Inequality Database (2020)

Therefore, in addition to understanding the political economy of skill systems, studying the cases of Mexico and Turkey will be helpful to realise the implications of global dynamics and national institutions for high-road development in MICs. In summary, through studying these two countries and their firms, this book investigates (i) the patterns of convergence in skill systems due to the similar links of the two countries with the global economy; (ii) the patterns of divergence in national skill systems due to the varying state roles; and (iii) the links between skill systems and development outcomes because of their diverging development experiences.

1.2   The three lines of inquiry

For studying the political economy and the implications of multilevel skill systems, this book benefits from and cross-fertilises three main lines of research. These include the research on (i) GVC governance and convergence of skilling practices, (ii) national institutions and divergence of skilling strategies, and (iii) the outcomes of skill systems regarding workers' income and career progression, and smaller firms' access to skilled workers.

1.2.1   GVC governance and convergence of skilling strategies

This line of inquiry focuses on the pressures on Mexican and Turkish supplier firms in global AACs, and elaborates whether these pressures bring convergence in supplier firms' skilling practices, namely their hiring, training, and employee development practices. This discussion draws from the claims about the convergence of economic behaviour due to the rise of globalisation in the literature on GVC governance and strategic HRM. The GVC researchers and convergence arguments, in general, suggest that globalisation brings free movement of capital and goods and intensifies global competition, which gives companies greater ability to 'escape' their 'restrictive' national institutional 'constraints' and easily move their activities to other locations (Campbell and Pedersen, 2001; Wilkinson et al., 2001). However, firms move *only some* of their activities—not all—to a number of different locations, which creates GVCs that are managed by a small number of 'lead firms' (Gereffi and Korzeniewicz, 1994; Gereffi, Humphrey, and Sturgeon, 2005). These lead firms and governance structures along the GVCs are argued to become the main elements shaping the activities of supplier firms within these chains, while national institutions become 'irrelevant' to firm behaviour (Giddens, 2003; Gereffi, Humphrey, and Sturgeon, 2005). The researchers focusing on the workers in GVCs, moreover, have argued that this diffusion of production across the world, with substantial power held by the lead firms, generates a 'race to the bottom', with deteriorating labour conditions in supplier firms, especially from developing countries (Moody, 1997; Rudra, 2008; Barrientos, 2013).

In contrast to the GVC scholars, researchers in the strategic HRM literature have had more optimistic views about the globalisation of production and convergence of employment practices. These researchers argue that firms are forced to improve their employment practices in order to remain competitive in the global economy, and the High-Performance Work Systems (HPWSs)—which comprise several elements such as recruitment, training, employee development, and employee voice—create the 'best outcomes' for firms (MacDuffie, 1995; Ohmae, 1995; Appelbaum, 2000). Furthermore, these HRM 'best practices' are argued to diffuse across the world through several channels such as competition and learning in GVCs, and HRM education practices in management schools. As a result, the researchers of strategic HRM maintain that all firms will start adopting similar 'human resource bundles' that will lead to a convergence towards HPWSs (MacDuffie, 1995; Appelbaum, 2000).

Based on this background, the book investigates the convergence of skilling practices of Mexican and Turkish suppliers towards a 'race to the bottom' or HPWSs due to their participation in global AACs. It scrutinises the pressures on supplier firms in the global AACs and investigates the ways the suppliers respond to these pressures with regards to their hiring, training, and employee development practices.

1.2.2 National institutions and divergence of skilling strategies

The second main line of inquiry focuses on national institutions in Mexico and Turkey and the impact of these institutions on firms' skilling practices. The research for this draws from the literature on CCs, and particularly on CPEoSF, and the research in organisation studies and international business. The researchers in these fields acknowledge the pressures of globalisation on national institutions and economic behaviour. However, they oppose the claims of convergence of national institutions and economic behaviour. Researchers of the CCs literature argue that although national institutions may go through some changes due to the pressures of globalisation, these changes are path dependent, namely are shaped by previous institutional arrangements (Streeck and Thelen, 2005; Thelen and Kume, 2006; Hall and Thelen, 2009; Thelen, 2014). Therefore, these researchers argue national institutions continue to vary across countries, influence economic activity in specific ways, and lead to distinct national capitalist systems with distinct outcomes (Hall and Soskice, 2001).

While studies in the CCs literature claim firms to be the centre of analysis, they have mostly focused on studying the national institutions and their complementarities, rather than understanding the linkages between institutions and firms' activities. The latter one has been more the focus of organisation studies and international business literature, and particularly the discussions in the literature on ESs and international HRM address this issue. These researchers emphasise the importance of national institutions that surround firms for firm-level hiring, training, and employee development practices. According to these researchers, the application of HRM 'bundles' depends on the national institutional context, and, thus, there is no one model encompassing 'best practices' in HRM (Ferner, 2000; Edwards and Ferner, 2002; Almond et al., 2005; Webster and Wood, 2005; Demirbag et al., 2014; Horwitz and Budhwar, 2015; Jürgens and Krzywdzinski, 2016; Dibben et al., 2017; Singh et al., 2017). Despite their contribution to our understanding about the role of institutions for HRM practices, the empirical work of these studies has focused only on the HRM practices of MNC subsidiaries in different locations, without explaining the practices of supplier companies in GVCs.

Building on this background, the book studies the impact of national institutions on the hiring, training, and employee development practices of supplier firms in Mexico and Turkey. Based on in-depth empirical research on macro-level institutions and micro-level skilling practices, the book investigates the institutions that are studied in the CCs literature, which include the national VET systems and labour market structures. In addition to these, the book scrutinises other elements that influence labour market dynamics and thus influence firms' skilling strategies, such as firms' geographical location and public transportation facilities which influence the accessibility of firms to workers and vice versa.

1.2.3 Outcomes of skill systems and development prospects

The third main aspect of inquiry in this book concerns the implications of skill systems for high- or low-road development in Mexico and Turkey. The discussion here draws from the arguments in the CCs literature about the implications of different capitalist systems for economic performance and levels of inequality, and the debates in the GVC literature about the upgrading possibilities of supplier firms within GVCs and the impact of GVC governance on workers. However, in contrast to the focus on macro-level indicators in the CCs and GVC literature, the book generates inferences about the implications of skill systems for the two countries' development experiences based on the micro-level evidence about the influence of skill systems on workers and firms in the AAIs of the two countries.

The institutionalist research in the literature on CCs on advanced capitalist countries links the economic performance of and levels of inequality in these countries with their institutional configurations (Streeck, 1989, 1991, 1992a; Whitley, 2000, 2007; Hall and Soskice, 2001; Estevez-Abe, Iversen, and Soskice, 2001; Amable, 2003; Thelen, 2004; Busemeyer, 2015b; Schneider and Paunescu, 2012; Witt and Jackson, 2016). These researchers argue that due to the strong VET systems in coordinated market economies (CMEs), these countries have comparative advantage in sectors requiring specific skills, such as manufacturing. In contrast, because the skill systems in liberal market economies (LMEs) tend to generate general skills, these countries excel in sectors requiring general skills, such as financial services. While countries with these two categories of capitalist system are argued to have strong economic performance, the mixed-market economies that stand in between are claimed to have poor economic performance (Hall and Soskice, 2001; Hall and Gingerich, 2009).

Similar to the case of economic performance, researchers in the CCs literature relate the levels of inequality to the capitalist systems in advanced economies. Because of the importance of intermediate skills in CMEs, these countries have had strong VET systems, and the costs of training are shared among firms, the state, and individuals (Ryan, 2000; Mohrenweiser and Zwick, 2009). VET systems in these countries are argued to give important opportunities to individuals from lower income groups and with lower levels of education for career progression and to increase their income. Furthermore, the VET systems are argued to create a group of workers with intermediate skills and income, and thereby reduce income inequality (Estevez-Abe, Iversen, and Soskice, 2001; Thelen, 2014; Busemeyer, 2015a).[5] In contrast, more general skills are needed in LMEs—both low and high general skills— and individuals have the main responsibility for financing skill formation in these capitalist systems (Fleckenstein et al., 2011; Busemeyer, 2015a). This is argued to create a small group of workers with high general skills and high incomes, on the one hand, and a large group with low skills and low income, on the other, which lead to high levels of inequality in LMEs (Rueda and Pontusson, 2000; Fleckenstein, Saunders, and Seeleib-Kaiser, 2011; Schneider and Makszin, 2014; Thelen, 2014; Busemeyer, 2015a). Furthermore, researchers focusing on the CPEoSF argue that VET systems with different levels of state commitment and firm involvement have distinct implications for income inequality in CMEs (Busemeyer, 2015b).

The implications of governance structures in GVCs constitutes a major area of discussion in the GVC literature. Researchers in this literature argue that the

---

[5] Here, I talk only about income inequality but not educational inequality, which has been widely discussed in the educational sociology literature (Pfeffer, 2008).

governance structures in GVCs determine the upgrading prospects of firms in these chains, and thus affect the development prospects of countries (Gereffi, Humphrey, and Sturgeon, 2005). These researchers argue that based on the type of governance, lead firms in GVCs have different types of relations with and expectations from their suppliers, which determine suppliers' prospects for product, process, functional, and intersectoral upgrading (Humphrey, 2000; Humphrey and Schmitz, 2002). Furthermore, several researchers in the GVC tradition have discussed the impact of GVC governance on the employment conditions of workers and social upgrading in supplier firms (Barrientos, Dolan, and Tallontire, 2003; Riisgaard and Hammer, 2011; Mayer and Phillips, 2017; Mayer, Phillips, and Posthuma, 2017).

This book utilises the approaches found in the CCs and GVC literature to understand the possibility of high-road development for Mexico and Turkey. However, different from research in the CCs and GVC literature, the book looks at the micro-level outcomes of these practices for workers and firms. Firstly, the book elaborates what types of skills are generated in the skill systems of Mexico and Turkey. Secondly, it investigates how the skills systems affect individuals' access to different skills, and the opportunities of shop floor workers for career and income progression. Thirdly, the book examines the accessibility of skilled workers to different firms, especially the SMEs.

1.3 The main argument

Figure 1.14 presents a summary of the arguments of this book. The book suggests that the state plays the main role in skill systems, and capitalist systems with higher state involvement in the economy are more likely to promote high-road development. This argument consists of three subarguments that are based on three main lines of inquiry showing the linkages between the pressures in the global economy, national institutions, firm-level skilling practices, and the outcomes of those practices:

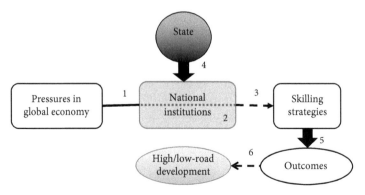

Figure 1.14 The skill system

1. *National institutions matter*: Although firms' participation in GVCs creates similar pressures on supplier firms (Arrow 1 in Figure 1.14), these pressures are mediated by national institutions (Arrow 2 in Figure 1.14), which results in distinct skilling strategies at the firm level (Arrow 3 in Figure 1.14). More specifically, the governance structures in AACs put similar pressures on the Mexican and Turkish suppliers and result in similar skill needs in these firms. However, the pressures in AACs do not directly influence how firms address their skill needs. Instead, the national institutions modify these pressures and become the main factors that influence firms' skilling practices. Therefore, although Mexican and Turkish firms need workers with similar types of skills, they have distinct strategies to address their skill needs because of the distinct national institutional arrangements. The pressures in AACs, moreover, have higher influence on firms' skilling practices in Mexico, where the national institutions are looser, which leaves more room to the Mexican firms to shape their activities in line with the expectations from their clients in AACs.

2. *The state plays the main role in skill systems*: The state's involvement in the economy (Arrow 4 in Figure 1.14) not only defines the characteristics of VET systems, but also determines the institutions affecting the supply of and demand for different types of workers, which then influence firms' skilling strategies (Arrow 3 in Figure 1.14). The higher state involvement in Turkey results in a statist VET system with some firm collectivist elements, strict labour market regulations with certain flexibilities and the rigorous implementation of these regulations, and high wages and high mobility of workers. In contrast, the low state involvement in Mexico leads to a liberal VET system, strict labour market regulations with weak implementation, and low wages and limited worker mobility. Because of the institutional arrangements, Turkish firms tend to use the public VET system to generate the skills they need, while Mexican firms develop these skills mostly within the firm.

3. *Higher state involvement is more likely to lead to skill systems for high-road development*: The skilling strategies that are shaped by the pressures of global competition and national institutions have distinct outcomes for workers and firms (Arrow 5 in Figure 1.14) and thus implications for countries' development prospects (Arrow 6 in Figure 1.14). The skill systems in locations with low state involvement, and therefore with looser institutional arrangements, like in Mexico, tend to generate specific skills through firm-level training. Such skill systems limit both firms' and workers' access to general skills, constrain workers' career and income progression, exacerbate labour market segmentation, and restrict smaller firms' upgrading and growth prospects. In contrast, skill systems with higher state involvement, like in Turkey, generate more general and more standardised skills, in addition to the specific ones, and these skill systems are accessible to both workers and firms. Therefore, the book proposes that workers in MICs with high state involvement in skill systems will have important opportunities for career and income progression.

This then will limit segmentation in the labour market and promote development that is more inclusive. Furthermore, in such countries, smaller firms' access to skilled workers will facilitate these firms' economic upgrading prospects in GVCs and will promote their further economic growth, which will be key for continuous development.

1.4 The structure of the book

Following this introductory chapter, Chapter 2 presents a detailed review of the literature and an explanation of this study's theoretical approach. It starts with a discussion on the firm-level determinants of recruitment and training behaviour, which is based on human capital theory. Later, it introduces the literature on institutions, summarising different research strands within the institutionalist literature and their approach to the study of skilling activities. The focus here is on CCs and the CPEoSF. This is followed by a discussion on the globalisation literature, where claims about the convergence of firm behaviour are explained, drawing from the literature on GVC governance. The debates on national institutions and GVCs are followed by the micro-level approaches analysing firm behaviour and the outcomes of skilling practices for firms and workers, which draws from the literature on ESs and on HRM. This chapter is concluded by outlining the overall theoretical approach of the book, namely the 'cross-fertilisation' of CCs, GVCs, HRM, and ESs research, and their distinct benefits for the analysis.

Chapter 3 introduces the empirical cases. It explains the rationale behind studying the AAI, the functioning of global AACs, and the participation of Mexican and Turkish AAIs in these chains. Additionally, this chapter charts the general development of the AAI in Mexico and Turkey, and the main lead firms in the two countries. It also introduces the interviewed companies, outlining the interview process and the sample of interviewed firms, as well as explaining the interviews with the stakeholders. Finally, the chapter describes the main positions on the production floors of the studied companies.

After these, the book presents the three aspects of inquiry in Chapters 4, 5, 6, 7, and 8. Chapter 4 discusses the role of globalisation and explains how governance structures in global AACs influence Mexican and Turkish firms, and their skill needs and skilling strategies. Chapters 5 and 6 turn to national institutions and explain the national institutions that complement the skill systems of Mexico and Turkey, and emphasise the role of the state for these complementarities. Chapters 7 and 8 explain the influence of national institutions on firms' skilling practices and discuss the outcomes of skill systems for workers and firms. Based on the outcomes of the skill systems, these chapters draw inferences about the implications of the Mexican and Turkish skill systems for high-road development prospects of these countries. Chapter 9 provides a comparative discussion of the two countries and concludes the arguments.

1.5 Contribution and further areas of inquiry

With its conceptual framing and empirical richness, the book aims to contribute to a variety of debates on globalisation and convergence of economic behaviour, the persisting role of national institutions and continuing diversities between capitalist systems, and development in MICs, especially in upper-middle-income ones, which currently comprise 56 countries in World Bank's classification.

The book maintains the importance of the state and national institutions for economic behaviour and rejects the arguments on the convergence of economic activity in global capitalism. With this, it supports the arguments in the literature on CPEoSF about the role of the state for skill systems. However, in doing this, it goes beyond the traditional institutions studied in the CCs literature through offering a multilevel analysis of skill systems that includes a study of macro-level institutions, macro/meso-level analysis of GVC governance structures, and micro-level research on firm activity and outcomes of this activity for workers and firms. Furthermore, the book contributes to the debates on development and argues that high state involvement in regulating the economy is more likely to promote high-road development in MICs by improving the opportunities for both workers and firms.

When concluding this introduction, it is perhaps important to mention what this book is *not* about and what further inquiry this book may lead to. Regarding the impact of GVCs, it would be interesting to see whether lead firms from different home countries have different impact on local auto parts suppliers in AACs. Indeed, this was initially one of the objectives of the research project conducted for this book, as Mexico and Turkey are located at the periphery of advanced capitalist economies with distinct capitalist models (i.e. the LME of the United States and CME of Germany and other European countries). However, addressing this question proved to be difficult because the local suppliers from both Mexico and Turkey sell to multiple lead firms from various locations simultaneously, and not only to those from their neighbouring countries. Therefore, it has not been possible to separate one lead firm's impact from another (see Chapters 3 and 4). For that reason, this book does not explain how lead firms from different home countries affect suppliers in Mexico and Turkey.

Furthermore, when understanding the role of globalisation, the book focuses only on the governance structures in GVCs, and does not discuss other elements that could lead to the convergence of skilling practices such as the role of managers studying in global MBA programmes or with work experience in MNCs. This is first because an analysis on GVCs is helpful to understand both the indirect influences of globalisation on firm-level practices, such as by shaping the demand for different types of workers, and direct ones, such as firms' recruitment and training practices through links between suppliers and lead firms. Therefore, the focus on GVCs helps to realise both direct and indirect influences of global economic competition and patterns of convergence. Secondly, this book is concerned with the development implications of global economic competition, and the GVC literature offers extensive analysis in this regard, namely about the economic and social upgrading prospects of supplier firms in GVCs, which will help to understand the development implications of skill systems. Thirdly, the unit of analysis in this book is the firm, and this is to understand the differences or similarities *between* Mexican and Turkish firms. An analysis on managers could be helpful to understand variations between firms *within* Mexico or Turkey, or to show similarities *between some* Turkish and Mexican firms. But the role of managers in firms' skilling practices is not within the scope of this book.

In terms of the discussion of national varieties of skill systems and the role of the state, the book aims to understand *which national institutions influence firms' skilling strategies* and *what kind of skilling practices these institutions lead to*. However, it does not explain *why these institutions came into place*, historically, although the development of certain institutions is briefly mentioned in certain parts of the book when discussing the role of the state. Therefore, this book considers firms, for now, as 'institution takers' rather than 'institution makers', and does not include an in-depth historical analysis of political dynamics shaping the institutions. One may legitimately argue that such an approach is 'too static' and cannot explain changes in the past or the future. Nevertheless, the purpose of this book is to provide a 'snapshot' of the linkages between skilling strategies and national institutions, and GVC governance structures *at a given period*, namely when the fieldwork for this book was conducted. Therefore, the discussion in this book is based on the research about firms' skilling strategies and relations with lead firms in July 2014–November 2015, and the institutions and regulations that were affecting firms' activities in this period.

None of this is to deny that institutions are formed through historical processes in which firms play a role as 'institution makers', and both institutions and firm behaviour can change in the future. Numerous elements may be responsible for the divergence of the state's role, and, thus, the differences of national institutions between Mexico and Turkey, such as differing domestic political coalitions or variations in each country's integration with the global economy (Sancak and Özel, 2018; Sancak, 2020). Nevertheless, answering these questions would require in-depth historical research. This book rather hopes to initiate a discussion on globalisation, institutions, and skill systems and their implications for development in MICs like Mexico and Turkey, which can be followed by other studies on the historical and political origins of these institutions and their change in the future.

2
The theoretical approach

A 'multilevel analysis of economic action' (Lane and Wood, 2009, p. 18) is key to understand the multiple levels of skill systems and the implications of skill systems for development. This book follows such an approach and brings together the macro approach of the studies on comparative capitalisms (CCs), macro-meso approach of global value chains (GVCs), and the micro approach of research on employment systems (ESs) and human resource management (HRM). Skill formation has an important role in the studies in these fields, which have made substantial contribution to our knowledge in this regard. Nevertheless, each field has remained separate from one another, creating important bottlenecks when studying skill systems. The lack of communication has been especially high for the studies carrying out only one level of analysis without explaining the linkages between different levels. For example, the research on CCs has focused on national institutions only, and has not empirically shown how national institutions are linked to what goes on at the firm level (Vincent and Thompson, 2010; Wood, Dibben, and Ogden, 2013; Allen, 2014). Similarly, the research on GVCs has centred its inquiry on the governance structures of GVCs and has overlooked the influence of these structures on firm-level skilling practices (Lakhani, Kuruvilla, and Avgar, 2013; Zhu and Morgan, 2018). On the other hand, the studies with a micro-level focus, including the ones in the fields of ESs and HRM, have explored firm-level recruitment, training, and employee development, have overlooked how the interactions between GVC governance structures and national institutions influence firm-level practices (Wilkinson, Wood, and Deeg, 2014b; Hotho and Saka-Helmhout, 2017).

Another shortcoming of the studies in the fields cross-fertilised in this book, namely the research on CCs, GVCs, ESs and HRM, concerns their focus on rich, advanced industrialised countries and firms from these countries, and their lesser interest on late-industrialising countries and firms from such countries. Because the late-industrialising countries—including middle-income and low-income countries—have experienced industrialisation and global integration at very different stages of their development, they have unique national institutional structures and distinct relations with the global economy. Therefore, a study on late-industrialising countries may challenge or support the arguments in the CCs, GVCs, ESs, and HRM studies, and thus will make theoretical contributions to these fields.

This is not to say that late industrialisers have never been the concern of researchers in the aforementioned fields. For example, some studies in the CCs tradition have included a number of late industrialisers in their analysis, and have

Global Production, National Institutions, and Skill Formation: The Political Economy of Training and Employment in Auto Parts Suppliers from Mexico And Turkey. Merve Sancak, Oxford University Press. © Merve Sancak 2022.
DOI: 10.1093/oso/9780198860655.003.0002

developed further regional types of capitalism such as Latin American, East Asian, Eastern European, and Southern European models of capitalism (Amable, 2003; Hancke, Rhodes, and Thatcher, 2007; Nölke and Vliegenthart, 2009; Schneider, 2013a; Witt et al., 2018). Furthermore, studying the impact of governance structures on firms and workers from late-industrialising countries has constituted a central agenda in the GVC literature (Barrientos, Dolan, and Tallontire, 2003; Selwyn, Musiolek, and Ijarja, 2020). Similarly, several studies in the ESs and HRM literature have studied the HRM practices of MNCs in developing countries (Webster and Wood, 2005; Wood, Dibben, and Meira, 2016; Dibben et al., 2017). Despite their contributions to our understanding about capitalist systems in late industrialisers, the studies in each field have been disconnected with the studies in the others and, hence, have provided only a partial view about how capitalist structures work in late industrialisers and the outcomes of these structures for inclusive development. This book is different: it proposes that 'cross-fertilising' macro- and micro-level research will enrich our understanding of multilevel skill systems in middle-income countries (MICs). Through such cross-fertilisation, the weakness of each field is addressed by the strengths of the other, which then provides a comprehensive analysis of skill systems and their outcomes.

This chapter first summarises the theoretical arguments of each field of study and explains the critiques towards these fields. It then explains how each research informs the book's conceptual approach. The chapter begins with the discussion on the firm-level determinants of skilling decisions, namely firms' preference for either hiring skilled workers or training unskilled workers, which is based on the studies in the field of labour economics. After this, discussions on national institutions and the CCs are introduced, and the arguments on globalisation and the convergence of economic activity are explained. These debates with macro- and meso-level approaches are followed by the elaboration of micro-level studies on skilling practices—namely the research on ESs and HRM. The last section elucidates the cross-fertilisation of the different research strands.

2.1 Inside the firm

The studies on firms' skilling activities in the field of economics provide valuable insights and an important starting point to understand multilevel skill systems. In general, these studies argue that firms have two main options to generate the skills that are necessary for them (Blatter et al., 2016). The first is *hiring workers with skills that match the requirements of the position*, whilst accepting that these workers may still need some time for adaptation and some training to develop the required firm-specific skills. The other option for firms is *hiring unskilled workers and developing their skills within the firm* through on-the-job learning and/or organised training (Thelen, 2004; Blatter et al., 2016). As firms are believed to be rational actors, their choice between hiring skilled workers and training unskilled workers is held to depend on the costs and benefits of each option (Stevens, 1994). *Hiring costs* mainly include the cost of advertising the position, the time spent by firm personnel in evaluating the candidates, and the production loss due to the absence of needed skilled workers (Dionisius et al., 2009).[1] *Training costs*, moreover, involve firms' funding of training activities, the expenses related to on-the-job learning, and the excess salary paid to trainees when they are not working to their full capacity.

Labour economists propose a number of factors that affect firms' costs of hiring skilled workers and of training unskilled ones and, thus, influence their decisions on skilling. These factors, in general, include the skill types needed by the firm (i.e. specific or general skills), firms' capacity to train and hire workers (referring to the number of their employees, their technological and managerial capacity, and their access to skilled workers), and the wages of, turnover, and retention rate for skilled and unskilled workers. Furthermore, firms consider their skilling costs for both *today* and *in the future*, and make a decision on skilling *today* in order to have skilled workers in the *future*. Therefore, if the training costs today are lower than the hiring costs in the future, firms are expected employ unskilled workers today and train them for the future (Oatey, 1970; Lindley, 1975; Merrilees, 1983; Stevens, 1994). Conversely, firms are expected to prefer hiring skilled workers in the future if current training costs are higher than the future hiring costs (Stevens, 1994). Figure 2.1 summarises the arguments about the costs of and decisions on training and hiring.

Gary Becker's work (1993) pioneers in the area of firms' skilling activities in the field of labour economics with a neoclassical approach. Focusing on skill types and their transferability, Becker argues that firms will train workers to generate only *specific* skills while they will hire workers with *general* skills, it being left to the individual worker to invest in the development of general skills. Becker describes specific skills as those that are used only at a specific company and that cannot be transferred to other workplaces. As these skills are firm-specific, they do not exist or are difficult to find in the labour market, and hiring costs for these skills will be very

---

Assumption: Firms will need skilled workers in the future
Cost of training (train$_{today}$**)**= today's hiring costs for unskilled workers plus today's training costs
Cost of hiring (hire$_{future}$**)**= future hiring costs for skilled workers
If **train**$_{today}$ < **hire**$_{future}$ → **firm-level training**
If **train**$_{today}$ > **hire**$_{future}$ → **hiring**

Figure 2.1 Costs of and decisions on training and recruitment
Source: Author, based on Oatey (1970); Lindley (1975); Merrilees (1983); Stevens (1994).

---

[1] There is also an additional cost that stem from new workers' integration into the firm and the induction provided to them.

high (Mohrenweiser and Zwick, 2009). Similarly, the risk of poaching, and hence labour turnover, is low for workers with specific skills, which reduces firms' training costs (Becker, 1993). As a result, firms needing specific skills are expected to recruit unskilled workers and train them in the firm (Becker, 1993). In contrast to specific skills, Becker (1993) argues, general skills can be used in different firms, and workers with general skills can be easily poached by other firms. This increases the turnover of workers with general skills and raises firms' training costs, thereby reducing firms' likelihood to offer training for general skills, and workers are expected to develop these skills themselves. As such, costs for hiring workers with general skills will be low because such workers will be available in the labour market, and, thus, firms needing general skills are expected to prefer hiring to training.

Firm size is another important factor that is argued to affect skilling costs according to labour economists studying firm-level skilling decisions. This is for three principal reasons. Firstly, hiring costs and the number of employees have a convex relationship while training costs and employee number have a concave relationship. This means that because large firms need to hire many workers at once, they may incur substantial costs for hiring skilled workers, as it will be difficult to find many workers already possessing the skills necessary for the firm (Dube, Freeman, and Reich, 2010; Blatter, Muehlemann, and Schenker, 2012; Muehlemann and Pfeifer, 2016). By contrast, the cost of training per worker will be lower when training a large group workers due to the increasing returns to scale (Blatter, Muehlemann, and Schenker, 2012; Bellmann et al., 2014). Secondly, because larger firms have more resources to dedicate to training, they can provide training also to improve the general skills of their workers, in addition to the specific ones, while training in small firms is usually oriented towards generating specific skills only. Thirdly, larger firms face lower risks of poaching, and firm-level training grants firms greater control over workers (Mares, 2003; Culpepper, 2007). As a consequence, it has been argued that large firms are more likely to prefer developing skills in the firm rather than hiring skilled workers (Culpepper, 2007). In contrast to large firms, small firms are argued to prefer hiring skilled workers because the cost of hiring is lower than training for these firms (Stevens, 1994; Culpepper, 2007; Muehlemann, Ryan, and Wolter, 2013; Blatter et al., 2016).

Worker wages and employee turnover constitute other important elements affecting firm-level skilling decisions. Firms may invest in training unskilled workers because they expect these workers to remain within the company and to have higher productivity in the future. It follows that firms will invest in training if they are confident that they will retain their trainees as skilled workers. Furthermore, firms may accept the costs of training unskilled workers in cases where they can pay lower wages to these workers (Dionisius et al., 2009; Bellmann et al., 2014). Through this they can recoup those additional labour costs stemming from the lower productivity of the trainees, as well as their cost to train them (Bellman et al., 2014). Table 2.1 summarises the arguments of labour economists regarding firm-level decisions on training and hiring.

Table 2.1 Firm-level factors of skilling activities

Skilling decision	Skill type		Skill level		Firm size		Wage difference		Worker turnover	
	specific	general	high	low	large	small	high	low	high	low
Train unskilled workers	x			x	x		x			x
Hire skilled workers		x	x			x		x	x	

2.1.1 Critique of the labour economics perspective on skill formation

While the arguments in the field of labour economics provide important insights about firm-level training and hiring decisions, they are not sufficient to understand the functioning of skill systems for several reasons, some of which are highlighted by the labour economists themselves. One line of critique relates to the complexity of calculating the costs and benefits of skilling, and the difficulty for firms to have full information on these aspects (Stevens, 1994; Ryan, 1998; Wenzelmann et al., 2015). As firms do not have all information that is required to measure their training and hiring costs, their skilling decisions are not based solely on cost calculations (Acemoglu, 1996; Acemoglu and Pischke, 1998, 1999). For example, although training may be costly for firms, especially when the labour turnover is high, firm-level training can increase workers' attachment to the company and reduce employee turnover, and thus firms' training costs, and encourage firms to train unskilled workers rather than hiring skilled ones (Muller and Jacob, 2008; Mohrenweiser and Zwick, 2009).

Another criticism is related to assumptions on skill types. In contrast to Becker's claims, it is not possible to make any clear or rigid distinction between specific and general skills, and hence about the costs of generating those skills. There are no skills that are either completely specific or general, and any training for a specific skill will also endow the trainee with certain general skills (Stevens, 1999). Furthermore, the specificity of skills does not always reflect the content or portability of skills. For instance, the possession of general skills does not necessarily correspond to having high skills, and these skills can also be gained through basic education, such as literacy skills (Fleckenstein, Saunders, and Seeleib-Kaiser, 2011; Streeck, 2012). Similarly, some specific skills, when they are in high demand, can bring important job mobility, such as in the case of brain surgeons who possess very specific skills but also enjoy high job mobility (Streeck, 2012).

The focus of labour economists on the firm only also creates important problems for their arguments on skilling strategies. Firms are not independent economic actors, and they do not operate in perfectly competitive markets but within national and global political and economic structures, which influence their skilling practices in distinct ways. There are national institutions which make the competition in labour markets imperfect and thus influence firms' skilling decisions. For example, collective bargaining structures affect wages and mobility of trainees and full-time employees and thus shape firms' hiring or training choices (Acemoglu and Pischke, 1998, 1999). Likewise, business chambers can resolve issues of collective action among employers and reduce the risk of poaching, which will increase firms' likelihood to train (Olson, 1965; Streeck, 1992b).

In addition to national institutional structures, the dynamics in the global economy will influence firms' skilling strategies. Many firms today have links with GVCs, where lead firms and governance structures in these chains shape the activities of all firms operating within these chains (Gereffi, Humphrey, and Sturgeon, 2005). For instance, global standards required by lead firms in GVCs, such as certification by the International Organisation for Standardisation (ISO), have been influencing the operations of supplier firms in these chains (Nadvi and Wältring, 2004). Similarly, linkages and power relations between lead firms and suppliers vary across different GVCs, which creates distinct mechanisms for the lead firms to influence the training and hiring practices of suppliers (Lakhani, Kuruvilla, and Avgar, 2013; Taylor, Newsome, and Rainnie, 2013; Zhu and Morgan, 2018).

2.1.2 The use of the labour economics approach in the book

Although the economic approach to training and hiring decisions suffers from important shortcomings, it is an important starting point to realise firms' concerns and expectations when training and hiring workers. Figure 2.2 summarises the firm-level calculations about training and hiring costs that affect firms' training and hiring decisions, which is the main use of this approach for the book. The book considers these dynamics when examining the skill systems to prevent any bias that may occur due to firm-level characteristics, such as firm size or skill type. This approach is then complemented with the research approaches that consider the impact of other micro- and macro-level dynamics on skill formation explained in the following sections.

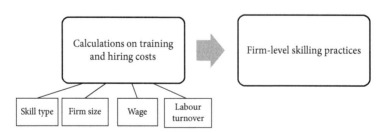

Figure 2.2 Firm-level dynamics and skilling practices

2.2 Institutions and skill formation

Firms and workers operate within wider societal structures, and these structures have substantial influence on the behaviour of both workers and firms. Societal structures have been the main focus of the CCs literature, which has investigated the evolution and complementarities of institutional arrangements in different countries, and examines how these arrangements affect actors and societies. Skill systems have been central in various strands of the CCs research, where the discussion has mainly focused on the variation of vocational education and training (VET) systems across countries (starting with Finegold and Soskice, 1988). In general, these researchers argue that national VET systems vary across countries due to the differences in societal structures that complement VET systems, and these structures have distinct influence on the behaviour of firms and workers, including their training, hiring, and employment preferences.

2.2.1 The institutionalist literature on skill systems and development

When studying the institutions that complement national VET systems and influence firms' skilling strategies, this book brings together two main strands within the CCs research: the comparative political economy of skill formation (CPEoSF) and the political economy of development. On the one hand, the former has provided an extensive analysis of skill systems but has focused on the case of advanced industrialised countries. On the other hand, the studies on the political economy of development have investigated the institutions that promote or prevent development in MICs, but have not provided an in-depth analysis on skill systems. Therefore, bringing these two strands together will be important when studying the national institutions that complement the skill systems in Mexico and Turkey, and their implications for development.

Before explaining the literature on the CPEoSF and political economy of development, it is important to discuss the term 'complementarity' and its meaning for this book. The use of 'complementarity' has been contentious in the institutionalist literature (Crouch et al., 2005; Deeg and Jackson, 2007; Lane and Wood, 2009, 2011). The discussions, and the disagreements, have concerned the origins of complementarities, their functioning, and their change. A major understanding of complementarity has been 'functionalist', which is the case in the varieties of capitalism (VoC) studies, where researchers build on rational choice theory and argue that institutions complement each other when 'one (or more) institution(s) [that] may enhance the effects of another institution (or of several others)' (Hall, 2005, p. 373). Others have criticised the functionalist view on institutions, and pointed out their contingency and dysfunctions (Crouch, 2005b; Wood and Frynas, 2006). For example, Crouch

(2005b) suggests that there may not always be a logic in the coexistence and 'complementarity' of institutions, and institutions that do not affect each other but form a 'whole' together can be complementarities of that whole. Jackson's (2005) approach towards 'complementarity', moreover, allows a multilevel understanding of complementarities. Jackson argues that complementarities between institutional domains (such as A and B) can take different forms: two domains influencing each other (A→B; B→A; making A and B complementary institutions), and two domains together influencing a third phenomenon ([A&B]→C, where A, B, and C are complementary) (2005, p. 378).

The aim of using the institutional approach in this book is to understand which institutions in Mexico and Turkey affect firms' skilling practices and how these institutions interact with one another. Therefore, this study goes beyond the functionalist approach to complementarity, and it adopts a comprehensive and multilevel approach, benefiting from the discussions of Crouch (2005) and Jackson (2005). Jackson's approach will be especially useful to recognise the complementarities of skill systems at macro, meso, and micro levels. At the macro-level, this approach will inform how different institutional domains, such as VET systems and labour regulations, influence each other. At the meso level, it will help us to realise the interactions between the macro-level institutions and GVC governance structures. Last, at micro-level, it will help to understand the implications of the macro- and meso-level domains for firms' skilling practices. Therefore, the macro, meso and micro-level domains complement one another, and become the complementarities of skill systems.

2.2.1.1 Institutional research on skill systems in advanced industrialised countires

The study of skill formation systems has constituted an important part in the CCs literature. In general, the studies on CCs argue that different capitalist systems lead to distinct skill systems due to specific institutional complementarities in those systems. The main institutions that complement skill systems include interfirm relations, labour unions, industrial relations, financial system, corporate governance structure, welfare system, innovation structure, and the state (Whitley, 1999, 2005; Schmidt, 2003, 2009; Hancke, Rhodes, and Thatcher, 2007; Hancke, 2009; Morgan et al., 2010). Amongst all institutions, those that resolve the coordination problems of firms and workers, namely business associations and labour unions, are particularly important for skill systems. This is because union structures and types of collective agreements affect the wage levels and mobility of different types of workers, and hence influence firms' training and hiring decisions (Franz and Soskice, 1995; Acemoglu and Pischke, 1999; Dionisius et al., 2009). Moreover, business associations, especially the all-encompassing ones, can resolve the coordination problems among firms and reduce the risk of poaching and noncompliance to training among firms (Streeck, 1997; Hall and Soskice, 2001).

According to researchers within the VoC tradition, different institutional complementarities lead to skill systems with distinct comparative advantages. These researchers argue that there are strong VET systems in coordinated market economies (CMEs) due to the institutional arrangements that facilitate 'strategic coordination' between different actors. It is argued that the strategic coordination in CMEs creates 'beneficial constraints' and leads to skill system that generates mainly industry- or firm-specific skills (Streeck, 1991, 1997; Hall and Soskice, 2001). Therefore, these researchers argue that CMEs have advanced in 'diversified quality production' and have developed comparative advantage in sectors requiring more specific skills such as the manufacturing of medium-technology intensive goods (Streeck, 1991; Hall and Soskice, 2001). In contrast, coordination in 'liberal market economies' (LMEs) is market-based, which results in skill systems generating more general skills. This is argued to bring comparative advantage in sectors that require general skills, such as the high-tech software industries (Hall and Soskice, 2001). The main examples of CMEs in the VoC literature have been Germany and Japan, which grew substantially in the 1970s and 1980s and challenged the LMEs, namely the United States and the UK (Streeck, 1997; Sorge and Streeck, 2018).

Although the arguments of the VoC studies have received several aspects of criticism, such as the functionality of institutions and its inability to explain change, the VoC literature provides important insights for understanding the role of national institutions for skill systems. Indeed, later studies in the VoC strand have responded to many aspects of the criticism. The Growth Models Perspective, which is the more recent research in the CCs tradition, has constituted an important body of research for addressing several shortcomings of the VoC studies, particularly their 'static' approach to institutions and complementarities, and the role of politics for institutions. These studies also include skill systems in their analysis, although at a much lesser extent compared to the original VoC, and argue that 'consumption-led growth' models create 'favourable' conditions for unskilled workers, while 'export-oriented' growth models require a greater number of workers with better skills (Baccaro and Pontusson, 2016).

The research on the CPEoSF forms the main body of research focusing on skill systems within the CCs tradition, which provides several insights about the development of skill systems in advanced industrialised countries, as well as the outcomes of these skill systems. Bringing together the firm-centred research on VoC and labour unions-centred research on welfare systems (Esping-Andersen, 1990; Pontusson, 2005), the researchers of the CPEoSF literature investigate the political economic dynamics that lead to distinct skill systems in advanced economies, and the socioeconomic consequences of these skill systems. The work of Kathleen Thelen and Marius Busemeyer has made important contributions to our understanding in this regard. Thelen (2004) focuses on the state's 'bureaucratic' role and discusses the state as one of the key actors, along with businesses and labour unions, who have led to distinct VET systems in Germany, the United States, the UK, and Japan.

Busemeyer and Trampusch (2012b) provide a comprehensive discussion on the state's commitment to and firms' involvement in distinct VET systems in advanced industrialised countries and explain the differences between countries that are classified as CMEs in the VoC literature. They define four neuralgic points for analysing the VET systems: the state's commitment to and firms' involvement in (i) providing VET, (ii) financing VET, and (iii) controlling VET, as well as (iv) the permeability between VET and general education. According to these authors, VET systems with higher state commitment, and lower firm involvement, such as the one in Sweden, lead to 'statist' VET systems that generate more general skills compared to 'collectivist' VET systems with lower state commitment but higher firm involvement, like in Germany (Busemeyer and Trampusch, 2012b). Countries with low state commitment and low firm involvement, such as the UK and United States, are defined as 'liberal' VET systems, whilst low state commitment and high firm involvement are argued to lead to 'segmentatlist' VET systems, like in Japan. Thelen (2014) adds the continuing-VET systems to the initial-VET programmes to the analysis by Busemeyer and Trampusch (2012b), and relabels the categories, although the example countries remain the same. Other studies in this tradition also have pointed out the 'political' role of the state, in addition to the 'bureaucratic' one, and emphasised the importance of electoral systems and partisan coalitions for distinct VET systems (Iversen and Stephens, 2008; Dobbins and Busemeyer, 2015). Lastly, the different skill formation systems have been linked to varying levels of income inequality in advanced economies (Estevez-Abe, Iversen, and Soskice, 2001; Busemeyer, 2014; Busemeyer and Iversen, 2014).

2.2.1.2 Institutional research on MICs

Research with the CCs approach provides important insights about the national political economies of skill systems in rich, advanced industrialised countries while overlooking the case of late industrialisers including the MICs. Focusing their analysis on ideal types of capitalism, many researchers in the VoC literature have described countries outside the CME or LME archetypes as 'mixed-market economies' with 'weak', 'fluid', 'less mature', or 'not perfectly coupled' institutional structures (Hall and Soskice, 2001; Hall and Gingerich, 2009; Lane and Wood, 2011; Demirbag et al., 2014; Dibben et al., 2017; Singh et al., 2017; Wilkinson and Wood, 2017; Fainshmidt et al., 2018). They have argued that the mixed-market economies will have lower levels of economic growth compared to the countries with perfectly complementary institutions, and have focused their empirical analysis on the latter (Hall and Soskice, 2001; Hall and Gingerich, 2009).

The paucity of studies on the countries in the Eastern and Southern Hemispheres of the world creates important challenges for the CCs literature and has been defined as 'one of the major shortfalls of the existing literature' (Wood and Frynas, 2006; Wood, Dibben, and Ogden, 2013; Wilkinson, Wood, and Deeg, 2014a). Furthermore, the term 'mixed-market economies' includes a wide range of countries with diverse institutional structures, political struggles, and experiences of internationalisation, economic growth and social development, making the arguments of the CCs litera-ture on ideal models seem incapable of accounting for the capitalist systems in most of the world. Many countries that are outside of the ideal types have developed their own institutional structures and have complementarities of their own, which will shape the labour market dynamics and affect the costs of training and hiring in dis-tinct ways (Brewster, Mayrhofer, and Cooke, 2015; Horwitz and Budhwar, 2015; Witt et al., 2018). A few studies in the regulation school and business studies have included some of the later industrialising countries, and developed new typologies for these countries. For instance, Amable (2003) includes some Asian and South European countries and develops five types of capitalist structures. Later studies in the CCs literature define the Central and Eastern European countries as 'dependent market economies', where the economy is heavily reliant on MNCs (Nölke and Vliegentart, 2009), the East Asian countries as 'familial capitalism' (Carney, Gedajlovic, and Yang, 2009; Steier, 2009; Tipton, 2009), and the Latin American countries as hierarchical market economies (Schneider, 2009b; Schneider and Soskice, 2009).

Despite the abovementioned studies, research on later industrialising countries in the CCs literature remained rather limited until the 2010s—especially the late 2010s, when the rapid economic growth of emerging market economies (EMEs) led to curiosity about the capitalist systems of these countries. Several monographs and edited volumes have been published focusing on in-depth analysis of certain EMEs (Bohle and Greskovits, 2012; Walter and Zhang, 2012; Becker, 2013; Schneider, 2013a; Nölke, 2014; Witt and Redding, 2014; Bizberg, 2015b, 2019; Demirbag and Wood, 2018; Nölke et al., 2019). In addition to the work with a regional focus on Central and Eastern Europe, Latin America, and East Asia, a few studies with a quantitative approach have carried out cross-regional comparisons. In 2020, the prominent journal *New Political Economy* dedicated a special section on CCs in EMEs and discussed the strengths and blind spots in the CCs literature in this regard (Wood and Schnyder, 2021).

The role of the state has constituted a common focus in the recent discussions on CCs in EMEs. While some of the earlier research on EMEs has overlooked the role of the state, the economic growth of countries with different forms of state involve-ment in the economy, particularly China, India, and Russia, has pushed many researchers to discuss the state's role in capitalist systems.

Previous studies on governance and development have argued that even though many late industrialisers have strict regulations, there have been issues with their implementation due to the capacity or willingness of the state in these countries (Bhagwati, 1995; Elliott and Freeman, 2003; Estache and Wren-Lewis, 2009). Focusing on the state's ownership of certain industries, regulation of markets, indus-trial policies, and relations with different socio-political groups, the recent studies with the CCs approach have come up with new models of capitalism including 'state capitalism', 'state-permeated capitalism', 'authoritarian capitalism', 'crony capitalism', 'patrimonial capitalism', and 'international outsourcing capitalism' to describe different types of state involvement such as the 'developmental state' and the 'predatory state' (Schlumberger, 2008; Sánchez-Ancochea, 2009; Robinson, 2011; Becker, 2013; Buhr and Frankenberger, 2014; Carney and Witt, 2014; Becker and Vasileva, 2017; Bizberg, 2019; Nölke et al., 2019; Alami and Dixon, 2020; Allen et al., 2021; Sallai and Schnyder, 2021; Schedelik et al., 2021). In fact, the role of the state has been a main point of controversy in the CCs literature for a long time, including the studies about advanced industrialised countries. While the earlier work of VoC has overlooked the state's role in capitalist systems, some researchers in the CCs tradition, and particularly that on national business systems and regulation theory, have argued that the state has a key role in capitalist systems leading to variation between them (Hollingsworth and Boyer, 1997; Whitley, 1999, 2005; Amable, 2003). The state is argued to have a key role in capitalist structures though not only its involvement in markets, but also its *power to intervene* and its *encouragement of intermediary organisations* (Crouch, Finegold, and Sako, 1999; Whitley, 1999; Schmidt, 2003; Deeg and Jackson, 2007).

Notwithstanding the growing literature on the capitalist systems of late industrialisers, and the state's role in them, there is still very little research on the *skill systems* of these countries. Most institutionalist research on late industrialisers focus on other institutions, such as financial systems and state-business relations, while many late industrialisers such as those in Latin America are argued to be in a 'low-skills bad-jobs trap' (Schneider, 2009b, 2013a; Schneider and Soskice, 2009; Schneider and Karcher, 2010), or have a 'low-wage regime with an education system in which the vast majority of the population receives only a secondary education and enjoys only a low level of class mobility' (Nölke et al., 2015, p. 562). This description is oversimplistic and cannot account for the variation of skill systems between different EMEs or MICs, which has led to different social, political, and economic dynamics in these countries. For instance, for Mexico and Turkey, although the education statistics may be similar at first instance with similar levels of enrolment, a more detailed analysis shows important differences between the two countries, such as the very different shares of VET within upper-secondary education (Sancak, 2020). Similarly, Jürgens and Krzywdzinski (2016) show that the different VET systems in Brazil, Russia, India, and China play an important role in the varying employment practices within these countries.

There are a few recent studies that form important exceptions to the neglect of skill systems in the research on late-industrialising countries. The recent contribution of Doner and Schneider (2016, 2020) on the politics of the middle-income trap links the lack of improvement in skill systems in MICs with the institutional structures in these countries. They argue that in many MICs, the economy has been dominated by national conglomerates and international MNCs, which have developed competitive advantage thanks to state subsidies and low labour costs in these countries, while they have the capacity to provide firm-level training when necessary. These businesses, moreover, have been the most organised political actors with links to the state, and they have preferred policies that keep labour costs down, and have not created pressures on governments to increase investment in the public education and training systems (Doner and Schneider, 2016). The groups that would push for state investment in education and training, including workers and SMEs (Thelen, 2004; Culpepper, 2007), have not possessed the necessary means to organise and represent their interests in many MICs, leading to weak VET systems in these countries (Doner and Schneider, 2016). Others have focused on the countries that have managed to develop vocational and general education policies, namely Turkey and Malaysia, and have emphasised the importance of political alliances between the governing political party, SMEs, and labour market outsiders, and the role of persistent governments for the development of education policies in MICs (Doner and Schneider, 2020; Sancak, 2020).

2.2.2 The shortcomings of the CCs literature

The CCs approach has provided important insights for understanding the complementarities and varieties of national skill systems However, this approach contains two main shortcomings that would prevent us from fully understanding multilevel skill systems. This subsection focuses on two aspects of criticism related to studying multilevel skill systems, which are addressed in this book through the cross-fertilisation of the CCs approach with the other fields of study (for a more comprehensive discussion on the institutionalist research and its critique, see Deeg and Jackson, 2007).

Firstly, because of its focus on the complementarities of skill systems *within only national contexts*, the CCs approach does not consider how the dynamics in the global economy, such as the *connectedness between firms across nations*, influence skill systems. With the abolishment of barriers on the movement of capital, many firms, especially those from advanced industrialised countires, have shifted (some of) their activities to new locations while keeping the others in home locations. This shift has led to a global division of labour, forming GVCs/global production networks (Gereffi and Korzeniewicz, 1994; Gereffi, Humphrey, and Sturgeon, 2005; Henderson et al., 2002; Coe et al., 2004). Therefore, the way the national economies—and the firms from these economies—are integrated into the world economy will influence the capitalist systems and firms within these countries. In the global economy, firms operate not at national level only, but at 'multiple spatial scales' including regional, national, and international ones (Dicken et al., 2001). Indeed, the regulation school, which forms a key strand of the CCs research, has emphasised the multiple scales of economic activity and the hierarchy between the institutional realms (Hollingsworth and Boyer, 1997; Boyer, 2005; Boyer and Saillard, 2005; Jessop and Sum, 2006; Jessop, 2011, 2015). Nonetheless, there has been very limited empirical research on MICs following such an approach, which continues to be an important void in the literature. There are a few recent studies that address this issue and consider the integration of national economies to the global economy as a key determinant of national capitalist structures in EMEs (Nölke and Vliegenthart, 2009; Bizberg, 2019; Schedelik et al., 2021). Nonetheless, these studies have focused on the impact of 'openness' or 'closedness' to the global economy, without explaining the *content of connection* with the global economy. While countries' openness/closedness is important, it is not sufficient to understand their links with the global economy and the impact of these links on the countries, and firms and workers within these countries. For instance, the types of products being produced in and exported from a country and different governance structures adopted in different GVCs are important to determine the place of these countries in the global economic hierarchy. More specifically, for example, the links of countries exporting commodities and those exporting manufactured products within the global economy will be very different, leading to distinct influences of globalisation on these countries and their development experiences.

The second shortcoming of the CCs literature is that the researchers have been 'overly concerned with explaining institutions and institutional processes, [...] rather than with using them to explain and understand organizations' (Greenwood, Hinings, and Whetten, 2014, p. 1206; Lakhani, Kuruvilla, and Avgar, 2013; Wilkinson, Wood, and Deeg, 2014b; Hotho and Saka-Helmhout, 2017). Even though the researchers of the CCs literature claim that their unit of analysis is the firm, and they aim to understand the linkages between national institutions and firm behaviour, their empirical research on the latter has been limited. These researchers have rather focused on studying the macro-level institutions, interactions between these institutions, and the implications of these institutions measured through macro-level indicators such as growth in gross domestic product and the Gini index on inequality. Nevertheless, they have been much less occupied with explaining how these institutions are interpreted and experimented with at the level of the firm, which would influence the 'feedback' to those institutions, and hence bring institutional change due to endogenous pressures (Allen, 2004, 2013; Crouch, 2005a; Morgan, 2007; Kristensen and Morgan, 2012a; Wood, Dibben, and Ogden, 2013; Wilkinson, Wood, and Deeg, 2014b).

2.2.3 The use of the institutional approach in this book

Despite its shortcomings, the institutional approach in the CCs is helpful to understand which national institutions influence firms' skilling strategies. These studies are also useful to analyse the state's direct and indirect role in skill systems, and to draw linkages between national institutional structures and their implications for high-road development. This book uses the four neuralgic points developed by Busemeyer and Trampusch (2012) when analysing the public VET systems in Mexico and Turkey. Unlike Busemeyer and Trampusch (2012a), who focus only on initial-VET (IVET), the analysis in this book also investigates continuing-VET (CVET) programmes, including the public retraining programmes (for the

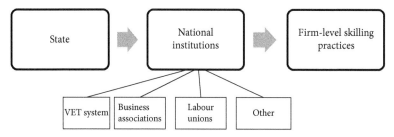

Figure 2.3 National institutions and skilling practices

unemployed) and skill standardisation and certification systems.[2] This is because CVET is increasingly becoming a key mechanism for skill formation in the postindustrial era and should be studied when understanding skill systems (Thelen, 2014). The other divergence of this book from the CPEoSF literature is the inclusion of 'other institutions', which have not been in the focus of this literature (Figure 2.3).

In addition to the tools for analysing the public VET systems, the discussions on complementarity in the CCs literature helps to examine the multilevel complementarities of the multilevel skill systems. Particularly, the discussion is helpful to realise how different institutions (A and B, such as VET system and business associations) become complementarities because they influence a third phenomenon (C, such as the firm-level hiring and training practices) (Jackson, 2005); and how different institutions are complementary to each other not because they affect each other, as it is claimed in the functionalist approach to complementarity, but they form the parts of a 'whole' together (such as the skill system) (Crouch, 2005b).

2.3 GVCs and impact on firm practices

This book benefits from the studies on GVCs in order to understand how countries and firms with variegated forms of integration into the global economy influence their capitalist systems, and the outcomes of these systems for workers and firms. The GVC literature is important for this as it focuses on different governance structures in GVCs, which then affect the firms in these chains in distinct ways. This literature starts with Gereffi and Korzeniewicz's (1994) prominent work on global commodity chains (GCCs), which is based on the world systems theory and emphasises the linkages between firms in global production, where the output of one node of the chain constitutes the input of the next one. These researchers argue that with globalisation, '[t]he way firms do business in the global economy […] is determined to an increasing extent by their position in GCCs, not their national origins' (Gereffi

---

[2] Although the skill standardisation system is not a method for developing skills by itself, it is important to discuss it as part of the public VET system because it constitutes a critical part in lifelong learning, determines who has the control over VET and skills, and influences workers' mobility (Busemeyer, 2015b).

and Korzeniewicz, 1994, p. 433). The term 'global commodity chain' was replaced with 'global value chain' in later work (Gereffi, Humphrey, and Sturgeon, 2005) which has introduced the transaction cost economics into the analysis and has paid more attention to the 'value' created in each node of a production chain. The work on global production networks (GPNs), however, criticises the focus on linear linkages between supplier and buyer firms in GVC studies and gives attention to both horizontal and vertical links between firms in the global economy (Dicken et al., 2001; Henderson et al., 2002).[3]

The researchers of GVCs argue that there are three main elements that determine the governance structures across value chains, which then shape the activities of firms throughout these chains. These three elements are (i) the sector of economic activity, (ii) the complexity of products and codifiability of product information, and (iii) the capacities of supplier firms (Gereffi, Humphrey, and Sturgeon, 2005). These researchers emphasise the role of power dynamics in GVCs and argue that GVCs are 'governed' by lead firms, which are 'a group of firms in a particular functional position (or positions) [that are] able to shape who does what along the chain (and at what price, using what standards, to which specifications and delivering at what time)' (Ponte and Gibbon, 2005, p. 5).[4] Therefore, the three elements shaping governance structures and lead firms governing these chains become the main determinants of activities throughout GVCs, including the activities of supplier firms in lower tiers.

Gereffi et al. (2005) suggest five types of GVCs, each with a different governance structure and degree of influence on suppliers. The first type is *market-based chains*, where products are simple and easily codified, relations between suppliers and buyers are at arms-length, and suppliers do not need much guidance from lead firms. The second type is *modular value chains*, where products are specialised and more complex than those in market-based chains, but are easily codified. Suppliers are capable of carrying out the necessary activities while they are required to comply with certain international standards relevant to their industry. These lead to arms-length relations between suppliers and lead firms, and hence a low level of lead-firm influence over suppliers (Gereffi, Humphrey, and Sturgeon, 2005). The third type of governance in GVC is *relational*. Production along these chains is more complex and

---

[3] This book adopts the term 'GVC' when exploring the impact of firms' linkages with the global economy since it aims to understand the influence of relations between *suppliers* and *lead firms*, and how the dynamics of power relations between the two affect suppliers' skilling activities. This is not to deny that the supplier firms' horizontal links with other firms may influence their activities. Additionally, while the GVC approach may give a static view on value chains and relations across the chains, this term is useful for the book, which aims to realise the impact of relations between the suppliers and buyers *at a certain point in time*, namely when this study was conducted—while I acknowledge these relations could have been different in the past and can change in the future.

[4] It is important to point what is meant with the terms 'lead firms' and 'multinational corporations' (MNCs). While before 'MNC' would signify a company that has assets in more than one country, the definition has changed based on GVCs, and now 'MNC' means a firm that coordinates and controls operations in more than one country, although they may not necessarily have assets in the other countries (Dicken, 2007).

requires a high level of tacit knowledge, which necessitates close cooperation between suppliers and lead firms (Sturgeon, Biesebroeck, and Gereffi, 2008; Plum and Hassink, 2011). The cooperation between suppliers and lead firms brings inter-dependence between these firms, and both parties can influence the activities of the other. Fourth, in *captive chains*, production is highly complex and easily codifiable, but suppliers' capacity is low. Therefore, buyers have important power over the sup-pliers in these chains via monitoring and controlling (Gereffi, Humphrey, and Sturgeon, 2005). Finally, *hierarchical value chains* relate predominantly to firms' in-house activities carried out by separate divisions, such as the research and develop-ment centres of MNCs (Gereffi, Humphrey, and Sturgeon, 2005). The products in these chains are highly complex and difficult to codify, which causes these activities to remain mostly in-house, under the heavy control of lead firms.

The governance structures and lead firms of GVCs can influence suppliers' skill-ing practices through two main ways. Firstly, they can affect these practices directly, through regulations about and intervening in supplier firms' HRM practices (Okada, 2004). Secondly, the GVC governance structures can influence suppliers' skilling practices indirectly through their general expectations from the suppliers, such as the expectations about the quality and price of the product, which will then affect suppliers' skill needs and thus their methods to address those needs.

2.3.1 Critique of the GVC literature

The literature on GVCs provides important insights about the functioning of the global economy, the power dynamics between lead and supplier firms, and the out-comes of these dynamics. Nonetheless, this line of research has three main short-comings, among other ones, for it to explain the role of these chains for skill systems in MICs. The first is related to the neglect of national institutional structures in the analysis of lead firms' and suppliers' economic activity. While the debates on GPNs consider firms as actors embedded in local, national, global, and political contexts, there is limited empirical research on the impact of national institutions together with GVC governance structures. Although firms compete in a global economy, which creates important pressures on their activities, they still operate within national and even regional contexts. However, the studies on GVCs do not consider the role of national institutions in their focus on governance structures in these chains.

The second shortcoming of GVC studies is related to the neglect of studies on the impact of GVCs on the activities of supplier firms in *lower tiers of these chains* (Quintanilla and Ferner, 2003; Morgan and Hull Kristensen, 2006; Brewster et al., 2007; Lane and Probert, 2009; Kristensen and Morgan, 2012b). In fact, the majority of GVC studies have focused on *lead firms* and *their* strategies to manage supply chains, while the empirical research on supplier firms has taken a backseat. Similarly, the very few studies investigating the interactions between national institutions and

GVC governance structures have centred their analysis on lead firms and these firms' home countries (Lane and Probert, 2009). Nevertheless, research on *suppliers' institutional environment* and the influence of this environment on supplier firms' activities is very limited. The capacity of lead firms to influence suppliers will depend in no small measure upon the suppliers' home country institutions as 'being located in specific institutional contexts [...] [which will] provide particular sorts of resources [...] that shape how the firm can participate in particular global supply chains' (Zhu and Morgan, 2018, p. 511). For instance, it has been argued that in locations with tighter institutional complementarities, lead firms would have fewer mechanisms to influence supplier activities while suppliers will have less room to manoeuvre in their activities when addressing lead firms' expectations, as compared with suppliers in locations with looser complementarities (Rosenberg, 1992). Similarly, the governance structures in supply chains can be supplementary or complementary to national institutions, resulting in different supplier activities in these chains (Locke, 2013; Zhu and Morgan, 2018).

Such disregard of supplier firms and the institutions surrounding them have left an important gap in the GVC studies for two main reasons. On the one hand, not considering the suppliers' institutional environment prevents these studies from fully understanding how GVC structures can influence suppliers' activities, as these structures will have different influence on suppliers in different contexts. On the other hand, the focus of the GVC literature mainly on lead firms and top-down governance structures limits these studies' ability to explain the activities of firms from MICs because most firms from MICs participate in GVCs as suppliers in lower tiers, and these firms have very different experiences of globalisation from advanced industrialised nations. Although there are several studies about the impact of GVCs upon local firms' learning and upgrading opportunities in the literature on international development, as well as the impact of GVC governance on working conditions in suppliers, research on how the governance structures and lead firms in GVCs affect local firms' skilling practices has been very limited (Okada, 2004; Ramirez and Rainbird, 2010; Lakhani, Kuruvilla, and Avgar, 2013).

The third main shortcoming of the GVC studies is about their macro-level focus, as is the case for the CCs literature. The research on GVCs has mainly been occupied with defining different value chain structures, and '[a]lthough the firm is clearly—and explicitly—the central actor in all analyses it is, invariably, treated as a black box [...] [A]ll of the attention in the GPN/GVC literature focuses upon interfirm relationships to the almost total neglect of intrafirm relationships and of the ways in which the internal structures and relationships inside firms play a critical role in how GPNs [or GVCs] operate and have their impact' (Coe, Dicken, and Hess, 2008, p. 277). Although the research on the influence of GVC governance structures on casualisation and feminisation of labour, and wages and work conditions in lower tiers has been important exemptions addressing this gap (Barrientos and Kritzinger, 2004; Nadvi, 2004; Dolan, 2005; Crane et al., 2019), the focus on labour conditions has not been sufficient to explain how the pressures in GVCs are interpreted at the firm level and affect their skilling practices, given that these firms operate in a distinct institutional environment and will act differently.

There have been a small number of recent studies focusing on the interactions between GVC governance structures and firm-level employment relations (Ramirez and Rainbird, 2010; Lakhani, Kuruvilla, and Avgar, 2013; Wood, Dibben, and Meira, 2016; Zhu and Morgan, 2018; Wright and Kaine, 2015). The article by Lakhani et al. (2013) is an important one in this regard, where the authors suggest a 'configurational framework' to explain the influence of both GVCs and national institutions on suppliers' employment relations. The authors argue that the activities of supplier firms will be shaped by three sets of factors: the nature of the task requirements (as discussed in the literature on GVC governance), the lead firms in GVCs (and their home country institutions), and local firms' institutional environment. For example, because the level of coordination between the lead firm and supplier is limited in market-based GVCs and the tasks are not complex, lead firms' influence on suppliers' ESs are expected to be low (Lakhani et al., 2013). Instead, supplier firms and their national institutional environment will be the main determinants of training and hiring practices in these chains.

The configurational framework by Lakhani et al. (2013) makes a significant contribution for understanding both the complex interactions between global and national economies and their impact on employment systems of supplier firms. Nonetheless, there are two main issues in the framework that warrant careful consideration. Firstly, the authors view suppliers as a single homogenous group and do not consider the tier of suppliers or the role of institutional arrangements in supplier countries, which creates serious problems for their arguments. Suppliers' operations will vary depending on their tier of activity *and* their home country institutions. With respect to their tier of activity, the influence of lead firms on suppliers' behaviour will be different for firms at the lower and upper ends of value chains (Cattaneo et al., 2013). Furthermore, the capacity of lead firms to influence suppliers will depend in no small measure upon the suppliers' home country institutions. In locations with tighter institutional complementarities, suppliers will have less room to manoeuvre in their activities—as compared with suppliers in locations with looser complementarities—when addressing lead firms' expectations (Rosenberg, 1992). Furthermore, the lead firms may also shape their expectations from suppliers according to the institutional structures in supplier locations. For instance, the presence of a public VET system in Brazil has had a significant impact on the hiring and training practices of a Volkswagen plant in this country (Jürgens and Krzywdzinski, 2016).

Secondly, Lakhani et al. (2013) provide a general framework about lead firms' influence on suppliers' ESs, yet they do not discuss the *characteristics* or *strength* of this influence. For instance, the authors argue that in relational chains, both lead firms and local institutions will affect suppliers' employment relations. Similarly, bringing the GVC literature together with the institutional approaches to studying employment systems, Zhu and Morgan (2018) argue that the 'combination of [...] pressures from the global supply chains and the local institutional environments create potential gaps between *what is required and expected by the lead firms* and *what is feasible within the supplier firms given the resources and constraints in their local institutional environments*' (pp. 511–12, emphasis is mine). While these studies provide important insights to understanding the intersections between GVC governance and firm-level employment relations, the authors discuss employment relations in general and do not specify the impact of global and national dynamics on *skilling practices*, namely recruitment, training and employee development, as compared with other elements of employment relations. The impact of GVC governance can vary across different elements of employment relations, such as industrial relations and training, depending on the institutional environment surrounding the firms (Jürgens and Krzywdzinski, 2016). For instance, Jürgens and Krzywdzinski (2016) show that the influence of global OEMs on industrial relations has been much more limited in their subsidiaries in the BRIC (Brazil, Russia, India, China) countries while the headquarters had more control over shop floor organisation in those plants.

2.3.2 The use of the GVC approach in this book

This book utilises the approach in the GVC literature in its exploration of how Turkish and Mexican firms' operations in auto parts-automotive value chains (AACs) affect their skilling practices, and thus become a part of the multilevel skill systems. Through studying the functioning of global AACs and the governance structures in these chains, the book discovers *in what ways* and *how much* these governance structures pressurise the supplier firms. Centring the analysis on local firms at lower tiers of GVCs, the book explains how the governance structures in GVCs influence firm-level skilling practices both directly, through affecting suppliers' hiring and training activities, and indirectly, through shaping suppliers' skill needs. Figure 2.4 summarises the incorporation of the GVC research into this book.

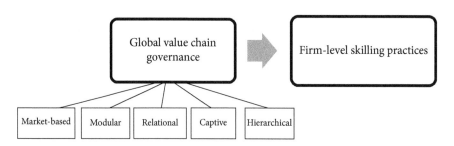

Figure 2.4 GVCs and skilling practices

2.4 The micro-level approach: firm-level skilling strategies and their outcomes

A common criticism towards both the CCs literature and studies on GVCs is their overlook to how macro-level institutions and governance structures are interpreted and reacted to at firm level, namely *what really goes on inside the firm*. To address this issue, this book incorporates the micro-level approach of organisation studies and international business literature which focus on the behaviour of firms and the elements that influence this behaviour (Muller, 1994; Harzing and Sorge, 2003; Tempel and Walgenbach, 2007; Brumana and Delmestri, 2012; Quack, 2016). Particularly the studies on ESs and HRM are key for this book since they focus on firms' hiring, training, and employee development practices, in addition to other firm-level employment practices—such as pay structures and firm-level industrial relations. Therefore, this book draws from the studies on ESs and HRM to develop better insights into how national institutions and governance mechanisms in GVCs are interpreted at firm level and affect firms' behaviour, whether institutions continue to determine firms' activity, and whether it is possible to observe a convergence of behaviour between firms in different national contexts but with comparable links to GVCs. The micro-level analysis also helps to assess the outcomes of different skill systems for workers and firms—such as through understanding the skill profile of firms' employees and realising different workers' career development prospects—and thus, it will be useful to draw inferences about the development implications of skill systems.

2.4.1 Convergence and divergence of firm-level skilling practices

The studies on ESs and HRM comprise several distinct, and contrasting, arguments about the determinants and outcomes of firm-level training regarding the commonalities and differences of skilling practices across nations, industries, and firms. The main two camps in these discussions include those claiming the global *convergence* of HRM practices and those arguing the persistence of *variation* of HRM systems between countries, regions, and cultures.

2.4.1.1 Convergence of employment practices

The convergence argument, in general, maintains that the employment practices of firms across the world are becoming similar due to globalisation production and consumption. This *globalist* camp includes both pessimistic and optimistic arguments about the convergence of employment practices. According to the *pessimists*, the rise of GVCs and governance structures in these chains leads to a 'race to the bottom' in employment practices, with frequent labour exploitation and minimal investment in workers' skills (Moody, 1997). This has been extensively studied by the researchers of labour standards in GVCs, and particularly the workers in the supply chains of MNCs.[5] Many researchers in this area have argued that the governance gaps in global supply chains, and the unequal power balances between MNCs, developing country states, and the developing country supplier firms often result in feminisation and exploitation of workers in supplier firms (Barrientos, Dolan, and Tallontire, 2003; Phillips, 2013; Rubery, 2015). Similar to the MNCs' impact on the workers in supply chains, the researchers focusing on the practices of MNC subsidiaries have emphasised the power of these firms to disseminate 'hard HRM strategies' that include contingent employment and anti-union practices (Cooke et al., 2019, p. 68).

In contrast to the pessimists, the *optimists*, including researchers mainly in the strategic HRM literature, argue that globalisation, increased competition, and technological advancements will lead to convergence towards HRM 'best practices', and namely High-Performance Work Systems (HPWSs) (MacDuffie, 1995; Ohmae, 1995; Appelbaum, 2000). Focusing on transaction costs, these researchers argue that the 'logics of industrialization produce common values, beliefs and systems of organization despite different ideologies, politics and cultures' (Brewster and Mayrhofer, 2009, p. 286). Since the HRM best practices—or 'the good HRM'—are argued to be the optimal practices that will help firms to achieve their goals and 'organisational effectiveness', firms are expected to develop similar HRM strategies regardless of their location (Wright and McMahan, 1992; Schuler and Jackson, 2008, 2014).

According to the optimistic globalists, the HRM best practices will diffuse across the world through several channels, in which MNCs have the major role (Meyer, 2000; Cooke et al., 2019).[6] An important way for the MNCs to trigger the convergence towards 'good HRM' is argued to be the management strategies implemented by the MNC headquarters in their subsidiaries, and the extensive research in the international HRM literature has argued that global MNCs have standardised HRM strategies across their subsidiaries in different locations (Muller, 1994; MacDuffie and Helper, 1997; Jürgens and Krzywdzinski, 2016). Furthermore, MNCs are argued to affect the HRM practices of firms elsewhere also indirectly. For example, MNCs' interactions with firms from or in other locations, such as those in their supply

---

[5] Here, the term 'MNC' is used for both companies with subsidiaries in other countries and lead firms in GVCs, which may not necessarily have subsidiaries but are multinational—or *transnational*—because they operate in more than one national territory.

[6] There are additional ways of spreading HRM 'best practices'. For instance, many suppliers from late industrialisers use global consultancy services for HRM to meet the demands within GVCs and improve their performance, which has resulted in extensive adoption of similar HRM practices in different locations (Lakhani et al., 2013). Similarly, management education programmes across the world have been promoting the standard HRM practices as 'best practices', and the individuals completing such training usually implement these methods when they are employed as HR managers or employees in HR departments (Jürgens and Krzywdzinski, 2016). Supranational institutions such as the European Foundation for the Improvement of Living and Working Conditions, as well as rating agencies, are argued to facilitate the convergence of HRM strategies towards HRM 'best practices' for increasing competitiveness (Meyer, 2000; Brewster and Mayrhofer, 2009; Jürgens and Krzywdzinski, 2016).

chains, can result in a spill-over of their practices to the firms they interact with (Okada, 2004; Nathan and Kaplana, 2007; Jensen, 2009; Cattaneo et al., 2013; Wood, Dibben, and Meira, 2016). MNC practices can spread to other firms in host locations also through expatriation or the turnover of the managers, who can transfer MNC HRM practices to local firms (Contreras, Carrillo, and Alonso, 2012).

The auto parts-automotive industry (AAI) has been one of the most notable industries to be influenced by globalisation and the convergence pressures on HRM practices due to the mechanisms already mentioned. It has been argued that the convergence in the AAI has been expected to be towards HPWSs, and not a race to the bottom, because of the requirements of this industry (Pil and MacDuffie, 1996; Appelbaum, 2000): the responsibilities of workers in mass production and lean manufacturing diverge greatly, and as more firms shift from mass to lean production in the AAI, they are expected to change their ESs too, and adopt HPWSs (Womack, Jones, and Roos, 1990; Kenney and Florida, 1993; MacDuffie, 1995; Pil and MacDuffie, 1996; Appelbaum, 2000; Lawler and Hundley, 2008; Frege and Kelly, 2013; Katz and Wailes, 2014; Jürgens, Malsch, and Dohse, 1993). In mass production, operations of firms are labour intensive and require low-cost workers without complex skills (MacDuffie, 1995; MacDuffie and Kochan, 1995). Hence, the shop floor is hierarchically organised while employer-employee relations are at arms-length, and work contracts are short-term (MacDuffie, 1995). In contrast to mass production, lean production systems require ESs characterised by higher and more polyvalent worker skills, as these firms need to quickly respond to the changes in the global economy and keep up with technological developments (MacDuffie, 1995). Therefore, the studies concerning the AAI argue that as globalisation and competition intensify, firms move away from mass to lean production, which is expected to lead to the convergence towards HPWSs in the global AAI (MacDuffie and Kochan, 1995; Jürgens and Krzywdzinski, 2016).

2.4.1.2 Divergence of ESs

In contrast to the globalists, several studies within the comparative HRM, international HRM, and ESs literature maintain the diversity of firm-level HRM practices due to the variation in national institutions, regional contexts, and cultural attitudes (Hofstede, 1980; House et al., 2004; Wilkinson, Wood, and Deeg, 2014a). According to these researchers, HRM practices are not only strategic choices but depend on several factors that are endogenous and exogenous to the firm, and thus having only one form of HRM 'best practices' is not possible. The researchers of the comparative HRM literature have highlighted the importance of local, regional, and national labour markets; the state; and labour unions as key elements that influence the firm-level HRM practices. Focusing mainly on the HRM practices of firms within different national contexts, the comparative HRM researchers have emphasised the variation of HRM practices across countries, regions, and cultures (Brewster, Mayrhofer, and Morley, 2004; Brewster and Mayrhofer, 2009). For instance, instead of convergence towards 'good HRM', these researchers argue that firms only in LMEs will be able to apply such 'hard' HRM due to more flexible institutional structures, while firms in CMEs are argued to develop 'softer' HRM that is mediated by the context in which the firms are embedded (Brewster, Mayrhofer, and Morley, 2004; Wilkinson and Wood, 2017). A few researchers have argued that although there may be some 'directional convergence', such as the rise of flexible contracts and contingent pay, this does not lead to a 'final' convergence, and variation between key HRM aspects continue, including firms' training and employee development practices (Brewster, Mayrhofer, and Morley, 2004; Brewster and Mayrhofer, 2009; Mayrhofer, Morley, and Brewster, 2011).

Centring their analysis on MNCs, the researchers of international HRM have also emphasised the variation of HRM practices across countries. These researchers have discussed how the home country and host country institutions of MNCs influence their ESs, and have argued that HRM practices vary across MNC subsidiaries not only because of the specific strategies of each subsidiary, but also due to national institutions of host countries that surround these subsidiaries (Ferner, 1997; Ferner, Quintanilla, and Varul, 2001; Edwards and Kuruvilla, 2005; Ferner, Almond, and Colling, 2005; Farndale and Paauwe, 2007; Ferner, Edwards, and Tempel, 2012). Others have focused on the impact of MNCs' country of origin on the strategies of these MNCs to organise the activities, including HRM practices, of their subsidiaries, as well as firms in their supply chains (Quintanilla and Ferner, 2003; Ferner et al., 2004; Lane and Probert, 2009; Ferner, Edwards, and Tempel, 2012). These researchers argue that cheap labour is not always the main motivation of MNCs to disperse their activities across the world, and MNCs with different countries of origin are found to follow different strategies when moving their activities to elsewhere(Lane, 2008; Lane and Probert, 2009).

In addition to their insights about the factors shaping firm-level employment relations and firms' skilling activities, the micro-level approach of studies on HRM and ESs helps to understand the *outcomes* of different skilling practices for firms and workers. Many researchers in these fields argue that HPWSs are more likely to bring high-road development compared to HRM practices applied in mass production (Jürgens and Krzywdzinski, 2016).[7] According to to these researchers, the higher commitments of both employers and employees in HPWSs will bring 'high employment security, teamwork and engagement in improvement activities in small groups, greater transfer of responsibility to the shop floor (empowerment)' together with higher level of training (Jürgens and Krzywdzinski, 2016, p. 31). The HPWSs, on the one hand, are argued to give important responsibilities to workers and provide

---

[7] Sengenberger and Pyke (1992) explain the distinction between high- and low-road development as follows: 'The 'low-road' [development] [...] consists of seeking competitiveness through low labour cost, and a deregulated labour market environment. [...] [T]he 'high road' [development, however, is] based on efficiency enhancement and innovation; that is, through economic gains that make wage gains and improvements in social conditions feasible, as well as safeguarding workers' rights and providing adequate standards of social protection' (pp. 12–13). Therefore, it can be argued that high-road development brings more continuous and inclusive development, while the experiences in low-road development may be more temporary and exclusive.

opportunities for career development. On the other hand, the HPWSs provide firms higher flexibility in their HRM strategies, which will help firms' economic growth (Jürgens and Krzywdzinski, 2016). Similarly, according to studies on ESs, 'function-centred' employment systems with a training approach will provide important benefits to both workers and firms as they generate more polyvalent skills and hence a more flexible skill profile (Marsden, 1999). Workers with higher and polyvalent skills, moreover, are argued to have higher horizontal and vertical mobility, namely more opportunities to move between different companies and for career progression, which helps to reduce workplace hierarchy, improve workers' influence on production, and enhance workers' power on the shop floor (Appelbaum, 2000). Having employees with more flexible and polyvalent skills is also expected to facilitate continuous growth of firms through giving these firms greater opportunity to respond to the competitive pressures in the global AAI, adapt to changes in demand and technology, and prevent problems in production.

2.4.2   Limitations of the HRM and ES approach

While the research on ESs and HRM help to realise the firm-level dynamics of skilling practices and their outcomes, they have not studied how the intersections between national institutions and GVC governance structures influence firm-level skilling practices (Ferner, 1997; Brewster, 1999, 2004; Sorge, 2014; Wood, Brewster, and Brookes, 2014; Hotho and Saka-Helmhout, 2017). Another critique towards the international/comparative HRM literature, which is a common critique towards the international business literature, is its 'thin' view on institutions, where 'institutions are studied largely as single "variables" that impact directly on firms' (Jackson and Deeg, 2019, p. 5). Therefore, this view on institutions does not consider the interaction between multiple institutions and the impact of this interaction on firms, which will be helpful to explain not just 'differences of degree but of kind' (Jackson and Deeg, 2019, p. 5). Last, the majority of the studies on ESs and HRM focus on the same components of employment relations, particularly on industrial relations and pay systems, while the research on recruitment and training of employees is limited.

2.4.3   The use of the ESs and HRM approach in this book

This book adopts the micro-level approach of ESs and HRM studies first to examine *firm-level* skilling practices and to understand the elements that influence firm-level decisions about hiring, training and employee development. This will help to make linkages between firm-level skilling practices, on the one hand, and national institutions and GVC governance structures on the other. Furthermore, the micro-level analysis, which is summarised in Figure 2.5, will help to evaluate how different skilling practices impact workers' opportunities for career progression and firms' growth

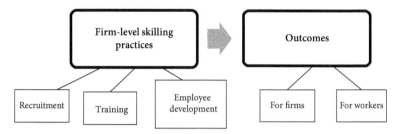

Figure 2.5 Firm-level analysis and skilling outcomes

prospective, which will help to draw inferences about the implications of skill systems for high-road development.

2.5 Cross-fertilisation

In analysing the skill systems of Mexico and Turkey, this book cross-fertilises the macro-level approach of institutional research and the macro and/or meso focus of GVC studies together with the micro-level approach of the literature on ESs and HRM. This book aims to develop a bridge between different fields of study and views firms as *actors embedded in national and global networks* whose actions are shaped by *pressures in global markets* and the *institutional arrangements surrounding them*. Bridging different fields of study and their 'cross-fertilisation' has been suggested by various researchers to enable a more comprehensive analysis on contemporary capitalism (Campbell and Pedersen, 2001; Busemeyer and Trampusch, 2011; Hotho and Saka-Helmhout, 2017), yet there have been few empirical studies following this approach.

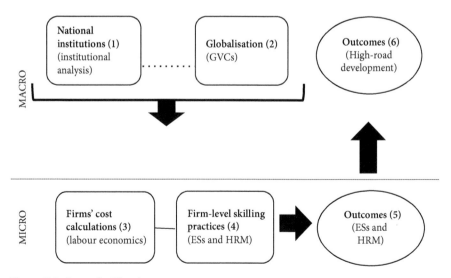

Figure 2.6 Cross-fertilisation

Figure 2.6 summarises how each field of study is cross-fertilised in understanding the working of skill systems and their outcomes. The institutionalist approach helps to study the national institutions that complement the skill system (point 1 in Figure 2.6), while the GVC approach helps to understand the pressures on firms in the global economy (point 2). Furthermore, the analysis built on labour economics helps to realise, and control for, the role of training and hiring costs (point 3), and ESs and HRM research helps to investigate the firm-level skilling practices (point 4). The micro-level research also helps to examine the outcomes of skilling practices for firms and workers (point 5). By looking at the micro-level outcomes of skill systems for workers and firms, this book offers substantial empirical evidence about the macro-level implications of skill systems for high-road development (point 6).

3

The auto parts-automotive industry in Mexico and Turkey as the study case

The aim of this chapter is to familiarise the reader with the Mexican and Turkish auto parts producers operating in global auto parts-automotive chains (AACs) (Peters, 2012). The chapter starts with elaborating why the auto parts- automotive industry (AAI) is an important industry when seeking to understand the impact of global and national dynamics on firm behaviour and skill systems in middle-income countries (MICs). In this regard, the chapter lays out the current situation of the industry in Mexico and Turkey, with a brief history of its development, production and export dynamics, and main original equipment manufacturers (OEMs) operating in the two countries. Then, it goes on to explain the research method, data collection process, and the interview process of the research used in the book. Last, the chapter defines the key characteristics of interviewee firms, including their capacity, products, and the necessary skills in their production functions.

3.1 The AAI and AAC as the focus of analysis

The AAI forms an important case to examine the impact of globalisation and national institutions on firm behaviour and hence to assess patterns of convergence and divergence. Similar to other global value chains (GVCs), the activities of global AACs have dispersed to different parts of the world. Firms from advanced capitalist countries have specialised in higher value-added activities as lead OEMs or global Tier-1 suppliers, while firms from MICs have focused on lower value-added manufacturing operations at lower tiers of these chains. Furthermore, because of the potential of the AAI to increase technology investments, employment opportunities, and the level of economic value-added in the industry, many governments in MICs have paid specific attention to improving the AAI. MICs have been competing also amongst themselves to attract investments from global OEMs (Humphrey, 2000; Robertson, 2003; McGrath, 2007; Sturgeon, Biesebroeck, and Gereffi, 2008; Biesebroeck and Sturgeon, 2010).

The spatial globalisation of AACs, compared with other industries, has been more limited, which makes the AAI and the firms in the industry more exposed to national institutional arrangements compared to sectors with higher spatial dispersion, such as the textile industry (Sturgeon, Biesebroeck, and Gereffi, 2008; Lane and Probert, 2009;

Global Production, National Institutions, and Skill Formation: The Political Economy of Training and Employment in Auto Parts Suppliers from Mexico And Turkey. Merve Sancak, Oxford University Press. © Merve Sancak 2022.
DOI: 10.1093/oso/9780198860655.003.0003

Sturgeon and Biesebroeck, 2011). There are at least four reasons for the regionalisation of the AAI. Firstly, the manufacturing activities in the AAI require 'tacit' and 'synthetic' knowledge that is more difficult to codify or transport (Sturgeon, Biesebroeck, and Gereffi, 2008; Plum and Hassink, 2013). Production requiring such knowledge, moreover, is argued to necessitate a high level of coordination between firms at different levels of the production chain (Plum and Hassink, 2013, p. 209). Secondly, the AAI is a 'bulky' and 'heavy' industry with high investments in capital, and the parts and components required for production, as well as the end products, are costly to transport (Biesebroeck and Sturgeon, 2010, p. 219). This 'heavy' nature, and the increasing adoption of just-in-time delivery principles in supply chains necessitate supplier and buyer firms in the AAI to be located close to one another. Thirdly, the sensitivity of the AAI industry for governments has limited the global dispersion of the industry. Many MIC governments, including the ones in Mexico and Turkey, have recognised the AAI as critical for their development, and initially restricted the imports of finished products in the industry, which has led to foreign OEM investments towards these countries (Humphrey and Memedovic, 2003; Sturgeon and Biesebroeck, 2011). Fourthly, the finished products in the AAI need to be adapted to different markets because of factors such as differentials in income, standards and regulations regarding automotive production, driving conditions, tax regulations, and different consumer preferences (Humphrey and Memedovic, 2003). Resultantly, many OEMs and Tier-1 suppliers have located their plants in key places to access markets in specific regions, which has led to the emergence of regional AAI clusters in North America, South America, Europe, and South Africa (Sturgeon, Biesebroeck, and Gereffi, 2008; Biesebroeck and Sturgeon, 2010; Plum and Hassink, 2013).

Despite the spatial concentration of AACs in regional clusters, the AAI is considered as one of the 'most globalised' industries since it is dominated by very few OEMs and Tier-1 suppliers from advanced capitalist economies, namely the United States, Germany, and Japan, and the entry costs to the industry are extremely high. The AAI is also considered to be highly globalised due to the similar strategies adopted by the very few OEMs, leading to convergence of management and production practices in the industry (Dicken, 2007; Wad, 2009). It has been suggested that OEMs have increasingly been shifting to lean manufacturing, which leads to convergence in the ways they organise their supply chains and their human resource management (HRM) strategies. With the shift to lean production, the OEMs are argued to reduce the number of their direct suppliers and to develop more 'relational' coordination with them (see Chapter 4) (Gereffi, Humphrey, and Sturgeon, 2005; Sturgeon, Biesebroeck, and Gereffi, 2008). Similarly, these OEMs, and their suppliers, are argued to adopt HRM 'best practices', namely High-Performance Work Systems (HPWSs) (MacDuffie, 1995; Appelbaum, 2000; Jürgens and Krzywdzinski, 2016).

In contrast to the convergence claims, several authors have pointed out the continuing variations in supply chain management and HRM strategies in the global AAI (Turnbull, Oliver, and Wilkinson, 1992; Wood, 1996; Cooney, 2002; Dyer and

Chu, 2011; Lanz, Miroudot, and Nordås, 2013; Jürgens and Krzywdzinski, 2015, 2016; Krzywdzinski, 2017). One reason for this variation has been linked to the different institutional structures in the home countries of lead OEMs, which have resulted in different forms of value chain governance and HRM practices (Lane and Probert, 2009; Jürgens and Krzywdzinski, 2016). Other researchers have emphasised the role of OEM managers and supplier firms' strategies which result in different supply chain structures and HRM practices (Zhu and Morgan, 2018; Dibben et al., 2020).

Due to these local and global dynamics, the AAI constitutes an important case to study the patterns of convergence and persisting divergence in the skilling strategies of supplier firms from MICs. On the one hand, the globalisation of the AAI, and the concentration of the industry on very few lead OEMs adopting similar strategies will create similar pressures on supplier firms from different countries and hence, can lead to a convergence in their skilling practices. On the other hand, the limits to spatial globalisation of the AAI and the focus of the industry on regional markets exposes the industry to national institutions and the influence of these institutions on firms' activities.

In addition to its importance for understanding the effects of global and national dynamics on supplier firms, the AAI is particularly relevant for studying suppliers' skilling practices with regard to intermediate skills, which are key for the development of MICs (Tripney and Hombrados, 2013; Doner and Schneider, 2016). The AAI comprises a variety of activities that require low, intermediate, or high skills at different levels of the production chain. The AAIs of many MICs have initially focused on labour-intensive, low-skill production, and hence have faced the danger of a low-road development with discontinuous economic growth and a race to the bottom in their employment practices (see Chapters 1 and 2). Therefore, shifting production from labour-intensive activities to the ones requiring higher skills in the AAI, namely upgrading in AACs, has been key for MICs for a high-road development, and moving to production functions that require intermediate skills constitutes a critical first step in this regard.

Some may argue that the focus only on AACs may not bring findings that are generalisable to other industries. For example, commonalities between the Mexican and Turkish auto parts suppliers' activities—if any—may signal a convergence in AAI only, and the firms in AAI might be different from those in other industries within the two countries. Therefore, an application of skilling practices that promote a high- or low-road development in the AAI, such as HPWSs or exploitative employment relations, may not happen in other industries. Nonetheless, despite its difference from other sectors, the AAI constitutes a major share of the manufacturing production and employment in both Mexico and Turkey. Furthermore, the employment practices adopted in such a critical industry may spread to other industries.

Another challenge of studying the AAI can relate to the advancements in automotive production and the changes in global AACs. One may argue that worker skills will not be as important for manufacturing in the AAI due to the increase of

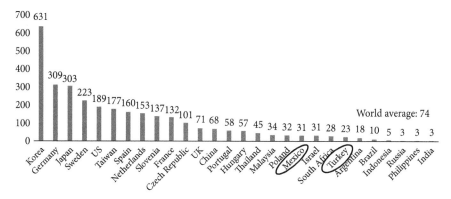

Figure 3.1 Number of installed industrial robots in the manufacturing industry (2016)*
* Per 10,000 employees
Source: International Federation of Robotics (2018)

automated machinery. Nevertheless, while the claims on increased automation and its challenges for labour dynamics may be true for advanced industrialised economies, the level of automation is still very limited for many MICs. For example, Figure 3.1 shows that the level of automation has been very low in many MICs, and the number of industrial robots per the thousand employees in Mexico and Turkey were well below the world average. Furthermore, the next section shows that both Mexico and Turkey have comparative advantage in producing medium value-added parts, which requires intermediate skills, rather than low value-added parts, which are more labour-intensive and hence face a higher risk of automation. Therefore, workers and intermediate skills still constitute an important element for the manufacturing industry of these countries.

3.2 The AAI and AAC in Mexico and Turkey

Mexico and Turkey have a number of similarities regarding their AAIs and the links of their AAIs with global AACs, which makes the AAI an important case to study the impact of globalisation and national institutions on Mexican and Turkish firms' skilling practices. Different from many MICs, both Mexico and Turkey have developed comparative advantage in cars and vehicle parts production,[1] and the AAI has an important place in the economies of the two countries. For instance, in 2016, the AAI formed about 3 per cent of the gross domestic product (GDP) of both countries (Milliyet, 2017; OECD, 2021a), while AAI exports constituted the second largest share in exports for the two countries (UNCTAD, 2017). Furthermore, medium

---

[1] The 'revealed comparative advantage' (RCA) scores were 2.5 for Mexico and 2.1 for Turkey for car production; and 2.2 and 1.6, respectively, for parts production (http://atlas.media.mit.edu/en/visualize/tree_map/hs92/export/mex/all/show/2013/).

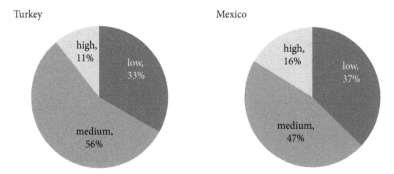

Figure 3.2 Share of exports of the Turkish and Mexican AAI according to the value added (2010)
Source: Author, based on UN Comtrade Data and the method developed by Pavlinek et al. (2009)

value-added goods have constituted the main share of the Mexican AAI and the Turkish AAI, followed by low value-added products, while high value-added activities comprise the lowest share (Figure 3.2).

The links of the Mexican and Turkish AAIs with the global economy also have important similarities. One similarity stems from the investments by global OEMs in these countries, which have brought comparable impact on the local AAI. For example, it is argued that the OEMs investing in countries with large domestic markets like China and India have cooperated more with local companies with the aim of developing new designs that can address domestic market demands (Biesebroeck and Sturgeon, 2010; Herrigel, 2013). In contrast, the OEMs in Mexico and Turkey are argued to mostly have aimed to sell to the neighbouring economies, including the United States and Latin America for Mexico, and Europe, the Middle East, and North Africa for Turkey (Biesebroeck and Sturgeon, 2010). Therefore, they have not always adapted their original designs to the local markets in Mexico and Turkey and have more limited interaction with the local industry (Biesebroeck and Sturgeon, 2010).

As a result of their location and relations with global OEMs, the Mexican and Turkish AAIs have important similarities regarding their links with the global AACs. For instance, the length index, which is used to measure the level of production stages of a GVC in one country,[2] was very similar for the AAI in the two countries in 2009 (De Backer and Miroudot, 2013). Moreover, the levels of domestic and foreign content in the products produced in the industry are also very close in Mexico and Turkey (De Backer and Miroudot, 2013). The Mexican and Turkish AAIs have developed substantial linkages with the rich capitalist economies located nearby, often making the former's economy dependent on the latter. Mexico has 'enjoyed' being the sole late industrialiser sharing a lengthy border with the United States, which has led to the 79 per cent of Mexican AAI exports being to the United States in 2015 (UNCTAD, 2017). This has created a vulnerability for the Mexican AAI and its

---

[2] For more comprehensive explanation of the length index, see De Backer and Miroudot (2013).

dependence on the US economy with possible negative consequences, such as the huge negative impact of the 2008 global financial crisis on the Mexican AAI (PwC Mexico, 2014). Similarly, the majority of Turkish automotive and auto parts exports are to the European countries (73 per cent of Turkey's exports were to the EU-27 countries in 2015), making it vulnerable to—and dependent on—the European economy (UNCTAD, 2017).

The historical development of the Mexican and Turkish car industries shows important similarities. Both received their first OEM investments during the state-led import substituting industrialisation (ISI) period, when the OEMs produced for the large domestic markets and enjoyed trade protection. The first investments in the AAI took place as joint venture investments because of the local content requirements, which aimed to develop a domestic auto parts industry, although the actual happening of this has been dubious since most OEMs initially preferred in-house production rather than engaging with local firms (Jordaan, 2011). The arrival of the first OEMs happened much earlier in Mexico—in the 1930s—while Turkey continued importing vehicles until the late 1950s. The first investment in both countries was by Ford, which was followed by other North American, European, and Japanese OEMs in later years during the ISI (General Motors, Chrysler, Volkswagen, and Nissan in Mexico; Fiat and Renault in Turkey). These OEMs gained access to the markets in neighbouring countries when the ISI model was abandoned and when these countries joined regional trade agreements in the 1990s, namely the NAFTA and Customs Union, which has made these two countries even more important locations for the AAI investments to reach the regional markets.

Despite these similarities, there are two main differences between the Mexican and Turkish AAIs that stem from the variation in their geographical size and location, which should be considered. Firstly, Mexico and Turkey face different levels and types of competition in global AACs due to their location. Mexico is the only late industrialiser that is in a proximate location to the United States and Canada, sharing a lengthy border with the former. This gives an important advantage to Mexico in trade and FDI compared to other late industrialisers due to the regional cluster-based nature of the AAI and thus, many OEMs and Tier-1 suppliers have located their investments in Mexico for accessing the North American market. In contrast to Mexico, Turkey has faced important levels of competition from the Central and Eastern European countries for both attracting FDI in the AAI and for selling to the lead firms based in Europe. As a result, Mexico has had much closer trade relations with the United States compared to Turkey's relations with Europe. For instance, in 2016, exports from Mexico constituted the largest share in the auto parts imports of the United States, while the AAI imports of the EU from Turkey formed a much smaller share (UNCTAD, 2017). Furthermore, thanks to its geographical advantage, Mexico has continued attracting new FDI in the AAI, and OEMs including BMW, Audi, and Toyota made substantial amounts of investments (billions of dollars) in Mexico in the last decade (Althaus and Boston, 2015; Bernstein and Alper, 2015). In contrast, the FDI inflows to the AAI in Turkey have been more limited, and Turkey has not attracted major OEM investments in recent years (Interview Notes).

Secondly, the AAI in Turkey is much more geographically concentrated than the one in Mexico due to both their land size and political administrations. The land size of Mexico size is more than twice that of Turkey, and Mexico has a federal system that has allowed a variation of policies between different states and has facilitated competition between the states in Mexico to attract FDI in the AAI (Rothstein, 2005). Due to its size and varying administration, the AAI has developed in several regions in Mexico. Lauridsen et al. (2013) argue that there are at least 14 clusters in Mexico, the ones in the northern and central regions being the oldest and most important ones. While the central region has focused on producing for the local market, the northern companies aim to sell to the markets in North America (Lauridsen et al. 2013). As a result, Lauridsen et al. (2013) argue, the firms in the central region have managed to shift from producing low value-added products in the AAI to higher value-added activities, while firms in the north have continued producing labour-intensive goods with low value-added.

The geographical area of Turkey is much smaller than that of Mexico, and its public administration is much more centralised, which has limited the dispersion of the AAI in the country. Currently, the AAI is clustered mainly in one region, Marmara, located in the north-west of the country. Although new industrial clusters have emerged in different parts of the country in the last 2 decades, the Marmara region remains the main AAI cluster in Turkey, producing for both national and international markets. In order to prevent a potential bias that may stem from the differences in the geographical size of Mexico and Turkey, and the variation between regions in Mexico, supplier firms from both the central and northern regions of Mexico are included in this study, while the research about Turkey focuses on firms located in the Marmara region.

3.3 Interviews in Mexico and Turkey

The research in this book is based on qualitative analysis of in-depth interview data from face-to-face meetings with representatives of 39 firms, as well as with the stakeholders of the AAI and skill systems in Mexico and Turkey, and an analysis of primary and secondary documents.

3.3.1 The interviewee sample

The sample comprises firms producing plastic or metal parts from Mexico and Turkey, as these two constitute the main sectors of auto parts production in the two countries. In order to prevent bias that can arise due to firm-level characteristics, 'almost identical' firms from the two countries were included in the interview sample, namely firms producing similar products and with similar capacity.

The firms in the sample were selected through multiple methods. One method was a search of the databases of firms developed by the Union of Chambers and Commodity Exchanges of Turkey (*Türkiye Odalar ve Borsalar Birliği*—TOBB) and the Mexican Business Information System (*Sistema de Información Empresarial*—SIEM). Potential interviewee firms were identified according to their location and products, and firms described as 'manufacture of motor vehicles, trailers and semi-trailers' were searched for.[3] Furthermore, firms from the cities in the predetermined clusters were identified and included in the sample. However, the databases by the SIEM and TOBB were not up-to-date and were missing some information about the firms. Also, a significant number of firms producing plastic and metal parts for AACs were not included in the identified product classification as they were grouped in other categories such as metal manufacturing. Therefore, additional methods were applied to expand the sample. Requesting the names and contact details of supplier firms from the local offices of business chambers and industry associations was a key method for identifying more firms. Media resources and news items related to the AAI were scanned for finding more firms in selected regions. Additionally, snowball sampling was utilised where interviewees were asked for names and contact details of other firms in the local AAI. Overall, with these methods and based on the knowledge developed during the interviews, as well as on reports and articles published on the AAI in the two countries, it can be confidently assumed that the sample includes almost all key local Tier-1 and Tier-2 suppliers in Mexico and Turkey.

Approximately two representatives from each firm were interviewed, with most interviewees being from the human resources (HR), sales, and quality departments. For smaller companies, plant managers and company owners responded to the questions regarding both skilling activities and firms' relations with their clients. In the end, a total of 86 individuals from 39 firms (20 firms and 38 interviewees from Turkey, and 19 firms and 48 interviewees from Mexico) were interviewed (see Appendix 2). Although the possibility of interviewing shop floor workers was considered at the start of the project, this was not pursued after pilot interviews with some workers. This was because the workers were contacted via the administrative staff in the firm, which caused the interviews to take place in the presence of a representative from these departments, mainly the HR department. This restricted the confidence of workers to respond freely to questions and made them uncomfortable, causing them to not answer some questions or to give short answers. Therefore, and to not to put workers under such pressure, worker interviews were dropped.

In addition to representatives of local supplier firms, interviews with several actors related to the AAI and the skill systems were conducted. These include representatives of national and local business chambers and industry associations, labour unions, Mexican Secretary of Public Education (*Secretaría de Educación Pública*—SEP), Mexican Secretariat of Labour and Social Welfare (*Secretaría del Trabajo y*

---

[3] NACE Rev. 2 product codes were used for Turkey and product names for Mexico when identifying the firms.

Previsión Social—STPS), Turkish Ministry of National Education (*Milli Eğitim Bakanlığı*—MEB), Turkish Ministry of Labour and Social Security (*Çalışma ve Sosyal Güvenlik Bakanlığı*—ÇSGB), organisations related to vocational education and training (VET) in the two countries (the International Labour Organisation and the German-Mexican Chamber of Commerce (*Cámara Mexicano-Alemana de Comercio e Industria*—CAMEXA) in Mexico, and the Istanbul International Centre for Private Sector in Development and the Education Reform Initiative (*Eğitim Reformu Girişimi*—ERG) in Turkey), in addition to academics and policy experts working on VET and AAI (see Appendix 2).

3.3.2 The interviews

Most firms in the sample were contacted via email and then phoned. Additionally, some interviews were arranged by a third party providing the link to the firm, such as the local office of a business chamber or a representative of another firm. Another important method to contact the interviewees was LinkedIn, which is a popular online social platform focusing on businesses and employment. Some firms in the sample were searched through this platform, and their employees were invited for an interview.

Firms were informed about the project prior to the interviews. The invitation letter sent to firms requested to interview *representatives of the firm who can answer questions regarding their recruitment and training practices for shop floor workers*, as well as *representatives responsible for firms' relations with buyers*. The interviews were held on firms' premises, which provided the opportunity to observe the production floor, and to note down details in a fieldwork diary about production and working practices.

The firm interviews were semistructured, meaning that although they followed a specific structure, the questions were open-ended, giving the opportunity for collecting extensive qualitative data (Lane and Probert, 2009). This also made it possible to come across additional and unanticipated information, and to inquire new information further. Quantitative data were also requested from firms about their labour turnover, employees' average education level, and the distribution of workers between different departments. Although workers' wage levels were asked initially, some firms were reluctant to give information on this matter, which then interrupted the confidence of the interviewee when answering the subsequent questions. Therefore, the question on the wages was dropped, and the wages of employees were mentioned in a unstructured way, such as if and when it arose when talking about something else. Supplementary data about firms were collected from firms' websites and other online resources such as newspapers and business and automotive industry magazines. This inquiry has generated a comprehensive database that has helped to study various aspects of firm characteristics, their relations with buyers, their skilling activities, and the outcomes of skilling practices for firms and their workers.

Similar to the interviews with AAI firms, the interviews with the stakeholders took place in the premises of the relevant institution and were semistructured, although less structured compared to the firm interviews. These interviews included open-ended questions about the VET systems, labour regulations, the functioning of the global AAI, and the links of the two countries with global AACs. Additionally, semistructured interviews with representatives of one key OEM from each country were conducted for understanding the dynamics in AACs from lead firms' point of view, and these interviews are listed within the stakeholder interviews. In total, 42 stakeholder interviews were carried out (18 in Mexico and 24 in Turkey) (see Appendix 2).

While the interviews with firm representatives lasted between 40 and 70 minutes, the stakeholder interviews were of various lengths depending on the content of the interview. Anonymity was guaranteed to all interviewees, and, hence, firms are coded with first letter of their country and a randomly assigned number, such as T1 or M2, and referred to as such throughout the book. The stakeholder interviewees are referenced as TS (Turkey Stakeholder) [number] or MS (Mexico Stakeholder) [number], such as TS1 or MS2, and the institutional affiliation of these stakeholders is provided in the interview list in the Appendix 2. Last, more general information gathered through interviews is referred as 'Interview Notes' throughout the book. All, except three interviews,[4] were carried out in the local language (i.e. Spanish in Mexico and Turkish in Turkey), recorded, transcribed, and analysed using the software Atlas.ti, which was also utilised for analysing the primary and secondary documents.

A qualitative thematic analysis was conducted, where codes for major themes and subthemes were generated. The codes were first developed via utilising the existing literature. Further codes were added during the analysis of interviews. The main major themes and subthemes in the firm interviews comprised (i) *firm characteristics*, including ownership and management structures, location, main clients, and history of the firm; (ii) *relations with buyers*, such as the length of relationship with different buyers, buyers' requirements, quality certificates held, and the frequency and methods of communication with buyers; (iii) *employee characteristics*, including number of employees, the level of employee turnover, and average level of education; and (iv) *methods to recruit and train workers*, including whether they recruit already skilled workers or conduct firm-level training and the length of induction and training (see the table on themes in Appendix 1 and the questionnaire in Appendix 3). Furthermore, the analysis of elite interviews and published documents included generating major themes and subthemes such as *VET system* (i.e. links with the private sector, the education content, characteristics of practical training); *competitive advantages of the AAI* (i.e. proximity, quality, price, and competition with other countries and industries); *state involvement* (i.e. subsidies for VET, policies to

---

[4] Representatives of one firm in Mexico and two firms in Turkey did not agree to being recorded. Therefore, analysis of these interviews is based on the notes taken during the interviews.

encourage VET, VET for employment, VET for industrial development, and cooperation between state bodies). In total, eight major themes and more than 100 subthemes were developed (see Appendix 1).

3.3.3 Contextual issues

It is important to highlight some contextual issues that were faced when conducting a comparative field study in Mexico and Turkey with special reference to skill systems. The school system was one element in this regard, and is important to realise when reading this book. Schools below tertiary education in both countries can be summarised in three levels: primary, secondary, and upper-secondary. The primary and secondary education comprise 8 years of schooling in Turkey and 9 years in Mexico. The individuals finishing the upper-secondary education, which is called *Lise* in Turkey and *Preparatoria* in Mexico, finish 12 years of schooling in total in both countries. This book is about those workers who at most complete upper-secondary education (up to 12 years, namely ISCED 3)[5] and employed in direct production functions (see the following section). Therefore, it does not concern those workers with postsecondary education, such as postsecondary-nontertiary education or tertiary education and above (ISCED 4–8).

One important issue that needs mentioning is about the concepts used in the interviews and their translation to different languages (English, Spanish, and Turkish). The concepts to define 'technical workers' within firms do not correspond to the same term in the two countries, and it was necessary to clarify them in Mexico, where the investigation was conducted in a foreign language for the researcher. For instance, the term 'workers with technical skills' (*trabajadores con habilidades técnicas*) was perceived as 'technicians' (*técnicos*), who are typically the workers employed in maintenance departments and who have postsecondary education from Polytechnics (*Politécnicos)* or Technical Universities (*Universidades Tecnológicas*). In contrast, workers participating directly in production, who constitute the focus of this book, were not considered as 'workers with technical skills' by the interviewees in Mexico. In contrast, the translation of this term to Turkish corresponds to *teknik beceri gerektiren çalışanlar*, and comprises workers in both direct and indirect production functions. Therefore, the differentiation between direct production workers and maintenance workers was clarified in the interviews in Mexico.

The term 'certification' has also caused confusion in the interviews in Mexico. Mexican firms use the Spanish translation of 'certified workers' (*operadores certificados*) to explain that their workers have the necessary skills in accordance with the post description. However, this 'certification' is internal and happens via recording the workers' skill levels in company documents rather than through a standardised

---

[5] Based on ISCED 2011.

external certification system. Therefore, the concept of 'certification' needed to be clarified in the interviews.

3.4   The interviewee firms and their skill needs

Before proceeding to the chapters on skill systems, it is important to have a clear insight about the interviewed firms and their skill needs in production departments in order to understand the determinants of their skilling practices. This section summarises the characteristics of firms studied in this book and describes their employee profile.

3.4.1   Interviewee firms

The firm sample includes firms defined by the products they produce and their ownership structures, position in global AACs, and size/capacity. Most of the interviewed firms in Mexico and Turkey produce metal or plastics parts, are family owned, and are Tier-1 or Tier-2 suppliers, while some of them also produce spare parts of motor vehicles for the aftermarket. Although professional managers are in charge of some management departments, family members of the owners have key roles in management positions, which also reflects the general reality about the Mexican and Turkish firms (Vega, 2005; Özel, 2014).

Firms' size—or better said capacity—is an important element with important influence on skilling practices (see Chapter 2.1). The original aim at the start of the project was to include only small and medium-sized enterprises, where the criterion was going to be the number of employees in the company. However, the classification of firms' capacity based on the number of their employees has proven to be insufficient due to the ownership structure of firms in Mexico and Turkey and the role of automation in AAI firms. For instance, firms with more automation have fewer workers than firms with less automation. Therefore, a low number of employees in one firm does not automatically reflect a lower capacity for this firm to organise training or recruit skilled workers (see Chapter 2.1). Similarly, many AAI suppliers in Mexico and Turkey are a part of multisectoral conglomerates that have important power in the national and local economies. Therefore, while a firm belonging to a conglomerate may have small number of workers, it can still have a high capacity to recruit skilled workers and provide comprehensive training for its employees thanks to its relation to the group.

Because of the difficulties in describing firms based on only their number of employees, companies with different number of employees were included in the sample, and their *capacity* was determined based on four main criteria. The first criterion is firms' *ownership structure*, where the company's links to business groups were examined. The second criterion is the *level of automation*, which is assessed via firm interviews, exploring firms' webpages, and observing the production facilities during the plant visits.[6] The third criterion is *firms' position in AACs*, namely if they are a Tier-1 or Tier-2 supplier or a producer for the aftermarket, as well as their level of dependence on any buyer. The last criterion is the *number of employees*, as it is still an important variable to understand firms' capacity and preference for recruitment and training (see Chapter 2.1).

In the end, three main groups were developed to define firms' capacity: low-, medium-, and high-capacity companies. Low-capacity firms are mainly Tier-2 suppliers, while some of them also produce for the aftermarket. In general, they have a small number of workers, a low level of automation, and are not part of a business group. Medium-capacity firms are also mostly Tier-2 suppliers, while they may also act as Tier-1 suppliers for some OEMs, especially to those with modular relations (see Chapter 4). The level of automation is low in these companies, and is limited to only a few automated machines, while the number of employees is higher compared with low-capacity firms. High-capacity firms have large numbers of workers, are part of a multisector business conglomerate, and/or have a higher level of automation. Most firms in this group are Tier-1 suppliers, while some also have started acting as a Tier-2 when they were pushed to lower levels by the entry of multinational Tier-1 suppliers into the local economies. Based on these features, the term 'firms' capacity' refers to the categories developed through the four main criteria throughout the book, while term 'size' is also utilised throughout the book and denotes firms' capacity.

Tables 3.1 and 3.2 provide general information on firms in the sample and their capacities.[7]

3.4.2 Workers and skill needs

Workers in the interviewed companies are composed of two main groups, production workers and administrative workers, with the former also being divided into subgroups of indirect and direct production workers. Direct production workers are those directly involved in the manufacturing of a product, and the tasks for this

---

[6] My lack of knowledge about manufacturing precludes an in-depth judgement about automation. However, my aim here is to have a general idea about firms' automation level, and the analysis is based on observing the number of workers operating with regard to the size of the manufacturing plant and the amount of machinery used in manufacturing.

[7] At first glance, the tables may show important differences among the firms due to the variation in number of their employees. However, a closer look at the tables will reveal a better understanding about firms and their capacity. Firstly, despite the outliers with very few or many employees, most firms in the sample are in the middle range. Furthermore, as mentioned, the number of employees is not by itself sufficient to classify firms, and the four criteria are accounted for to truly understand a firm's capacity. For example, while M2 has a very low number of employees, it is a new company established through a partnership of some previous high-level managers from an OEM, and it possesses solely automated machinery. Similarly, T19 in Turkey belongs to one of the largest multisectoral conglomerates and has substantial capacity to organise training and recruit skilled workers despite its low number of employees.

Table 3.1 Interviewee firms in Mexico

Firm	Product	Year	Location	Tier	Number of Employees	Part of a Group	Assigned Capacity
M1	Metal	2001	Guanajuato	Tier-2	170	No	Medium
M2	Plastics	2011	Puebla	Tier-2	27	No	Low
M3	Plastics	1959	Mexico City	Tier-2, Tier-1	592	No	Medium
M4	Metal	1965	Monterrey	Tier-1, Tier-2	404	Yes	Medium
M5	Plastics	1964	Monterrey	Subcontractor, Tier-2	510	No	Medium
M6	Metal	1998	Monterrey	Tier-2	500	Yes	High
M7	Batteries	1953	Monterrey	Tier-1, aftermarket	3200	Yes	High
M8	Metal	2002	Guanajuato	Tier-2	110	No	Medium
M9	Plastics	1964	Queretaro	Tier-2	170	No	Medium
M10	Car covers, plastics	1988	Puebla	Tier-1	88	Yes	Medium
M11	Metal	1981	Mexico City	Tier-1	567	Yes	High
M12	Metal	1956	Monterrey	Tier-1	617	Yes	High
M13	Metal	1979	Monterrey	Tier-1	6400	Yes	High
M14	Metal	1980	Puebla	Tier-2, Tier-1	383	No	Medium
M15	Metal	1961	Mexico City	Tier-2	446	No	Medium
M16	Metal	1970	Mexico City	Tier-2, aftermarket	200	No	Medium
M17	Metal	1982	Puebla	Tier-2	25	No	Low
M18	Plastics	2002	Puebla	Tier-2, Tier-1	256	Yes	Medium
M19	Metal	1975	Monterrey	Tier-1, Tier-2	1800	Yes	High

Table 3.2 Interviewee firms in Turkey

Firm	Product	Year	Location	Tier	Number of Employees	Part of a Group	Assigned Capacity
T1	Metal	1999	Bursa	Tier-2	70	No	Low
T2	Metal	2011	Bursa	Tier-2	34	No	Low
T3	Metal	2003	Bursa	Tier-2	220	No	Medium
T4	Metal	1993	Bursa	Tier-2	241	Yes	Medium
T5	Metal	1981	Gebze	Tier-1, Tier-2	569	No	Medium
T6	Metal	1960	Bursa	Tier-1	2500	Yes	High
T7	Metal	1987	Bursa	Tier-2	169	No	Medium
T8	Metal	1968	Corlu	Tier-2, aftermarket	152	No	Medium
T9	Metal	1970	Gebze	Tier-2	265	No	Medium
T10	Metal	1972	Bursa	Tier-1, Tier-2	558	Yes	High
T11	Plastics	1979	Bursa	Tier-1	750	Yes	High
T12	Plastics	1974	Gebze	Tier-1	1400	Yes	High
T13	Metal	1973	Bursa	Tier-1, Tier-2	325	No	Medium
T14	Batteries	1955	Istanbul	aftermarket	953	No	High
T15	Plastics	2012	Bursa	Tier-2	n.a.*	No	Medium
T16	Metal	1978	Istanbul	Subcontractor, Tier-2	85	No	Medium
T17	Metal	1980	Bursa	Tier-2	376	No	Medium
T18	Metal	1970	Istanbul	Subcontractor, Tier-1	291	Yes	Medium
T19	Metal	1972	Istanbul	Tier-2, aftermarket	45	No	Low
T20	Metal	1992	Gebze	Tier-2	256	No	Medium

* n.a.: not available

group vary across companies according to the product they produce and firms' capacity. Indirect production workers are responsible for assuring uninterrupted and quality production, and comprise maintenance workers looking after the machinery and equipment, as well as those in the quality department in charge of ensuring product quality. This project focuses on the generation of skills only for direct production departments because this group constitutes the largest share of workers in companies, and the skills for these tasks are usually more difficult to find in the labour market due to their more specific character. While the types of workers and their skill needs are different across the plastic and metal parts producers, there are certain similarities regarding the organisation of shop floor workers and the recruitment and training patterns.

3.4.2.1 Plastic parts producers

The majority of production workers in plastic parts providers are injection operators, who are in charge of producing certain parts in plastic injection machines, as well as checking the quality of products and manually fixing the products with failure. The injection operator posts do not require a complex set of skills, and these skills can typically be developed on the job in a short time. These operators, however, still must possess certain basic general skills and personality traits to carry out those tasks. The essential skills for these posts include general writing and mathematical skills to record the required information about products, as well as attention to detail and problem-solving skills to recognise problematic products and rectify them. They also need to have certain manual skills to carry out the necessary corrections.

In addition to the injection operators, the plastic parts producers require direct production workers with some specific technical skills. The main share of these comprise the operators in charge of the plastic moulds, including their placement into the machine, arrangement of the machine settings, and maintenance of the moulds. These workers are required to have knowledge about the moulds used in the company and operating the relevant machinery. They also need to be physically strong, as they need to lift and place the heavy moulds, which is why the majority of workers in these areas are often male (Interview Notes).

While the abovementioned positions exist in all plastic parts producers, some companies performing additional tasks, such as painting and assembling, need other workers with certain technical skills for these departments. For instance, T12 has a painting department where painting operators form an important part of the production workers. Furthermore, T11 has assembly functions, and because the parts it produces are used for the exterior parts of a car that are more visible, the company requires workers with better manual skills for higher precision when producing such products.

3.4.2.2 Metal parts producers

The metal parts producers have various departments on their shop floor, which mainly include, but is not limited to, die-casting, welding, mould-making, and turnery. In die-casting, basic metal-shaping tasks are carried out which require basic general skills and some specific technical skills. Workers in these areas are called press operators, and the necessary skills for these tasks can be developed mainly on the job in a short period. Additionally, the press operators need to have basic visual and analytical skills to understand the process and pursue the task. Also because this department involves heavy machinery, it carries a high risk of work accidents that can result in permanent injury. Therefore, workers can start operating press machines only after having some training about the task, as well as after a thorough health and safety training.

The other production departments in the metal parts producers—including welding, mould-making and turnery—require more complex technical skills, as well as some general and analytical skills, with the types and levels of skill needs depending on the level of automation and the production department. Even though the interviewed firms have some automated machinery, which requires workers with more analytical and engineering skills, production is not fully automated in all interviewed firms, and these firms still need workers with manual skills. The necessary skills in each department also depend on the products of the company. For instance, firms producing smaller parts pay more attention to the aesthetics of the product and prefer workers who can carry out detailed manual welding. In contrast, for larger products, producing a high number of products in a short period is more important, and automated welding may be preferred.

3.5 Summary

This chapter has explained the importance of the AAI and AACs for studying the influence of national institutions and GVC governance structures on firms' skilling practices due to the globalisation of AACs led by few lead firms and more regional nature of the AAI. Furthermore, it showed the similarities and differences between the AAI of Mexico and Turkey, which make the AAI an important area for these countries and the for the purposes of this book. The following section of the chapter focuses on providing in-depth information on the interviews, which was the main data collection method of the study conducted for writing this book. The chapter finishes with information on the firms in the study sample, which helps to familiarise the reader of the book with its study subject.

PART 2

THE CONVERGENCE VERSUS DIVERGENCE OF SKILL FORMATION

4

Patterns of convergence: global auto parts-automotive value chains and suppliers' skill systems

This chapter discusses the patterns of convergence in the skilling strategies of Turkish and Mexican auto parts suppliers due to globalisation in the auto parts-automotive industry (AAI). In particular, it examines how the governance structures in global auto parts-automotive value chains (AACs) influence the suppliers' skilling practices, as global value chains are argued to put similar pressures on supplier firms and thus influence them in similar ways, leading to the convergence of their skilling practices. The chapter investigates if the convergence arguments are true, and if the globalisation of the AAI is leading to High-Performance Work Systems (HPWSs) or a race to the bottom in the AAIs of middle-income countries (MICs). The chapter is divided into two main sections. The first section focuses on the globalisation of AAI and the influence of globalisation on the Turkish and Mexican suppliers that participate in global AACs. The second section of the chapter explains the implications of globalisation for the skilling practices of supplier firms, and then demonstrates the patterns of convergence.

4.1 Globalisation in AAI and its impact on Mexican and Turkish suppliers

Globalisation and increased competition in the global AAI create important pressures regarding the price, quality, and in-time delivery of products for both Turkish and Mexican auto parts suppliers. Furthermore, the governance structures in global AACs have important influence on the activities of suppliers, which may lead to the convergence of these firms' skilling practices. This subsection summarises the general developments about the globalisation of AAI, and links this discussion to the production systems applied in the AAI. The following subsection then focuses on the Turkish and Mexican supplier firms, and explains how the elements discussed here are affecting the AAI firms from the two countries.

Global Production, National Institutions, and Skill Formation: The Political Economy of Training and Employment in Auto Parts Suppliers from Mexico And Turkey. Merve Sancak, Oxford University Press. © Merve Sancak 2022.
DOI: 10.1093/oso/9780198860655.003.0004

4.1.1 Globalisation of the AAI and channels for the convergence of skilling practices

With the globalisation in the AAI and the further concentration of automotive production on very few original equipment manufacturers (OEMs), increasingly, similar production and supply chain management strategies have been adopted in the global AAI. These strategies adopted in the global AAI are expected to influence the skilling practices of AAI suppliers—and may lead to the convergence of these practices. The two main production systems in the AAI, namely mass production and lean production, systems can affect supplier firms' skilling practices through two main channels. Firstly, the production system applied by lead OEMs affects these OEMs' strategies to manage their supply chains and, thus, shapes the impact of AAC governance structures on supplier firms. Secondly, the two production systems in the AAI require different types of workers and employment systems and, hence, will have substantial influence on supplier firms' recruitment, training and employee development practices. Because the governance structures of AACs and human resources management (HRM) practices adopted by AAI firms will together influence the skilling practices of supplier firms, it is important to understand the production systems and their influence on AAC governance and HRM when studying the patterns of convergence in the Turkish and Mexican AAI suppliers' skilling practices.

4.1.1.1 Mass production

Mass production, alias Fordist production, was the dominant production system throughout the twentieth century and was first adopted by the American 'Big Three' (General Motors, Ford, and Chrysler). Price is firms' main competitive advantage in mass production, and quality or delivery problems do not constitute major issues because of the 'buffers' that help to manage problems, such as the keeping of extra inventory in cases of faulty products (MacDuffie, 1995; Sturgeon et al., 2009). OEMs with mass production produce most of the parts and components in-house, and they buy a small number of parts from suppliers based on short-term contracts (Humphrey and Memedovic, 2003; Humphrey and Schmitz, 2004; Wad, 2009). They may buy the same part from multiple suppliers that compete on price, and these suppliers usually have low technological capacity.

Because the OEMs with mass production aim to maintain low-cost production, and because quality is not their priority, they often do not invest in their relations with suppliers and maintain arms-length relations with them. Therefore, the governance structures in AACs led by OEMs with mass production can be described as modular chains in the terminology of Gereffi et al. (2005) (see Chapter 2). Lead OEMs in these chains adopt standardised quality systems for maintaining the quality of products in their suppliers while having minimal interaction with their suppliers, which leads to limited information flow from the lead firm to supplier (Womack, Jones, and Roos, 1990; Humphrey, 2000; Humphrey and Schmitz, 2004; Liker and

Choi, 2004). While in the past each OEM had their own quality management system, they have increasingly adopted the ISO system, which is an international and standardised quality management system. The lead OEMs in the global AAI have been gradually requiring their suppliers to obtain the ISO/TS 16949 certificate in order to join their supply chains, which has made this certificate a major mechanism for OEMs to influence suppliers' activities in modular AACs.

The ISO/TS 16949 (hereafter, ISO/TS) was first introduced in 1999 by the International Automotive Task Force comprising the European and North American OEMs (Nadvi and Wältring, 2004).[1] The aim was to create a global and standardised quality system for the global AAI. This would combine the systems applied by different OEMs to better understand suppliers' capacity and achieve a unified system to govern supplier relations (Wad, 2006). ISO/TS is built on the general ISO 9001, which concerns companies' quality management systems, and includes special items about the AAI in line with lean manufacturing principles. It promotes continuous improvement and focuses on the prevention of defects along the supply chain. For this, the ISO/TS quality system sets a number of requirements for suppliers including the Advanced Product Quality Planning, Production Parts Approval Process, Failure Mode and Effect Analysis, Statistical Process Control, and Measurement System Analysis (Nadvi and Wältring, 2004). Accredited independent certification bodies carry out the certification process of the ISO/TS, during which they inspect firms' activities and performance. The inspection includes a revision of firm documents, as well as on-site inspection of production functions and administrative practices. The certification bodies also carry out periodical audits to ensure the continuation of firms' compliance with the requirements. The certificates are valid for 3 years, and the OEMs expect their suppliers to have up-to-date certificates.

In addition to the governance structure of the supply chain, mass production systems are argued to affect the HRM strategies of firms in the AAI, including both the lead firms and their suppliers. Because the main focus is on price, and because the quality and delivery expectations are not as crucial as they are in lean production, firms with mass production do not make large investments in HRM including their recruitment, training, and employee development practices (MacDuffie and Kochan, 1995). The shop floor workers in mass producing firms are expected to have specific experience and knowledge about the tasks they carry out, and are often not expected to possess some general skills such as problem-solving or knowledge about other parts of production. The skill needs for the shop floor positions are not complex since the production functions are composed of repetitive tasks requiring workers with low skills (MacDuffie and Pil, 1997). The workplace in mass production is administered via a centralised hierarchy, where a large group of workers with low skills are employed in specific tasks and are managed by a supervisor who has multiple skills, and is knowledgeable about and has experience with the production

---

[1] This was later replaced by IATF 16949:2016, yet after the interviews for this project were completed. This quality system includes very similar measures to that of ISO/TS.

processes in the relevant production department. Consequently, training and employee development practices are very limited in firms involved in mass production because of the division of labour and hierarchical organisation on the shop floor, as well as the skill profile of shop floor workers.

4.1.1.2 Lean production

Lean production, also labelled as the 'Toyota Way', is the other main strategy adopted in the global AAI. It started to become an alternative to mass production in the 1980s, when Toyota started to challenge the American Big Three. In contrast to mass production, buffers are minimal in lean production, and, thus, quality and in-time delivery are crucial. The production of a final good, such as an automobile, relies to a significant degree on quality-at-source and just-in-time delivery of products with 'zero-defects' (*jidoka*) throughout the supply chains.

OEMs with lean manufacturing manage their AACs very differently from mass production OEMs and hence will have a distinct influence on suppliers. These AACs are described as 'tiered system[s] of contractors and subcontractors' that include the OEMs and Tier-1 firms at the higher levels, and Tier-2 and Tier-3 suppliers at lower levels of the supply chain (Sturgeon, 2007, p. 5). The lead OEMs with lean production prefer tight relations with their suppliers in order to ensure the quality and in-time delivery of the products and to prevent problems in their supply chains due to the limited buffers.

With the globalisation of the AAI and the spread of AACs to new locations, maintaining tight relations for quality-at-source and just-in-time delivery with multiple suppliers became challenging for OEMs with lean production. The challenge is argued to have been higher in MICs, and late industrialising countries in general, where local supplier firms often lacked the necessary capacity to ensure the lead OEMs' expectations (Humphrey and Memedovic, 2003). Therefore, OEMs with lean manufacturing started asking their suppliers in home locations to follow them to new locations. These 'follow-source suppliers', namely the Tier-1 suppliers, which are also called catalogue suppliers or Tier-0.5 suppliers, have become the OEMs' only direct suppliers. These suppliers are highly competent, have substantial capacity for research and development, and participate in designing the products. The relations between OEMs and the follow-source suppliers are balanced and are based on inter-dependency and high cooperation, which will qualify them as *relational* chains (Gereffi, Humphrey and Sturgeon, 2005; Sturgeon, Biesebroeck and Gereffi, 2008).

The follow-source suppliers have become key lead firms in AACs since they provide modules to the OEMs, and are responsible for managing the rest of the supply chain through buying parts and components from lower tier suppliers. These lead firms are also responsible for maintaining the quality and delivery expectations of the OEM throughout the chain. In contrast to this high capacity of the follow-source suppliers, the suppliers at lower tiers have limited capacity, and they face important pressures from the lead firms, including both the OEMs and the Tier-1 suppliers, concerning quality production and in-time delivery. Furthermore, these suppliers in the lower tiers of AACs often do not carry out any R&D, and receive all information about the product from their clients. Lead firms in these AACs often provide training to suppliers to minimise problems and maintain the just-in-time delivery of parts and components. As such, the relations between the follow-source suppliers and the suppliers in lower tiers of AACs can be described as 'captive' in the classification of Gereffi et al. (2005) (see Chapter 2).

The characteristics of the shop floor workers and their organisation are also very different in lean manufacturing as compared with mass production. Because quality and in-time delivery of products are critical, and disruptions can cause big problems, workers' skills constitute a fundamental issue in lean production. Firms need workers that can identify disruptions and resolve problems efficiently and on the spot (MacDuffie and Kochan, 1995). Therefore, in addition to the specific technical skills for production, shop floor workers in lean manufacturing must have a thorough understanding of firms' production processes, and must possess certain general skills such as reasoning, problem-solving, and enterprise skills in order to be able to recognise problems and intervene to find solutions (Piore and Sabel, 1984; MacDuffie and Kochan, 1995). Furthermore, workers need to have polyvalent skills that enable them to work in different production functions, which gives firms higher flexibility when resolving problems and adapting to technological changes (Florida and Kenney, 1991; Kaplinsky, 1995).

As skills constitute a central issue for firms with lean production, firms with lean manufacturing are argued to invest to a significant degree in their human resources and are argued to start adopting certain HRM 'bundles' that generate 'best outcomes', which have been labelled as High Performance Work Systems (HPWSs) (Geringer and Hebert, 1991; MacDuffie, 1995; Kochan, Lansbury, and MacDuffie, 1997; Appelbaum, 2000). HPWSs differ from the HRM strategies of firms with mass production regarding their skilling strategies for shop floor workers, namely recruitment, training, and career development practices, along with other elements of HRM (Jürgens and Krzywdzinski, 2016). In an ideal form of HPWS, the shop floor workers are organised as teams, in contrast to the hierarchical management in mass production, and they need to have some analytical and high general skills, in addition to the specific technical skills. Therefore, the selection criteria for production workers is argued to be very demanding, the recruitment process is meticulous, and continuous training and employee development are central in firms with lean production principles (Appelbaum, 2000; Jürgens and Krzywdzinski, 2016).

4.1.2 The Turkish and Mexican auto parts producers in global AACs

Both mass and lean production systems have been affecting the AAI suppliers from Mexico and Turkey because of two main reasons. Firstly, although lean production principles have been increasingly adopted in the global AAI, this has not resulted in a uniform production system worldwide, and most firms still apply mass production together with lean production principles. The lead OEMs produce somewhere on a scale of mass-to-lean production, rather than fully moving to lean production (Sturgeon, Biesebroeck, and Gereffi, 2008), and the Mexican and Turkish firms simultaneously participate in the supply chains of multiple OEMs that operate on a scale of mass-to-lean production. Therefore, both lean and mass production strategies influence the governance structures of AACs in which the suppliers from Turkey and Mexico participate. Secondly, the interviews with representatives of Mexican and Turkish suppliers revealed that mass production continues to be the main strategy of these suppliers, although some suppliers have started applying certain elements of lean management. Consequently, the supply chain management and HRM practices related to both mass and lean production have been influencing the supplier firms in Mexico and Turkey, including their skilling practices.

Because the Turkish and Mexican suppliers sell to lead OEMs with mass and lead production simultaneously, the modular and captive relations constitute the main governance structures for the suppliers studied in this book.[2] There are two main elements in these AACs that characterise the relations between suppliers and lead firms: (i) the *rules of the game* (i.e. the expectations of lead firms from suppliers and the quality management strategies applied by the lead firms) and (ii) *the game in action* (i.e. the methods for implementing quality management strategies and the intensity of interaction between supplier and the lead firm). The rules of the game and the game in action in modular and captive AACs then together affect the Mexican and Turkish supplier firms' activities, including their skilling practices.

Before going into the analysis about the influence of global AAI on Mexican and Turkish suppliers, it is important to elaborate the relations between the supplier and buyer firms in global AACs: there are two main periods of relations throughout a contract between the supplier and the lead firm, in which the rules of the game and the game in action vary. The first period is the *contracting period*, which refers to the period before a contract is signed between a supplier and a lead firm, and involves activities such as the investigation of the supplier by the lead firm or third parties, the supplier's self-assessment about the feasibility of buyer firms' expectation, the development of a contract, and training provided to suppliers on various matters such as the product specifications. The second period is the *production period*, in which the production takes place in the supplier firm, and which includes everyday production and delivery of products. The rest of this chapter mentions the differences between the contracting and production period in relevant sections.

---

[2] The very large firms in the sample, such as T6, T12, M12, and M13, are Tier-1 suppliers (of OEMs with lean manufacturing) and hence their links with the OEMs can be described as relational.

4.1.2.1 Suppliers in modular chains

Modular relations constitute a key AAC governance structure that affects the Turkish and Mexican suppliers' activities. Modular relations influence these suppliers through the OEMs' price expectations from suppliers and their standardised quality management strategy for supply chains (rules of the game), as well as the arms-length strategies they adopt to ensure their expectations are met and limited interaction between suppliers and lead firms (game in action) (Table 4.1).

Rules of the game: price expectations and standardised quality management

The Turkish and Mexican suppliers that participate in modular AACs face important pressures for maintaining a low price of their product and although the quality and in-time delivery of products are also important, they rather take a back seat in these chains. The price expectations are explained to suppliers in the contracting period, when the suppliers agree to incrementally reduce the price of their products in the later years of the production period. This is because suppliers' costs are higher in the initial years of a project, when they make more mistakes, but they start making fewer mistakes in the later years of a project period as they gain experience. The lead firms in these AACs are aware of this situation and they require their suppliers to reduce the price of product in the later years of a contract.

For maintaining low prices, the lead firms in these AACs have an arms-length approach in managing their supply chains, and they do not make substantial investments in their relations with suppliers. Using standardised quality management systems, and particularly the ISO/TS system, suffices for most OEMs in both contracting and production periods. The AAI suppliers are required to obtain the ISO/TS certificate in order to start negotiating a contract with these OEMs (within the contracting period), and they are asked to be up-to-date with their ISO/TS certification throughout the production period. The suppliers from both Mexico and Turkey state that their clients in modular AACs, namely those focusing on price and having arms-length relations, do not typically have additional requirements from them. Almost all of the interviewed suppliers already held an ISO/TS certificate at the time of interview and have been receiving periodical audits to keep their certificate up to date.[3]

The game in action: arms-length interaction between lead firms and suppliers

The focus on price and the adoption of ISO/TS for quality management have led to an arms-length interaction between the Mexican and Turkish suppliers and their clients in modular AACs. The arms-length interaction in these chains has three key elements: maintaining quality expectations through third parties (i.e. the ISO/TS

---

[3] This is except for some small suppliers in the state of Guanajuato in Mexico, which have been producing plastic or metal parts for other industries and recently started producing for the AAI with the new OEM investments in this region. These suppliers were in the process of getting the ISO/TS while they already held the ISO 9001.

Table 4.1 AAC governance and mechanisms of influence

	Rules of the Game		Game in Action		Pressures on Suppliers
	Main expectations	Quality management systems	Strategies to maintain expectations	Intensity of interaction	
Modular	Price	ISO/TS	ISO/TS audits	Online platforms Rare personal communication	Pressures for low price ISO/TS requirements
Captive	Timely response Quality	Lead firm-specific quality standards Supplier-specific quality management	Supplier evaluation Activities for performance enhancement Training	Intense personal communication Frequent Limited use of online platforms	Pressures for quality and in-time delivery Specific requirements from clients Pressures for target scoring in evaluations by lead firms Training by lead firms Extensive information flow from lead firms from suppliers

auditing), limited training and assistance provided to suppliers by lead firms, and having minimal and indirect communication between suppliers and lead firms.

The Mexican and Turkish suppliers in modular AACs have been going through periodical audits carried by third-party companies for receiving and maintaining their ISO/TS certificate. Although some supplier firms might be subject to additional inspections by the lead firm in the contracting period, there are often no further mechanisms for reviewing suppliers' activities during the production period. The main strategy for evaluating the suppliers in the production period for these lead firms has been looking at the measures on suppliers' performance, such as the number and frequency of faulty products and delivery problems.

Suppliers in these chains mention that their clients do not typically make any investments for improving the suppliers' capacity nor do they provide any assistance to the suppliers at any stage of a project. For example, while obtaining and maintaining an ISO/TS certificate is a requirement, it is in the full responsibility of supplier firms and lead firms do not provide any financial or technical assistance in the process. Similarly, the OEMs and other lead firms in modular chains have not developed training systems or performance-enhancement programmes for their suppliers, which is different from the lead firms in captive chains. Although some suppliers stated that they receive training from their clients in modular AACs, this training is not specific to the supplier or its operations but is often about the lead firm, the product to be produced, or the use of the OEM's online supplier platform. Suppliers mentioned that they have more independence when making decisions about their activities since the lead firms in these chains do not interfere in suppliers' internal matters in any way during both the contracting or production period, and even in cases of substantial problems that are caused by supplier firms (which is very different in captive AACs). For example, the representative from the Quality department of T9 mention:

> When a problem occurs, this OEM sends the problematic part back and simply asks us to send a new product. And if they make any loss because of us, they also send the receipt of their loss and make us pay for it... This OEM only tells us that there is a problem with this product. But they don't tell us what the problem is. They don't help at all to resolve the problem.

In line with the arms-length quality management, the day-to-day interaction of Mexican and Turkish suppliers with their clients in modular AACs is limited and often indirect. While there is some direct communication between the suppliers and lead firms in the contracting period for new clients, such as face-to-face meetings and inspections of the suppliers, online supplier platforms constitute the main method of communication in the production period. Each OEM has its own online platform, and once the relations move from contracting to production period, the supplier firms are given access to the online platform by the OEM they sell to. All day-to-day issues, which range from the issues about orders and product delivery to reporting production problems, are managed through these platforms during the production period. Methods of more direct and personal communication (e.g. face-to-face meetings, phoning, or emailing) are not typically used in the production period even for issues that can create important disruptions in production or those that require immediate action.

Influence on suppliers

The focus on price and the lower importance of quality of the product, the use of ISO/TS system for managing the supply chains, and the arms-length interaction between the suppliers and lead firms in modular AACs put unique pressures on Mexican and Turkish suppliers participating in these AACs. Although the price expectations and ISO/TS requirements in modular AACs have had some influence on the Turkish and Mexican suppliers' activities, this influence has been lower and more indirect as compared to the AACs with captive relations. At first instance, the lower expectations and arms-length relations in these chains provide some flexibility to suppliers in their activities, including their skilling practices. Nonetheless, the pressures about reducing the price together with the arms-length approach to quality management have created important challenges for the supplier firms to remain competitive in the modular AACs. As the sales representative from T17 explained, '[h]aving an ISO/TS certificate is like having a driving license. You need a driving license to drive a car but then it doesn't mean that you are a good driver. You need ISO/TS to produce for an OEM [original equipment manufacturer] but it doesn't mean that you do it well'. When aiming to reduce their production costs, many suppliers also made important sacrifices in the quality of their product. This has resulted in a 'sectoral downgrading' for several small suppliers, which have been pushed out of these AACs and have switched their activities to new sectors with lower value added, such as producing metal parts for the furniture industry.

The management of supplier firms through the ISO/TS system has had some influence on the activities of suppliers—particularly the suppliers from Mexico due to the institutional structures in Mexico and Turkey, which are explained in the following chapters. The supplier firms mentioned that they have been organising their activities in accordance with the ISO/TS requirements in order to enter the supply chains of certain OEMs and to remain in these supply chains. For example, small firms from Mexico and Turkey mentioned that they have used the ISO/TS guidelines to conduct a feasibility analysis before getting into a new contract with a client. Furthermore, some suppliers state that they use the ISO/TS criteria to understand the general expectations in the global AAI, which then helps them to shape their activities accordingly to meet those expectations. Similarly, many suppliers have been keeping records about their physical and human capital, such as their employees' education and skill levels and their inventory, and they hold information about products with problems and client complaints since these are required in the ISO/TS system. These documents then have been helpful for supplier firms to analyse their performance, resources, and activities, and compare these with the requirements of the ISO/TS certificate (Interview Notes).

As well as the general influence of modular AACs explained in this subsection, the rules of the game and the game in action in these chains have distinct effects on suppliers' skilling practices, which are explained in Section 4.2.

4.1.2.2 Suppliers in captive chains

Captive relations constitute the other main form of governance in AACs for the Mexican and Turkish auto parts suppliers, and take place mostly in the supply chains of OEMs with more lean production principles. The expectations of lead firms and the strategies they apply to ensure that these expectations are met (i.e. the rules of the game and game in action) are very different in these chains, leading to unique forms of interaction between these lead firms and their suppliers.

Rules of the game: high-quality expectations and in-depth supply chain management

Lead firms in captive AACs have higher and more specific expectations from their suppliers regarding the quality and delivery of products, and they adopt detailed supply chain management strategies to ensure that these expectations are met. Firstly, although the price is also important for these AACs, the quality and in-time delivery of products are much more critical compared to modular AACs. In fact, many representatives of supplier firms from Mexico and Turkey emphasised that their speed to respond to lead firms' changing demands and their flexibility to adapt to unexpected circumstances have been the main priorities of lead firms in captive AACs.

Although the ISO/TS certificate is a minimum requirement for many OEMs in captive AACs, it is insufficient to ensure the higher and more specific expectations of lead firms in these chains. Therefore, the Mexican and Turkish suppliers are asked to comply with further requirements and more specific expectations, which are maintained through detailed supplier management strategies of lead firms. An important strategy for lead firms in captive AACs has been imposing additional requirements about not only the products being produced, but also suppliers' production functions, machinery, and performance. Some lead OEMs apply specific and standardised quality management systems for this, such as the VDA (*Verband Der Automobilindustrie*) for Volkswagen, which are similar to the ISO/TS but include additional and more specific measures to manage suppliers' activities. Other lead firms manage their supplier relations through more tailor-made measures rather than a standardised system like VDA (Interview Notes). The suppliers interviewed for this book mention that because their clients in captive AACs provide in-depth explanation about the product specifications, expectations regarding the product quality, suppliers' production processes, and storage and delivery of products, these suppliers have very limited flexibility for shaping their activities, as they organise these to address their clients' expectations.

The game in action: close interaction between lead firms and suppliers
In contrast to the arms-length interaction in modular AACs, the Mexican and Turkish suppliers in captive AACs have very close interaction with their clients who aim to ensure that their higher and more specific expectations are met. The close interaction between lead firms and suppliers happens through not only the additional strategies the lead firms carry out, but also more frequent and direct day-to-day communication between suppliers and lead firms.

The lead firms in captive AACs perform three main types of activities to ensure that their expectations are met. Firstly, and different from the lead firms in modular AACs, the lead firms in these chains carry out periodic evaluations, which include inspections of suppliers' inventory and activities by an employee of the lead firm, such as checking suppliers' machinery, raw material, employment relations, and performance indicators. In some cases, suppliers also get 'graded' in these evaluations and are expected to hit a certain target in the grading system, such as receiving at least a B mark in a system where the highest grade is A (Interview Notes). Scoring lower than this target, which is set by the lead firm, can create major problems for suppliers in these chains and their future relations with that particular client. For instance, low scores in successive evaluations can make it harder for suppliers to get into that OEM's supply chain in future projects and sometimes can cause a breach of contract before the project is completed (Interview Notes).

Secondly, lead firms in captive chains carry out several activities for enhancing suppliers' performance. Providing training to suppliers is a key method for this. Several suppliers in Mexico and Turkey mentioned that they receive training from their clients in the contracting period to ensure that they have the capacity to comply with the quality and delivery expectations of these clients. Some suppliers receive training also in the production period if they score low in the periodic evaluations carried out by the lead firms or cause successive problems. The extent and content of training provided by lead firms may vary across AACs, depending on the priorities and supplier strategies of lead firms. On the one hand, the representatives from the Turkish and Mexican suppliers mention that some lead firms provide training on more general subjects, such as lean management principles and quality production systems, where suppliers have the opportunity to learn also about their clients' production processes and quality systems. These training programmes are often voluntary and open to all suppliers of lead firms, and suppliers are expected to pay a certain fee to participate in this training (Interview Notes). On the other hand, other lead firms provide tailor-made training to suppliers that focus on improving certain aspects of suppliers' production functions. In this case, the employees of lead firms spend some time in the supplier facilities for training supplier employees from different departments, and suppliers are not expected to pay for such training (Interview Notes).

In addition to training provided to suppliers, the lead firms in captive AACs take certain measures in cases of problems to prevent the repetition of such problems in the future, which is a key aspect that differentiate the captive AACs from the modular ones. Lead firms in captive AACs have different approaches also when dealing with problems in their supply chains. Some lead firms adopt a looser approach and provide more independence and flexibility to suppliers when dealing with supplier-caused problems. While the suppliers are given more information about the problems, they are asked to realise the causes of those problems on their own, and they are expected to prepare plans to resolve them. In this case, the supplier needs to carry out a thorough investigation of its products and production processes, develop a detailed plan for improvement, and explain all details of the plan to the representatives of the lead firm from relevant departments while it does not receive any assistance from the lead firm (Interview Notes). Other lead OEMs and Tier-1 firms have a more hands-on approach for resolving supplier-related problems. The suppliers in the AACs of these lead firms not only face pressures for resolving problems and improving their production functions, but also receive assistance from their clients for these, which then allows the lead firms to interfere in suppliers' operations. The interviewee from T9 explains this as follows:

> We had a project with [Tier-1-x]. There was a problem in the product and they helped us resolve the problem. They tell you 'do this and this to find the cause of the problem, and do this to resolve it'. Then they come and check if we make any progress and if there is no improvement, they intervene. They check our processes and say 'these are the causes of the problem. Do this and this, and work on these matters etc.'. At least they make suggestions and these are very helpful when resolving the problem.   (T9 Sales)

Thirdly, the day-to-day communication of the Mexican and Turkish suppliers with their clients is more frequent and more direct and personal in captive chains, compared to the modular chains. The representatives of firms in the sample mention that they are in constant communication with their clients. Furthermore, this communication takes place through more direct methods such as emailing, phoning and face-to-face meetings. For instance, the owner of M5 stated:

> This one client, for example, they want to have the contact details of all of us, up to my personal phone number. For any problem, they talk to me on the phone. So, we resolve the problems very quickly.

Although some lead firms in captive AACs utilise online platforms, this is at a much lesser extent compared to AACs with modular relations. The frequent and direct communication between suppliers and lead firms in captive chains creates an important mechanism for lead firms to influence suppliers' activities. Such communication helps the suppliers to understand their clients' needs and expectations more clearly, according to which they can then shape their activities. Furthermore, the regular and direct communication enables information flow between the suppliers and their clients and facilitates suppliers' rapid response to the demands of their clients and to resolve the problems that may occur (Interview Notes).

Influence on suppliers
The higher and more specific expectations from suppliers, the detailed quality management systems, the strategies adopted for enhancing suppliers' performance, and the frequent and direct communication between suppliers and lead firms in captive AACs put important pressures on suppliers which have mixed effects on them. For instance, while the higher expectations from lead firms are challenging to address for the AAI suppliers, the more frequent communication between the lead firms and suppliers makes it easier for the suppliers to understand the expectations of these clients, which then improves the suppliers' ability to address those expectations.

Similarly, the varying strategies adopted by different lead firms for ensuring that their expectations are met, namely the more and less hands-on approaches, have mixed influences on, and challenges for, the suppliers from Mexico and Turkey. The representative from M8 explains the variation between different lead firms' approach as follows:

> [OEM-Y, with modular governance] does not really help us to improve. But then they also don't expect much. But working with [OEM-X] is very hard. They expect a lot and they don't tell us how we can do that. And it is completely different for [OEM-Z]. They expect high quality but they also help us to achieve that quality. It is hard to do a lot when you don't know how.   (M8 Quality)

Furthermore, the necessity to address the high expectations in captive AACs led by OEMs that do not provide assistance can create significant challenges for the Mexican and Turkish suppliers in the AAI. In fact, the high expectations of OEM-X in Mexico without sufficient assistance have led to the emergence of a common joke amongst Mexican AAI suppliers. The joke is as follows:

> A supplier of [OEM-X] asks his friend whether he has heard strange noises coming from his new car [Model-A]. The friend says 'yes, but I don't understand what it is'. The supplier replies 'these noises are the cries of all auto parts suppliers who are selling to [OEM-X] and trying to fulfil their requirements.   (MS2)

Despite the challenges, some suppliers state that complying with high expectations with minimum guidance can be rewarding and result in improvements in supplier firms that facilitate their competitiveness in AACs. For instance, the representative from the Quality department of M3 stated:

> This [the improvement process demanded by OEM-X] was a very difficult and stressful task for us. But at that time [when we did the revision and improvement],

we were about to apply for another project. And the examination of our processes and the improvement required by OEM-X [...] were actually very beneficial for us. With this, we revised all our activities, improved ourselves, and managed to win the next bid.

Some suppliers mention that even though their profit margin is smaller for lead firms in captive AACs, they prefer these clients to the ones in modular AACs because of the clearer expectations and guidance provided by the former who do not 'give [the supplier] a headache' (T10 Owner).

Overall, the distinct pressures and lead firms' strategies in captive AACs have substantial influence on suppliers. Furthermore, these pressures and strategies create important mechanisms for lead firms to influence their suppliers' skilling practice, which is explained in the next section.

4.2 AACs' influence on skilling practices

The Mexican and Turkish suppliers' participation in global AACs has important influence on their skilling practices. On the one hand, the governance structures in modular and captive AACs, and the suppliers' simultaneous participation in AACs governed by both of these structures, put multiple pressures on supplier firms, which then affect their activities in distinct ways. On the other hand, the application of mass production with some lean management principles in supplier firms influences these firms' recruitment, training, and employee development practices.

4.2.1 Indirect influence

The main influence of AACs on Mexican and Turkish suppliers' skilling practices happens indirectly, through lead firms' expectations from suppliers regarding price, quality, and delivery of products, as well as the strategies they adopt to ensure that these expectations are met. On the one hand, the pressures concerning the price of products push the suppliers to make limited investments in their employees and the training of these employees. On the other hand, the quality and in-time delivery expectations pressurise the supplier firms to employ workers with skills and thus, invest more in their skilling activities. The suppliers in Mexico and Turkey, which simultaneously participate in modular and captive AACs, organise their skilling practices to address these joint pressures, which then results in distinct skilling practices.

The firm representatives from the Turkish and Mexican AAI firms mention that they need to keep their labour costs minimal to address their buyers' price expectations. A key strategy for this for firms from both countries has been employing a group of temporary workers who do not have experience or technical qualification.

These workers are helpful in the first few years of a project with an OEM, when suppliers make more mistakes and need more workers to rectify the mistakes. These temporary workers are employed in labour-intensive tasks, and suppliers do not make substantial investments for their recruitment or training. When the suppliers start making fewer mistakes in the later years of a project and face pressures to reduce their price, some of these temporary workers are dismissed, which helps the suppliers to reduce their labour costs and hence to cut their price. The HR representative from T9 explains this as follows:

> In a project period [with OEMs], you need to employ more workers during the first years because you are inexperienced and sometimes you need to intervene manually in the production process when a problem arises. However, with years, the errors decrease and the product can be produced faster and more easily on the production line. So, we need fewer manual operators in the later years of a project.

The reduction in the number of workers can happen in two main ways in the later years of a production period. Firstly, some of the temporary workers leave themselves due to their lower pay and insecure working conditions, which helps firms to naturally reduce the number of workers. Firing is the second option since these workers are hired on temporary contracts and their dismissal does not create large compensations for suppliers—also because these temporary workers are often not unionised due to the weakened unions in the two countries (see Chapter 5 for Turkey and Chapter 6 for Mexico). Still, the practices and conditions of temporary employment vary between Mexico and Turkey due to the different institutional arrangements in these countries, which are explained in the following chapters of the book.

In addition to the price expectations in modular AACs, the expectations for quality and in-time delivery in captive chains have substantial influence on the Mexican and Turkish suppliers' skilling strategies. Several representatives of the supplier firms mentioned that having a workforce with analytical and technical skills has been a key strategy to respond to the quality and in-time expectations of their clients. For instance, the HR representative from T9 responded to the question '*Do your buyers have any expectations from you regarding your shop floor workers?*' as follows:

> Of course. They ask for products with zero defects. To attain this, we need to have good workers. We have some metrics to evaluate our workers, such as their education level, any training they have taken, and other issues like absenteeism. We try to ensure good scores on these matters so that we can have the necessary human resource to respond to our clients' demands.

Skilling practices have been shown as a major strategy for addressing clients' quality and delivery expectations by several suppliers. For instance, suppliers from Mexico and Turkey explain this situation as follows:

Our clients evaluate [our performance] and to succeed in that [evaluation], we need to have skilled workers. So, we develop training programmes to achieve that.   (M11 HR)

Our clients ask for products with good quality and they want them to be delivered on-time without any problems. For this, we need good workers with good technical training. If you want to produce high quality goods, it is very important that your principles are understood by employees at all levels of production. If you can't do that, you can't reach your aims about quality or in-time delivery. So, we pay a lot of attention to our [shop floor] workers starting from their recruitment. We only recruit those with relevant technical education.   (T18 Quality)

In sum, governance structures in both modular and captive chains influence suppliers' skilling practices in an indirect way through shaping their demand for different types of workers. While the modular chains put pressure on suppliers to reduce labour costs and result in the temporary employment of a group of inexperienced/untrained workers, the quality and in-time delivery expectations in captive chains push suppliers to employ some skilled workers. These together influence the arrangement of shop floor positions in both the Mexican and Turkish suppliers, and the skills necessary for these positions, which are explained in section 4.2.3.

4.2.2 Direct influence

In addition to the indirect influence on skilling through affecting labour demand, AAC governance has some, albeit limited, direct effects on suppliers' skilling practices, and this effect varies between the firms in Mexico and Turkey.

The quality management systems adopted by lead firms, including the ISO/TS system and the firm-specific quality management systems applied by some OEMs, have several elements that concern workers and their skills, and, thus, they have direct influence on suppliers' skilling activities. The ISO/TS system constitutes an important mechanism for direct influence since it involves several sections related to the management of shop floor workers and organisation of their skills. For example, the ISO/TS system requires firms to define the positions on the shop floor and specify the skills needed for these positions. Firms then need to employ workers complying with the post requirements and must prove that their workers have the specified skills. Therefore, with the aim of meeting these requirements, many suppliers have defined skill requirements for the shop floor positions and have been keeping detailed records about their workers' skills, which are then shown to ISO/TS auditors during evaluations. The HR manager from M16 explains this as follows:

We record all information about training and each worker's skill level. Because of the quality system requirements [of ISO/TS], we must have data about our workers and their skills, and this must be based on standardised measures. The ISO/TS is the reason why we record all information about our workers.

Skill matrices have been an important area of convergence of skilling practices in the global AAI, and both the Mexican and Turkish suppliers use 'skill matrices' for recording the information about their workers' skills and managing the skill profile in the company. The skill matrices contain detailed information about the skills of each worker in the company, such as their training, the tasks they can carry out, and their level of knowledge and experience in each task, which are aligned with ISO/TS skill requirements. These matrices are updated as workers gain experience and participate in training programmes. Because the skill matrices provide a detailed account of workers' skills, firms utilise these matrices when managing their shop floor workers and when making decisions about workers' career development. Firms use the skill matrices also to compare their existing skill profile with the skills required in post descriptions, which then helps them to realise the skill gaps and develop strategies to address those gaps.

The ISO/TS system and the skill matrices have provided important guidelines for HRM strategy particularly in the smaller auto parts producers in Mexico. Many firms in Mexico stated that they utilise the ISO/TS system when they organise the firm-level training and have 'certified' workers in accordance with the ISO/TS requirements.[4] Furthermore, the skill matrices have been very helpful for developing strategies to address the skill gaps in these firms. In contrast to Mexico, although the firms in Turkey also use the ISO/TS system and skill matrices, these have not been as critical since the firms organise their skilling strategies more in line with the institutional arrangements surrounding them (see Chapter 7).

In addition to the ISO/TS and skill matrices, the governance structures in captive AACs also have some direct influence on suppliers' skilling practices, particularly in Mexico. Some lead firms require their Mexican suppliers to employ workers with external certification for certain positions, such as welding and forklift operators. In these cases, suppliers need to employ workers certified by independent and accredited certification institutions. The methods of finding such externally certified workers vary considerably across suppliers in Mexico: Most firms mentioned that they send their current employees to external institutions for skill testing and certification because finding workers with such certification in the labour market is very difficult and expensive (Interview Notes). For example, the HR representative from M1 explains this situation as follows:

> We certified some workers externally because it was required by one of our customers. They wanted us to have welding operators with external certification. We were already training our workers to become welding operators and we were providing both theoretical and practical training. But then, we had to use the external certification institute only because our client asked for it.

---

[4] This is in fact the reason why the term 'certified workers' was confused in Mexico, as explained in Chapter 3. The 'certification' of workers in Mexico referred to the employment of workers with the skills explained in the job post, as required by ISO/TS.

The external certification is still limited to only a small group of employees working in the product lines of the specific buyers that require the external certification. Therefore, employees in other departments continue to acquire skills through firm-level training and/or on-the-job learning, and do not receive external certification. For instance, the owner of M14 stated:

> Our other clients [other than the one requiring certification] are not that demand-ing. They want our workers to be skilled and to be able to manage the required tasks. But we can ensure that ourselves through internal training. And that's suffi-cient for them.

4.2.3   Skilling implications of globalisation in the AAI: convergence of shop floor organisation and skill needs

The governance structures in both modular and captive AACs jointly affect the Mexican and Turkish suppliers due to the simultaneous participation of these firms in both types of the AACs. This leads to some similarities between the AAI firms in the two countries regarding (i) the (hierarchical) organisation of shop floor workers and (ii) the types of skills needed for the shop floor positions.

Juergens and Krzywdzinski (2016) describe the shop floor organisation as the division of tasks among direct production workers and the responsibilities and roles of superior and inferior staff., The Mexican and Turkish suppliers' participation in multiple types of AACs and their aim to simultaneously respond to their clients' price and quality expectations in these chains have resulted in a similar way of organising their shop floor workers. There are four main groups of direct production workers with distinct skill profiles in both the Mexican and Turkish AAI suppliers, and these workers are hierarchically organised in firms from the two countries, and not horizontally in teams as it is in HPWSs. The hierarchy between the workers is based on workers' level of experience, educational attainment, and participation in training. Although some supplier firms stated that they started organising their shop floor workers in line with lean management principles and as teams, which include team members, team leaders, and as groups that comprise a number of teams led by a group leader, such organisation has not been implemented. The main change has been in the labelling of workers, and the shop floor organisation has remained hierarchical. Therefore, the shop floors in both the Mexican and Turkish suppliers are similar and include a hierarchical organisation of auxiliary workers/trainees < operators/team members < foremen/team leaders < group leaders/shift supervisors.

The first group, the auxiliary workers/trainees, are the inexperienced and/or untrained workers. They carry out tasks requiring low skills, are employed through temporary contracts, and have lower wages compared to other employees of the firm. While some of these workers can become regular operators with experience and move to more secure contracts, many of these workers leave the firm after a short period or are dismissed when the suppliers need to reduce their costs in the later years of a project period (in the modular AACs). The education and skill profile and employment practices of auxiliary workers vary across Mexican and Turkish firms due to the different institutional environments surrounding these firms (see Chapters 7 and 8).

The second group of direct production workers in both Mexican and Turkish suppliers is the operators/team members. These workers have certain specific skills and are employed in tasks that range from simple manual jobs to operating certain machinery in production departments. These workers help to produce the goods in line with their clients' quality expectations (in captive AACs). Some of the auxiliary workers are promoted to the operator positions, while the recruitment of new workers with relevant experience or training is also possible for these positions.

The foremen/team leaders, which constitute the third group, are in charge of managing a small group of operators in each production department. They need to have experience in different functions in that particular department, and the capacity to train new and inexperienced workers. Additionally, they are expected to have some analytical skills such as problem-solving and independent decision-making, as well as managerial skills including leadership and team management. These workers are key for noticing problems in production and intervening to prevent problems, which are significant for the captive AACs.

Last, there are shift supervisors/group leaders who are responsible for the production in one shift.[5] These workers are required to know all production processes in the company, have higher analytical and managerial skills, and possess knowledge about multiple production functions. These workers oversee the production in a number of departments or the whole production on the shop floor, depending on the size of the company. In larger companies, a few number of teams form groups managed by the group leader, and a few number of groups form the whole production on the shop floor, which is managed by shift supervisor or production manager. In smaller firms, a group of teams is directly managed by a shift supervisor or production manager. These workers are responsible for a larger amount of tasks in production production and are important for the management of staff for producing products with the required quality and delivery specifications.

4.3 Conclusion

This chapter has explained the effects of globalisation in the AAI on firms' skilling strategies and shown the patterns of convergence. More specifically, it has examined how the production systems in the global AAI and governance structures in AACs affect suppliers' skilling practices directly and indirectly, and whether they lead to a convergence between the Mexican and Turkish AAI firms. The chapter has first

---

[5] Most of the interviewed firms have two or three 8-hour shifts a day.

Table 4.2 AAC governance and skilling practices

Value Chain Governance	Influence on Skilling Practices		Joint Skilling Implications of Modular and Captive AACs
	Direct influence	Indirect influence	
Modular AACs	ISO/TS sections about skill profile Skill matrices for the management of firm-level skill profile	Pressures on reducing price	Need for inexperienced and/ or untrained workers to reduce costs Need for trained and experienced workers to ensure quality
Captive AACs	Clients' direct requests about workers' skills, training, and certification	Pressures for quality production	Hierarchical organisation of shop floor workers Some but haphazard direct influence on training and hiring (in Mexico)

provided a general overview on the globalisation in the AAI, where it elaborated the different types of production systems that lead to distinct governance structures and HRM practices in AACs. It has shown how the governance structures put pressures on supplier firms and thus, influence their skilling arrangements, as well as examining the patterns of convergence to HRM also through suppliers' production systems.

Table 4.2 summarises the findings of this chapter. The discussion in the chapter has shown that the pressures in global AACs lead to similarities in the types of skills needed on the production floor, and the hierarchical organisation of the workers. Such similarities are due to two intersecting reasons. Firstly, there is no convergence towards lean production in the global AAI, and both lead firms and suppliers produce in a scale of mass-to-lean production. Secondly, because the Mexican and Turkish suppliers participate in multiple AACs that are led by OEMs with different production methods, their production is influenced by multiple governance structures, namely the modular and captive relations, which then jointly influence their skilling strategies.

The main influence in modular AACs happens indirectly through the lead firms' expectations about price, which pushes the suppliers to focus on reducing labour costs and thus to make limited investments in recruitment and training. The modular AACs also have some, although limited, channels for direct influence, through the ISO/TS sections about the skills of suppliers' employees and skill matrices. Captive AACs influence suppliers' skilling practices both directly and indirectly, and this influence is more intense compared to the modular AACs. The higher expectations of lead firms from suppliers regarding the quality and in-time delivery result in suppliers' employing skilled workers in critical positions on the shop floor. Additionally, lead firms' specific requirements regarding the suppliers' workforce and their skills create mechanisms for direct influence on suppliers' skilling practices

(Table 4.2). Although some firms in both Mexico and Turkey have started adopting lean management principles, there has not been convergence towards HPWSs.

Because of the distinct expectations in modular and captive chains and suppliers' participation in both types of AACs, the Mexican and Turkish suppliers need a group of unskilled workers to reduce their costs and address their clients' price expectations, as well as a group of skilled workers to ensure their clients' quality and in-time delivery expectations. This has resulted in four main groups of direct production workers that are hierarchically organised: auxiliary workers/trainees, operators/team members, foremen/team leaders, and shift supervisors/group leaders.

Despite the similar organisation of shop floor positions and the similar skills needed for these positions in the Mexican and Turkish suppliers, it is not possible to observe a convergence towards HPWSs or a race to the bottom in the firms from the two countries. There are important differences between the practices of the Mexican and Turkish firms to find workers for the shop floor positions, and these differences stem from their different institutional environments. The different skilling practices then have distinct outcomes for workers and firms in the AAI, and will lead to variation of development experiences in the two countries. The differences in skilling practices and outcomes are explained in the chapters following this one.

5

Institutions of skill formation in Turkey

the role of the state

After discussing the patterns of convergence between the Mexican and Turkish firms' skilling strategies due to their participation in auto parts-automotive value chains in previous chapter, the book now focuses on the national institutions that influence firms' skilling strategies in the current and following chapters. According to the studies with an institutional approach, the national institutions that surround firms are important determinants of firm activity and for the outcomes of this activity, even in the context of globalisation. The researchers with such an approach argue that even though globalisation puts important pressures on firms and affects their activity, there is no convergence towards one type of economic activity because of the national institutions. This chapter focuses on the case of Turkey, and it examines the institutions that affect the skilling strategies of Turkish auto parts suppliers. It studies the public vocational education and training system (VET) system, as well as the 'other institutions' that influence firms' skilling practices and thus become complementarities of the multilevel skill system in Turkey. The other institutions in this regard include the labour regulations and wage-setting institutions, firms' location and public transportation facilities around that location, and the military service requirement for men. The chapter starts with a thorough discussion on the VET system in Turkey, and the role of the state and nonstate actors. Later, it elaborates the other institutions that influence the firm-level skilling practices and explains their functioning. The last section then summarises the findings and the main arguments of the chapter.

5.1 The statist VET system

Public education and training systems constitute an important macro-level institution in the multilevel skill systems since they define the types of skills available in labour markets and outline the possible training instruments available to firms and workers. The public VET system in Turkey has been a significant instrument for skill formation especially for the auto parts-automotive industry (AAI), notwithstanding the problems of this system regarding the quality of training. There are four main types of institutions within the Turkish public VET system: Vocational High Schools (VHS) system, the dual apprenticeship system, the training programmes for the unemployed within the scope of active labour market policies, and the skill

Global Production, National Institutions, and Skill Formation: The Political Economy of Training and Employment in Auto Parts Suppliers from Mexico And Turkey. Merve Sancak, Oxford University Press. © Merve Sancak 2022.
DOI: 10.1093/oso/9780198860655.003.0005

Table 5.1 Public VET programmes in Turkey

Type	VET Programme	Year	Length	Training Content	Actors Involved
IVET	VHS	1986	4 years	Mainly at schools (minimum 8–15 per cent of training in a firm, depending on school type)	MEB, individual firms
	Apprenticeship	1986	2–4 years	80 per cent in firm, 20 per cent in MEM	MEB, TESK, individual firms
CVET	UMEM	2010	3–6 months	80 per cent in firm, 20 per cent in a VET institute (mainly VHS)	İŞKUR and TOBB (as managers); and MEB, TOBB-ETU University
	İşbaşı eğitim	2015	3–6 months	Only in firm	İŞKUR, individual firms
	Skill standardisation	2006	varied*	n.a.	MYK

* Depending on the necessity of additional training

n.a. Not available

standardisation and certification system (Table 5.1). While the first two constitute the initial-VET system (IVET), the latter two are parts of the continuing-VET (CVET) system.[1] This section analyses the Turkish VET system through the Thelen's (2014) version of Busemeyer and Trampusch (2012a) approach on the neuralgic points of VET systems (see Chapter 2).[2]

5.1.1 IVET programmes

The IVET system in Turkey is managed through the Apprenticeship and Vocational Education Law[3] (No 3308) (hereafter, the VET Law), which was introduced in 1986. This law explains the basic regulations regarding VET in VHSs and the apprenticeship system, and defines the responsibilities of the state and firms in both systems. This law remains to be the main regulation shaping the Turkish IVET system, although there were several changes and updates in the IVET system in the 1990s and 2000s.[4]

5.1.1.1 VHSs

VHSs constitute the principal VET institution in Turkey. These schools form the largest share of the VET system,[5] and are frequently used for developing skills for the

---

[1] Although the skill-standardisation system is not a method for developing skills by itself, it is import-ant to discuss it as part of the public VET system because it constitutes a critical part in lifelong learning, determines who has the control over VET and skills, and influences workers' mobility.

[2] For the skill standardisation and certification system, I focus the analysis on 'who controls' only, as this is the main element defining the division of responsibility between firms and the state.

[3] Its name was changed to Law on Vocational Education in 2001.

[4] 2000s corresponds to 2000–2010 throughout this chapter.

[5] In 2012, 75 per cent of those in all VET programmes were in VHSs (Sancak, 2020).

labour market (Table 5.1). VHSs are one of the three main school types in the formal education system at upper-secondary level in Turkey.[6] The VHSs have subcategories according to the sector of economy, such as Industrial VHSs and Tourism VHSs.[7] Industrial VHSs have been key institutions for developing skills for the AAI.

Who provides VET in VHS system?

The state has the main responsibility for providing VET in VHSs, while firms' involvement in VET provision is limited and regulated by the state. The main training in VHSs takes place at schools that are administered by the Ministry of National Education (*Milli Eğitim Bakanlığı*—MEB) and lasts 4 years. In the first year, the students receive an academic education on general subjects such as *Maths* and *Turkish Literature*, and the same curriculum is applied for the first-year high school students in the VHSs, *Anadolu Lisesi* and *İmam Hatip* schools (Grade 9 students). The training on technical areas specific to a vocational subject starts in the second year (Grade 10), and the students specialise in that subject in the third and fourth years (Grades 11 and 12).

Firms can get involved in the provision of VET in the VHS system through the practical training of VHS students. Firms' involvement in VET provision happens firstly because VHS students are required to conduct a minimum of 300 hours of practical training in a firm. Secondly, according to the VET Law, firms with more than 10 workers are obliged to provide training to VHS students, while firms with more than 200 workers are required to have a dedicated department and hire specialised personnel for the training of students from VHSs. Nevertheless, firms' overall involvement in providing VET in the VHS system is still limited because the time spent for practical training in a firm comprises a very small part of the total training in VHSs (i.e. about 20 per cent of the total education). Furthermore, although firms are obliged to provide training to VHS students, and students are required to have practical training in a firm to receive a VHS diploma, there are important problems regarding the actual happening of the firm-level training. This is primarily because many firms and students see the training requirements as a box-ticking exercise rather than a skill-development opportunity and show minimum commitment to this training (Interview Notes).

Who pays for VET in the VHS system?

The state is the main financier of VET in VHSs in Turkey, and the state commitment to the financing of VHSs has been high. VHS system constitutes a substantial share of the MEB's budget, and public spending for IVET in Turkey is much higher

---

[6] The other school types at this level are the general high schools (*Anadolu Lisesi*) that provide more academic training, and the Imam and Preacher Schools (*İmam Hatip Lisesi*) that focus on religious education. While the students with higher academic achievements prefer *Anadolu Lisesi*, the ones with lower grades study in either VHSs or *İmam Hatips*.

[7] These categories changed with the new legislations introduced in the late 2010s.

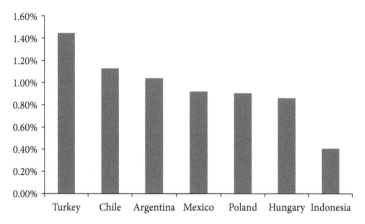

Figure 5.1 VET spending as percentage of gross domestic product in selected
MICs (2013)
Source: Sancak (2020)

than the spending in Mexico and other middle-income countries (MICs)
(Figure 5.1).

Firms' contribution to financing VET at VHSs happens mainly through employing trainees from these schools, as firms must pay a salary to the trainees—which
needs to be at least 30 per cent of the minimum wage according to the Labour Law,
and due to firms' expenses for the firm-level training, such as trainer personnel
expenses. Other expenses of VET at VHSs, such as students' social security contributions, are paid by the state and through the schools. Firms can also contribute to
the financing of training in VHSs through developing projects with these schools or
helping the schools to improve their infrastructure (Interview Notes). However, this
is voluntary, usually ad hoc, and depends on firms' willingness to make such contributions. When the limited amount of time spent at a firm for practical training is
considered, it can be argued that firms' contribution to financing the training in
VHSs is limited.

Who controls VET in the VHS system?

The state is the main controller in the VHS system in Turkey through the dominance
of the MEB in this system. The MEB centrally manages all VHSs in the country, and
all schools are obliged to abide by a standardised curriculum prepared by the ministry. Furthermore, the MEB controls the teaching material and the personnel of all
VHSs throughout the country, although individual schools may have some, albeit
limited, autonomy in these aspects. The MEB has control over the VHSs also through
the centralised and standardised certification of skills, namely the *VHS diploma* that
can be used as occupational certificates. Additionally, the VHS diploma can act as an
upper-secondary education diploma, which allows the graduates of VHSs to continue to further education in postsecondary-nontertiary or tertiary institutions.

Firms' control over VET in the VHS system is very limited in Turkey both at collect-ive and individual levels. The main mechanism for firms to get collectively involved in the VHS system is through their participation in the tripartite policymaking bodies via business associations. Business associations in Turkey, and particularly the Union of Chambers and Commodity Exchanges of Turkey (*Türkiye Odalar ve Borsalar Birliği*—TOBB), but also other associations including the Confederation of Turkish Tradesmen and Craftsmen (*Türkiye Esnaf ve Sanatkarlar Konfederasyonu*—TESK), have been included in several policy platforms that have influenced the VHS system, such as the National Education Council, the National VET Council, Provincial Employment and VET Councils, and the Vocational and Technical Education Strategy Paper and Action Plan. These platforms have provided important mechanisms to the business associations to influence the VHS system and have some control over VET in these schools. Still, the involvement of firms in managing VHSs is marginal when compared with the state's dominance in the VHS system, and the state remains to be the main controller over VET in upper-secondary education in Turkey.[8]

In addition to the weak firm control at the collective level, firms' influence over training in the VHS system is limited at the individual level and is regulated by the state. There are three main mechanisms for firms to have some control over VET in the VHS system at the individual level. Firstly, firms can influence the practical training of VHS students through the firm-level practical training of these students. Secondly, VHSs can develop projects with firms, such as projects to improve the school infrastructure, which gives firms an opportunity to shape the training pro-vided within these schools—for example, through offering training equipment and machinery to these schools and thus familiarising the VHS students with firm's machinery. Thirdly, according to a regulation introduced in 2012, firms receive a state subsidy to establish VHSs in Organised Industrial Zones (OIZ), which has encouraged many firms to set up such schools and thus, has provided the firms important mechanisms to influence the decisions on the infrastructure of and train-ing content in these schools (ERG, 2013; TE14). These all create important oppor-tunities for firms to influence the training of VHS students and shape this training in accordance with their needs.

Despite the abovementioned influence of firms on the VET in VHSs, this influ-ence is marginal, and the MEB remains to be the main controller of VET in VHSs. This is because the VHSs are still under the central administration of the MEB, and firms' involvement in the training is regulated by the Labour Law (Number 4857, Article 84 and Article 85).[9] Furthermore, the individual schools and local adminis-tration have very limited room to make independent decisions about the training

---

[8] The management of the VET system has changed in the later years and by 2019: the TOBB gained further control in the VHS system in Turkey. However, this happened after the field research for this book was conducted, and the impact of the higher control by TOBB had not influenced the Turkish VET sys-tem at the time of fieldwork.

[9] The Labour Law includes further particulars on other issues such as the number of trainees and the employment contracts and social security of trainees.

in VHSs, the power being concentrated on the central administration of the MEB. Lastly, although firms can develop projects with VHSs or establish new VHSs, firms' involvement in these is regulated by the state and firms cannot act independently from the MEB.

VHSs as a viable alternative to general education?

Despite the high state commitment to and some firm involvement in the VHS system, VET at upper-secondary level has not become a viable alternative to general education in Turkey. Although the participation to VHSs in Turkey has been much higher compared to many MICs and it has been increasing over the last decades, many graduates of VHSs do not join the labour market after they complete their studies but rather continue studying. This has substantial influence on the availability of workers with a VET certificate in the labour market and hence will affect the skilling strategies of AAI firms in Turkey, as discussed in Chapter 7.

VHSs have not been popular among students, families, or employers in Turkey for many years due to the problems in the system. Both public commitment to and firms' involvement in VET was low in Turkey until the 2000s, which created important issues regarding the quality of the training in VHSs. Furthermore, the 'ratio obstacle' (*katsayı engeli*), which was used for calculating VHS graduates' scores in the centralised national university entrance exam, was putting the VHS students at a disadvantage when they wanted to continue to higher education. Therefore, it has been argued that the ratio obstacle was a major factor decreasing the appeal of VHSs amongst the students of upper-secondary education (World Bank, 2008). In the end, the main participants of VHSs in Turkey have been disadvantaged students, namely those from poorer families and those with low academic scores, while these schools were usually unable to address firms' skill needs (Kenar, 2010; ERG, 2012).

The governments in the 2000s took several measures and collaborated with firms to increase the appeal of VHSs for both employers and workers (Sancak, 2020). Important changes were made in the VHS system to improve the quality of training and the responsiveness of VHSs to both workers' and firms' needs (Sancak, 2020). The possibility of 'direct transition' (*dikey geçiş*) was introduced in 2003, which allowed VHS students to study in the 2-year postsecondary-nontertiary institutions (*Meslek Yüksek Okulu*—MYO) without further requirements. Additionally, the 'ratio obstacle' was lifted in 2010, which increased the permeability between VHSs and higher education. These measures indeed have helped to raise the appeal of VHSs to students at upper-secondary level (Figure 5.2), and the share of VHS students amongst the new entrants of upper-secondary schools increased by 35 per cent in 2010–2013, right after the 'ratio obstacle' was lifted (ERG, 2014).

While the measures that were taken to improve the permeability between VHSs and higher education were successful to increase the number of students participating in VHSs, they have had unintended consequences. As a result of the increased permeability, many graduates of VHSs do not join the labour market but go to study in MYOs to get 'useless degrees' (TS8), even though the extra 2 years of education in

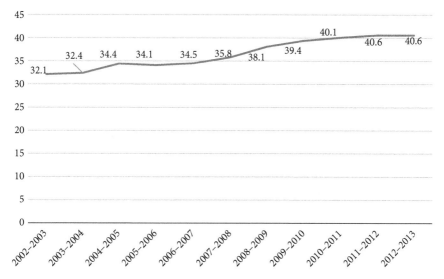

Figure 5.2 Share of VHS students in upper-secondary education (per cent)
Source: Sancak (2020)

MYOs does not provide substantial skills or give an opportunity for higher income. A graduate of a VHS explained this as follows:

> My foreman during internship told me that I was ready for work and that I shouldn't waste time with higher education. Yet, I still went for a 2-year higher education institution [MYO], where I haven't learned all that much as my high school provided better education. In the end, I started working at the same company upon graduation. I still think being a university graduate increases my status in life.   (Quoted in the report by Sayan and Yavçan (2013, p. 28))

Therefore, although the number of students participating in VHSs has increased in the 2000s, the number of VHS graduates in the labour market has not increased as much. For example, in 2008, 82 per cent of the students in VHSs aimed to study at a postsecondary or tertiary education institute once they complete their training (MEB, 2008). Furthermore, in 2010, 35 per cent of the graduates of VET programmes did not join the labour market after completing their studies (MEB, 2018).

5.1.1.2 The apprenticeship system
The apprenticeship system is the other main component of the Turkish public IVET system, although the share of this system in the overall VET system has been small. It is a dual-training programme similar to the German apprenticeship system, and individuals who have completed the mandatory basic education can participate in the apprenticeship system. Individuals enter the system as apprentices, and training as an apprentice takes from 2 to 4 years depending on the occupation. The standards

and requirements of training are determined and managed by the MEB for most occupations, while the Confederation of Turkish Tradesmen and Craftsmen (TESK) manages a small number of craft-based occupations that are not covered in the VET Law.[10]

Firms have the main responsibility of providing VET in the Turkish apprenticeship system: the participants spend 80 per cent of their time in a firm for practical training, and they receive theoretical training in a Vocational Training Centre (*Mesleki Eğitim Merkezi*—MEM) in the remaining 20 per cent of their training time. Firms partake the full responsibility for organising and providing the firm-level training, whilst the theoretical training is managed and provided by the MEB. At the end of the required training period, apprentices go through an examination organised by a MEM and receive a journeyman (*kalfa*) certificate. A journeyman can become a master (*usta*) after 5 years of experience as a journeyman, and completing the relevant examination requirements. The certification of skills and management of this by the MEB in the apprenticeship system gives the MEB an important power for controlling VET within the apprenticeship system.

Similar to the German system, the responsibility of financing VET in the Turkish apprenticeship system is shared between the firm, the state, and the apprentice. Firms are obliged to pay a salary to their apprentices, which is lower than the minimum wage but cannot be less than the 30 per cent of it. Furthermore, the state provides the financial resources for MEMs, which deliver the theoretical training and pay apprentices' social security contributions. Despite this infrastructure, state spending for the apprenticeship system has been low and has been decreasing over the years due to the declining participation rates in this system (Interview Notes).

The apprenticeship system has not become a viable alternative to general education in Turkey, and it is almost impossible for apprentices to switch to general education institutes or continue to higher education. Although the apprenticeship system is part of the IVET system, and is managed by the MEB, the apprenticeship certificates are occupational certificates, and are not formal education diplomas. Therefore, the apprenticeship certificates cannot be used to continue to higher education. Due to these restrictions regarding its permeability and the higher status attached to general and higher education, the apprenticeship system has not been popular amongst young individuals in Turkey (Kenar, 2009; MEB, 2009). Resultantly, apprenticeship has increasingly become a 'last resort' for young people with disadvantaged backgrounds, including those from poor families, those with low academic scores, and the dropouts of upper-secondary education institutes (Kenar, 2009).

5.1.2 Continuing-VET programmes

In contrast to the long legacy of IVET, CVET is much newer in Turkey but has started having an important role for skill development. The CVET system includes

---

[10] The apprenticeship system became also a part of the CVET in Turkey after the fieldwork for this book was completed.

retraining programmes for the unemployed and the skill standardisation and certification system, which have become important institutions in the Turkish VET system since the 2010s.

5.1.2.1 Retraining programmes for the unemployed

The retraining programmes for the unemployed were first introduced in the beginning of the 2000s as part of active labour market policies, and became a major social policy tool especially after the global financial crisis, which substantially increased the level of unemployment in the country. The Turkish Employment Agency (*Türkiye İş Kurumu*—İŞKUR), which is an institution under the management of the Ministry of Labour and Social Security (*Çalışma ve Sosyal Güvenlik Bakanlığı*—ÇSGB), is the main responsible body for managing the retraining programmes in Turkey, and these programmes include several elements that enable firms' involvement in them both at individual and collective levels.

When the fieldwork for this book was conducted (i.e. 2014–2015), there was one main retraining programme for the unemployed, which was called the Specialised Occupation Centres Programme (*Uzmanlaşmış Meslek Edindirme Merkezleri*—UMEM). This programme was developed in 2010, in the aftermath of the global financial crisis, when the country experienced high levels of unemployment.[11] The aim of this programme was to address the unemployment problem in the country while also responding to the SMEs' increasing needs for skilled workers (Sancak, 2020). The partners of the UMEM include the İŞKUR, TOBB, MEB, and the TOBB University of Economics and Technology (TOBB-ETU), which is a university established and managed by the TOBB. The İŞKUR and TOBB are the main managers of UMEM, with the İŞKUR being its main financier, as the İŞKUR manages the whole programme and pays for the trainees' daily allowance and social security contributions.

The courses within the UMEM include both theoretical training organised by the MEB, and practical training that takes place in firms. The TOBB plays a major role in deciding the type and location of the training courses through conducting surveys among its member firms, and determining the necessary courses to be opened. The TOBB is also responsible for managing the firm-level training through its local offices, which link the member firms with the unemployed. The successful participants of the UMEM courses receive an occupational certificate approved by the Vocational Qualifications Authority (*Mesleki Yeterlilikler Kurumu*—MYK) and firms employing UMEM trainees are obliged to offer a full-time contract to at least 50 per cent of the successful trainees.

Firms' involvement in the UMEM programme is high in terms of control, provision, and financing of VET both at individual and collective levels, although the state has the main responsibility in all aspects. Firms have important collective

---

[11] When the UMEM project finished in 2016, the İŞKUR and TOBB developed a more structured and longer-term partnership for the retraining of the unemployed. As the UMEM was still on-going when the fieldwork for this book was conducted, the discussion here focuses on the UMEM.

control over VET through the TOBB's partnership in the programme, and its power to determine the type and location of the courses. The TOBB has also assumed control over the content of training by managing the firm-level training through the local TOBB offices. Additionally, individual firms have control over the UMEM courses since firms are the main responsible bodies for organising and delivering firm-level training. Nevertheless, the UMEM is still a public retraining programme in which the state has remained as the main controller. This is firstly because the İŞKUR is the main body in charge of the UMEM programme, as it makes the ultimate decisions about the programme and regulates firms' involvement in it. Secondly, the trainees of UMEM courses go through a standardised examination and certification process organised by third parties that are accredited by the MYK.

Firms in Turkey have sought important roles regarding the provision and financing of training within the UMEM courses, although the state continues to have the main responsibility in both aspects. Firms' involvement in providing VET in the UMEM programme is very high, as the practical training, which constitutes 80 per cent of the whole training, takes place within firms, while the theoretical training—forming 20 per cent of total training—happens in a public VET institute.[12] Firms also have some responsibility in financing VET within the UMEM both at collective and individual levels: At the collective level, the TOBB and local chambers of commerce and industry have allocated important resources for the UMEM and dedicated special units and personnel for this programme. At the individual level, firms are responsible for financing the practical training within the firm through providing the necessary teaching personnel, materials, and equipment for this training. Some firms contribute to the financing of the UMEM training through paying additional salary to the trainees, in addition to the allowance they get from the İŞKUR. Even though firms get involved in providing and paying for the training in the UMEM courses, the state is the main financier of the UMEM, and the state's commitment to financing the retraining programmes has been increasing in Turkey (ÇSGB, 2016).

Notwithstanding the high commitment of both the state and firms to the UMEM, this programme was not popular amongst the unemployed, and participation in many UMEM courses remained very low (TurkStat, 2015). There are two main reasons for the low participation according to the interviews with different stakeholders of the UMEM programme. Firstly, most UMEM courses were offered in manufacturing-related occupations; however, the unemployed in Turkey prefer courses that provide skills that are more general, which then can be useful in more industries (Interview Notes). As a result, the courses providing general skills such as the ones on IT software have been over capacity while the courses related to manufacturing jobs, such as the ones on gas metal arc welding, could not be filled (Interview Notes).

---

[12] Although the theoretical training may also take place in a firm or a private training institute, it must follow the requirements developed by the MEB and MYK.

The second reason for the low participation in the UMEM courses is the daily allowance paid to the trainees. The trainees in the UMEM courses were receiving a daily allowance that was lower than the minimum wage, and many interviewees mentioned that the lower pay has discouraged the unemployed to participate in the UMEM courses, who instead have preferred having jobs that offer at least the minimum wage (Interview Notes). The problems due to the low daily allowance paid to the UMEM trainees were indeed noticed by the organisers of the UMEM programme, and this led to the raise of this allowance to the level of the minimum wage in the later years of the programme.

5.1.2.2 The skill standardisation and certification system

The skill standardisation and certification system is very new in Turkey, although its development started in the 1990s (Sancak and Özel, 2018). The system is administered by the MYK, which was established in 2006, and is responsible for the management of skill standardisation and certification system and the development of the National Qualifications Framework (*Ulusal Mesleki Yeterlilik Sistemi*—UMYS). By 2014, when the field research for this book started, the skill standardisation and certification system had become a major institution influencing firms' recruitment and training strategies in Turkey. The enforcement of the skill standardisation system has been rigorous in Turkey, where standards for several occupations have been developed, and numerous occupational certificates have been distributed (Sancak and Özel, 2018). The skill standardisation system has especially affected the occupations related to the AAI, since the MYK has focused on developing skill standards for occupations at ISCED levels between two and five, which concern many shop floor occupations in auto parts producers (Sancak and Özel, 2018).

There are several mechanisms for firms to influence the skill standardisation and certification system in Turkey at both collective and individual levels. The main bodies of the MYK—including the sector committees, the General Board, and the Executive Board—are tripartite bodies that include representatives of the state, firms, and workers, and they have become important platforms for firms to collectively influence the skill standardisation and certification system. For example, the sector committees are responsible for discussing and developing the skill standards for occupations. Representatives of individual firms and industry associations, such as the *Turkish Employers Association of Metal Industries* and *Uludağ Automotive Industry Exporters' Association*, have been highly influential in these committees and have affected the skill standards in several occupations that are key for the AAI (Interview Notes). Furthermore, the representatives of several business associations are members of the General Board and Executive Board of the MYK, which are respectively responsible for the management of the skill standardisation and ratifying the occupational standards developed by sector committees. Another way for firms to get involved in the skill standardisation system—at both individual and collective levels—is to establish certification institutes accredited by the MYK, by which they can carry out skill examination and distribute occupational certificates.

The TOBB has had an important role in the skill standardisation and certification system through both being a key member of all bodies of the MYK and establishing the 'Vocational Qualifications and Certification Centers Inc.' (*Mesleki Yeterlilik ve Belgelendirme Merkezleri A.Ş.*—MEYBEM), which are MYK-accredited institutions that carry out examinations and distribute occupational certificates in all cities throughout the country (TS24).

Although firms have considerable influence on the skill standardisation and certification system in Turkey, the state continues to hold the main control in this system. This is firstly because the MYK is not an independent institution but a public institution under the authority of the ÇSGB, and the chair of the MYK Executive Board is always someone from the ÇSGB. Furthermore, even though there are representatives of both firms and workers in the different bodies of the MYK, the representatives of the state dominate these bodies and their management. For example, in the governing body of the MYK, half of the members are from public institutions, while the remainder comprise representatives of different business associations, labour unions, and other nonstate actors such as nongovernmental organisations.

5.1.3 Defining the Turkish VET system

Table 5.2 summarises the study of the VET system in Turkey. It shows that the state is the main actor in the Turkish VET system. Although firms have some role at both collective and individual levels, the depth and breadth of this role is shaped by the state. Therefore, the Turkish VET system can be described as a *statist system with some collectivist elements*.

The state plays a central role in the Turkish VET system through not only its direct involvement in the VET system, as it is explained so far, but also its impact on the collective organisation capacity of firms and workers, and thus the involvement of these actors in the VET system, which is elaborated in this subsection. To start with, even though some institutions of the Turkish VET system are organised as tripartite bodies *de jure*, the *de facto* influence of both businesses and workers over these institutions is shaped by the state. For the case of business, the continuation of

Table 5.2 The statist VET system with some collectivist elements in Turkey

Type	VET Programme	State Commitment	Firm Involvement	Alternative to General Education
IVET	VHS	High	Medium-low	No
	Apprenticeship	High	High	No
CVET	Retraining for the unemployed (UMEM)	High	Medium-high	n.a.*
	Skill standardisation	High	Medium-high	n.a.*

n.a.* not applicable

corporatist structures in Turkey, and the close relations of the TOBB with the governing Justice and Development Party (*Adalet ve Kalkinma Partisi*—AKP) in the 2000s have been very important for the influence of the TOBB on the Turkish VET system (Sancak, 2020). The TOBB has been a major institution for representing the interests of businesses in Turkey due to its representational and financial power that comes through the corporatist structure in the country. Unlike Mexico (see Chapter 6), the corporatist structure has been maintained in Turkey in the neoliberal era, and membership to business chambers is still compulsory. Moreover, the local business chambers are collectively organised under the umbrella organisation, the TOBB, which is a semi-public institution with the membership of 365 chambers and 1.3 million firms across all cities in Turkey (Özel, 2021). In addition to its representational power that comes from its presence across the country, the TOBB has significant financial power as all firms pay a membership fee to their local chamber that is a part of the TOBB, which makes the TOBB the richest (semi-) public institution in Turkey (Özel, 2021). This representational and financial power has made the TOBB a major all-encompassing business association that vocalises the businesses' interests in policy platforms in Turkey.

In addition to the role of the corporatist structure, the TOBB has had important influence over the VET system in Turkey through its close relations with the governing AKP, as the TOBB's power to influence public policy has highly depended on its relations with the governing political parties in the country. Indeed, despite its representativeness and financial capacity since its establishment, the TOBB did not become a powerful institution for policymaking until the early 2000s, before when the state–business relations were dominated with the interests of large firms and the associations representing these firms, such as the TÜSİAD. However, the TOBB has gained important power during the AKP governments, when the dynamics of the state–business relations have been shuffled, and SMEs have gained important advantage to influence public policy. As a key business association representing the interests of the SMEs, the TOBB has gained significant political power and become a key representative of firms in public policy making (Özel, 2021; Sancak and Özel, 2018; Sancak, 2020).[13] With this, the TOBB has gained access to the public VET system in Turkey and has been involved in providing, financing, and controlling VET.

The TOBB's own interest in VET has also played a major role in its influence over the Turkish VET system. In order to address its members' increasing demand for skilled workers, the TOBB has dedicated certain departments and staff solely for VET, such as the Directorate for Education and Quality, which carries out the projects related to IVET and CVET programmes. Furthermore, the TOBB has frequently conducted research and published reports about the problems of the VET system in the country through its think-tank, the Economic Policy Research Foundation of Turkey (*Türkiye Ekonomi Politikaları Araştırma Vakfı*—TEPAV), and

---

[13] For more on the historical and political reasons of the change in political alliances, see Buğra and Savaşkan (2014) and Özel (2014).

through its university, TOBB-ETU. It has raised the issue of VET in critical policy platforms, and has put important pressure on the government for improving the VET system to address the skill shortages in the labour market (for more on TOBB's role in the VET system, see Sancak, 2020). This interest and investment of the TOBB in VET has facilitated its involvement in the Turkish VET system.

In contrast to firms' high collective involvement in VET through the TOBB, workers have not been involved in the VET system in Turkey. Labour unions have not become an influential actor for the Turkish VET system due to the state oppression and control of the union activity throughout the neoliberal era. Although the unions had important power in Turkey in the 1960s and 1970s, the neoliberal transformation together with the military coup in the 1980s curtailed the union power, and the labour unions in Turkey have not regained their power after the coup. The governments after the coup introduced new regulations that substantially restricted union activity through limitations on membership, strikes, and lock-outs, resulting in a significant drop in the number of unions in Turkey within only a decade (from 781 to 99 in 1975–1985) (Kuş and Özel, 2010). The labour unions in Turkey have been further weakened in the decades following the neoliberal transformation through regulations about both the union activity and work contracts, limiting unions' influence over industrial relations and public policies. Resultantly, union membership has reduced drastically and only 8 per cent of the workers in formal employment were union members by 2016 (ILO, 2020a). Even though unionisation is higher in the AAI, unionised workers constitute a marginal share of the AAI workforce in Turkey (16 per cent for metal workers were unionised in 2015 (ÇSGB, 2015)).

In addition to the state's influence on unions through anti-union legislation, the power of unionisation Turkey has been weakened further because of the divisions within the union activity. The unionised workers have been divided among three main confederations including the Confederation of Turkish Trade Unions (*Türkiye İşçi Sendikaları Konfederasyonu*—Türk-İş), Confederation of Progressive Trade Unions of Turkey (*Devrimci İşçi Sendikaları Konfederasyonu*—DİSK), and the Confederation of Turkish Real Trade Unions (*Hak İşçi Sendikaları Konfederasyonu*—Hak-İş). These union confederations have confrontational relations with one another due to the conflicts related to not only their approach to industrial relations, but also other political conflicts in the country, including the secular-religious conflict and the ethnic conflict with the Kurdish population (Interview Notes). This has resulted in the division of the unionised workers within the AAI between the Turkish Metal Workers Union (*Türk Metal*), United Metal Workers' Union (*Birleşik Metal-İş*), and the Iron, Steel, Metal and Metallic Products Workers' Union (*Özçelik-İş*), giving more limited membership and thus representational power to each union.

The unions in Turkey have not been key actors in the VET system also because VET has not constituted a major concern in their agenda. Regarding the unions of the AAI, the unions have focused their activities on other issues in industrial relations such as collective bargaining, formal employment, and health and safety at workplace, which constitute key areas of industrial relations conflict in Turkey.[14] In the interviews, the representatives of the industry-level unions of the AAI mentioned education and training only *vis-à-vis* educating workers about their rights, as well as training about the workplace health and safety. Nevertheless, training on occupational skills has not been a major concern for these unions, and neither the industry-level unions in the AAI nor the national union confederations have published documents to express their opinion about the VET system. Hak-İŞ, which is an umbrella union including *Çelik-İş* and has developed close links with the governing AKP, has been carrying out some activities regarding VET, such as providing occupational training to its members (Sancak, 2020). However, this interest has been ad hoc and restricted to providing specific VET programmes for its members, while a corporatist VET structure that includes the unions still does not operate (Sancak, 2020). Although some unions are *de jure* partners of the tripartite VET platforms, they have not become *de facto* influential actors in the VET system in Turkey. In fact, in the interviews, the representatives of the state and businesses described the labour unions as 'irrelevant' for the VET system (Interview Notes).

All in all, the state plays a key role in the VET system in Turkey through three main mechanisms. The first one is about the state's involvement in providing, financing, and controlling the public VET system, which then also shapes firms' involvement in this system. The second mechanism is related to the state's influence on institutions of collective business organisations, and its relations with these organisations. The continuation of the corporatist structure and the AKP's relations with the TOBB have played a major role in making this organisation the main representative of businesses in VET-related policy platforms. The third and last mechanism concerns the state's influence on collective organisation of workers: due to the state's oppression on union activity, the labour unions have been very weak and have not become influential actors in the VET system.

5.2 State regulations and the structure of the labour market in Turkey

In addition to the public VET system, there are several other institutions and regulations that influence firms' skilling strategies. This section focuses on these other institutions and regulations. It discusses how the other institutions are shaped by the state's involvement in them, and how they influence firms' skilling strategies and thus, become complementarities in the multilevel skill system. The main regulations and institutions in Turkey in this regard include the labour market regulations and wage-setting institutions, the arrangements that influence the geographical accessibility of different firms (i.e. firms' location and the availability of affordable public transportation around that location), and the military service requirement for young men.

---

[14] Still, the unions' focus on these issues will have indirect influence on the VET system.

5.2.1 Labour regulations and wage-setting institutions

Regulations about work contracts and the wage-setting institutions, particularly the minimum wage and occupational certificate requirement, are the main structures that influence the supply of and demand for skills in Turkey. On the one hand, the regulations on work contracts and the wage-setting institutions affect workers' willingness to invest in skill development and to work in jobs that require different skills and thus, they define the supply of different types of skills available in the labour market. On the other hand, the mandatory occupational certificate for workers carrying out 'heavy and dangerous jobs' influences firms' demand for workers with and without an occupational certificate.

5.2.1.1 Work contracts and labour market segmentation in Turkey
The types of work contracts have important implications for the labour market dynamics in Turkey, which makes the regulations on work contracts a key complementarity in the Turkish skill system. Although the OECD describes the labour market regulations in Turkey as 'strict' (2013a, 2020a), there are several elements in the Turkish Labour Law that create options for flexible employment, which leads to a segmentation in the labour market that includes several types of employment contracts with different levels of employment protection and social security (Sancak, 2011).

In line with the segmentation of the workforce in Turkey, the workers in the AAI are also categorised in segments, and there are three main groups of workers in this industry: the employees of smaller (subcontracted) firms, the nonunionised employees of larger firms, and the unionised employees of larger firms (in the order of their share within the labour market). There are three main reasons for such segmentation amongst the AAI worker groups. The first reason is the limited unionisation in the country and the substantial differences between the benefits of unionised and nonunionised workers. Although the AAI constitutes one of the industries with higher rates of unionisation compared to other sectors, the unionised workers comprise a very small share in all workers in this industry. Currently, for the AAI, the employees of large original equipment manufacturers (OEMs) and Tier-1 suppliers constitute the main group of unionised workers, and employees in lower-tier suppliers are often not unionised, although a few of the Tier-2 firms studied for this book mentioned that their workers were unionised. While the small group of unionised workers is employed through collective agreements, the majority of the AAI workers in Turkey are employed through individual contracts between the employer and employee. The contract terms and wages of the unionised workers are determined through collective bargaining between one of the three main industry unions and the employers' union, namely the Turkish Employers' Association of Metal Industries (*Türkiye Metal Sanayicileri Sendikası*—MESS). In contrast, the individual contracts are discussed between the employer and employee. Several interviewees from the Turkish firms mentioned that they follow the contract guidelines provided by the

MESS even when they are not part of a collective agreement, although this is voluntary and depends on the firms' willingness to do so. The different employment patterns result in important variation between the contractual terms of unionised and not unionised workers regarding their wages, job protection, and fringe benefits.[15] As a result, amongst the workers of the AAI, the unionised workers constitute the most advantaged yet the smallest group. For example, according to the DİSK, a unionised worker earned on average 60 per cent more than a nonunionised worker in 2017 (DİSK-AR, 2018).

The second reason of the segmentation amongst the AAI worker groups is the Turkish Labour Law, which has different requirements from firms with different sizes, firms with fewer employees being exempt from some of the requirements of the Labour Law.[16] For example, firms with fewer than 10 employees are exempt from the requirement of providing training to VHS students. Similarly, there are several exemptions in the Labour Law for smaller firms, which put fewer restrictions about hiring and firing practices of smaller firms compared to larger firms. While these exemptions may intend to provide certain flexibilities to SMEs in the employment practices, in order to facilitate their competitiveness against larger firms and in global markets (Interview Notes), they result in substantial insecurities for the workers employed in smaller firms, and create inequalities between the employees of larger and smaller firms.

The third main reason of the segmentation amongst the AAI worker groups is the possibility of subcontracting in the Turkish Labour Law, which has given an opportunity to large firms to avoid certain parts and restrictions of the Labour Law. Benefiting from the subcontracting possibility, large firms in Turkey have been employing a group of workers through subcontractors, which has helped these firms to curb down the union representation on the shop floor, and to avoid certain obligations to the workers, which they pass on to the subcontractors (Çelik, 2015). Subcontracting also helps large firms to look like they have fewer employees than they actually do, which then enables them to escape from certain Labour Law restrictions that apply to firms with higher number of employees.

Overall, the limited unionisation where the benefits of unionised and non-unionised workers significantly vary, the different requirements of the Labour Law for smaller and larger firms regarding their employment practices, and the 'strict' labour regulations together with the possibility of subcontracting have resulted in a segmented labour force in the AAI in Turkey. The state, moreover, has had a major impact on each of these elements through its influence on the unionisation in Turkey and the labour legislations it has introduced.

---

[15] There can also be some differences between the contracts of workers belonging to different unions.
[16] There are different regulations for firms with 1–9, 10+, 30+, 50+, or 100+ employees.

5.2.1.2 The role of the minimum wage

Minimum wage is a key macro-level complementary in the Turkish skill system because (i) it defines the wages of the majority of the working population, and (ii) it has been much higher in Turkey compared to other MICs. The minimum wage is a key complementarity as it is the *main mechanism for defining workers' wages*, and hence, the cost of training and hiring in the country, for three main reasons. Firstly, a significant share of formally employed workers in Turkey receive a minimum wage: in 2014, about half of the registered workers in Turkey were receiving the minimum wage, and Turkey has the highest proportion of workers earning minimum wage in Europe (DİSK-AR, 2018; Eurostat, 2020b). Secondly, the level of minimum wage affects the earnings of the trainees from public VET programmes since the salaries of the apprentices and the trainees from VHSs are based on the minimum wage (i.e. the salary paid to the apprentices and VHS trainees should not be lower than 30 per cent of the minimum wage). Lastly, the earnings of the informal sector workers are defined with respect to the national minimum wage, and is often lower than the minimum wage, which then creates pressures on firms when competing for inexperienced and/or untrained workers.

The minimum wage has been a significant institution for the Turkish skill system also because it has been 'very high', and much higher than many MICs including Mexico. For example, in 2015, the annual minimum wage in Turkey was about five times of the level in Mexico (Figure 5.3). The 'high' minimum wage that is paid to the majority of workers in Turkey has important implications for firms' hiring and training practices, and it creates challenges for the Turkish AAI firms when competing for workers with firms in other sectors. The interviewees from the Turkish suppliers mentioned that their ability to attract workers through offering a higher salary is limited because the minimum wage is already too high. Furthermore, the high minimum wage puts the AAI manufacturing firms particularly at a disadvantage compared to firms in the retail and service industries when

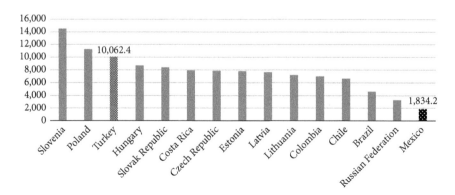

Figure 5.3 Annual real minimum wage in selected emerging market economies (2015; constant prices at 2015 USD purchasing power parity; annual)
Source: OECD (2020d)

recruiting young workers for entry-level posts. This is because the jobs in the manufacturing sector have been unpopular amongst young workers due to the work conditions in this industry: instead of the 'heavy' and 'unsocial' work environment in manufacturing firms, most young workers in Turkey are argued to prefer jobs in the service and retail industries, where the work is more sociable and 'less demanding', and they get paid the minimum wage as an entry-level worker (Interview Notes). The manager of the training institute of the Turkish Employers Association of Metal Industries stated:

> The working conditions are heavy in manufacturing. This industry isn't attractive [to young people]. Especially now, the retail sector and service sector are growing in Turkey. The young people prefer working in shopping malls, in better work environment with clean clothes rather than working in factories in greasy, rusty conditions…when you go to a shopping mall now, you will see lots of VHS graduates, especially in shops selling somewhat technical products. For instance, [...] I was buying a belt from DESA[17] in shopping mall the other day. The boy was making adjustments to the belt, using a screwdriver and we were chatting. I asked him where he graduated from. He said Şişli Industrial VHS. I told him, 'what are you doing here then?' He said 'the work here is better. And I earn the same money I would earn in a factory. At least this is a more relaxed work.'   (TS8)

The minimum wage is decided by the Minimum Wage Determination Commission (*Asgari Ücret Tespit Komisyonu*) in Turkey, which is a tripartite body that includes representatives of the state, employers, and workers. However, despite the *de jure* tripartite structure, the state has been the central actor in this Commission and has the highest decision-making power, whereas the influence of both business and labour representatives has been limited (Korkmaz, 2004; Erdoğdu, 2014). Through its domination in this Commission, the state in Turkey is argued to have promoted a high minimum wage, although this has been occasionally influenced by the political priorities of the governing political parties (Korkmaz, 2004; Erdoğdu, 2014). In fact, the major reason for the high level of the minimum wage in Turkey, in the absence of strong labour unions, is argued to be the high level of state involvement in determining the national minimum wage (Korkmaz, 2004). The state in Turkey is argued to have used the minimum wage regulation not only to protect the most vulnerable workers, which is the case in many countries, but also to provide a minimum welfare to the population in the absence of a generous welfare system, which is also in line with 'social neoliberalism' it has been adopting in the 2000s (Korkmaz, 2004; Öniş, 2012). Also because the majority of the population receive the minimum wage, the state in Turkey has aimed to provide basic living conditions to the population through maintaining a relatively high minimum wage (Korkmaz, 2004).

---

[17] A leather garments retailer.

5.2.1.3 Occupational certificate requirement

A more recent regulation that has substantial influence on firms' skilling strategies is the occupational certificate requirement in the Labour Law (No. 4857 Article 85), which was first introduced in 2009. According to this regulation, firms must employ only workers holding a 'valid' occupational certificate for 'heavy and dangerous' jobs.[18] The Regulation (*Tebliğ* no. 27417) also explains the risk classifications of different jobs and according to it, many jobs in the AAI are grouped as 'heavy and dangerous'. The 'validity' of a certificate, moreover, is ensured through it being from a certification body that is accredited by the MYK. Workers graduating from public VET programmes in a related subject area are automatically qualified to carry out the jobs classified as heavy and dangerous. This includes the graduates of relevant departments in VHSs, workers holding an apprenticeship certificate, and those successfully completing a public retraining programme such as UMEM. Workers who do not hold an occupational certificate but have relevant work experience are expected to go through a centralised and standardised examination, and get certified by accredited certification bodies. The accredited certification bodies comprise the public VET institutions, such as VHSs and MEMs, as well as private institutions that have received an accreditation from the MYK. For certification, the experienced workers may need to take additional theoretical and practical training if their skills and knowledge are not sufficient to receive the relevant certificate.

The introduction of the occupational certificate requirement and the rigorous implementation of this regulation have substantially increased the demand for workers with a VET certificate in Turkey, and particularly in the AAI firms (Interview Notes). Because of such increase in demand, as well as due to the challenges that are related to low supply of VET graduates in the labour market, it has become very challenging for the AAI suppliers in Turkey to find workers with a VET certificate. As a result, many of these firms have developed new strategies to address their skill needs while also complying with the occupational certificate requirement of the Labour Law, which are elaborated in Chapter 7.

5.2.2 Firms' location and public transportation services

The location and accessibility of firms via public transportation are important elements of the skill system as they shape the skill supply available to firms and jobs available to different workers. Moreover, in Turkey, the state has had a major influence on where the firms are located and how accessible they are. As in many countries, the manufacturing plants in the AAI are typically located in the outskirts of the cities and in remote areas in Turkey, mostly due to the lower land costs in these areas.

---

[18] The scope of jobs that require an occupational certificate was extended in the years after 2009.

Being in remote areas, nevertheless, can create challenges for firms, such as the underdeveloped infrastructure in and limited transportation links to these areas.

The state in Turkey affects firms' accessibility to workers, and hence workers' access to different employers, through its promotion of (i) OIZs and (ii) affordable public transportation networks. OIZs have been endorsed in Turkey since the 1960s as a key part of the industrial policy to facilitate the development of domestic firms and the local manufacturing sector (Mert and Akman, 2011; Örnek-Özden, 2016). OIZs offer several services to firms such as private security services, uninterrupted energy supply, and road infrastructure. One of the main services of OIZs in Turkey has been the free or low-cost transportation services provided to the workers employed in the OIZs, which has improved the links of firms in these zones with wider areas and workers residing in those areas.

Being located in OIZs also increases the labour turnover in firms located in these areas. This is mainly because there are many firms with similar production activities within or nearby the OIZs, and these firms need similar types of employees. Therefore, the workers of a firm located within OIZs have access to jobs in other firms within or near these zones, which increases their possibility of leaving their employer for a job nearby and, thus, raises workers' bargaining power against employers. Indeed, many interviewee firms mentioned that their workers have been poached by similar firms located within the same OIZ.

The public transportation networks in the regions with a well-developed AAI have been another key structure that increases the links between workers and firms in Turkey. The industrial areas that are located in the outskirts of the main cities of the AAI (i.e. Bursa, Gebze, and Istanbul) are well connected to the other parts of these cities through a wide network of affordable public transportation, which includes metro and light-rail systems, buses, and metro-buses. Furthermore, the availability of *dolmuş*, which are private minibuses operating in certain routes that are not covered by public transportation and are low-cost, increases the accessibility of further locations and improves the geographical mobility of workers while increasing firms' access to a wider range of workers. In addition to these, many firms in Turkey also offer free shuttle services to their employees who reside within a certain radius around the firm in order to compete with the firms in OIZs for workers, which then expands these firms' access to a larger group of (skilled) workers.

5.2.3 Military service requirement

A critical institution that influences the skilling strategies of Turkish AAI firms, and hence is a complementarity of the Turkish skill system, is the mandatory military service for men. The Turkish army is a conscript system, and all male Turkish citizens are obliged to conduct the military service at the age of 20 years. This service lasts about 15 months, while the compulsory serving in the military can be postponed to later years if the person is studying, or it can be cancelled if the person has certain health conditions.

Although the main aim of the conscript system is to preserve a strong army, and the military has been a key institution influencing the politics in Turkey, it has unintended consequences for the labour market. A major reason for this is the domination of the labour market by male workers, who must complete a military service, while the labour force participation of women, who are not required to conduct a military service, is extremely low in Turkey.[19] Male workers are prevalent particularly in the AAI, and almost all production workers in the interviewed firms in Turkey were men, except a small number of women employed as plastic injection machine operators.

As the male workers need to complete the military service when they turn 20, the military service requirement has substantial influence on firms' skilling decisions because both employers and workers see the military service as an interruption to workers' employment and career development. This then influences firms' decisions when recruiting and training new workers, and affects workers' employment choices. On the one hand, employers see the male workers who have not completed the military service as 'temporary employees' since these workers are expected to leave the firm to complete the military service. On the other hand, young male workers have this requirement in mind when they are deciding about their employment and skill training, which leads to distinct behaviour.

Those who have not completed the military service are typically the recent graduates of VHSs and/or new entrants to the labour market, and these young workers know that it is 'basically impossible' for them to find a permanent job before completing this service (Interview Notes). These young individuals are also aware of the challenges with finding a decent job with good salary and employment conditions before they complete the military service. Therefore, these workers do not have much bargaining power against the employers before completing the military service, and, consequently, many of these workers end up accepting work in more precarious conditions and with fewer benefits compared to those who have completed the military service. Furthermore, as the workers know that their work before the military service is temporary, they are often not fully committed to their employer before the military service, which creates high labour turnover amongst the new labour market entrants (Interview Notes). Many of the workers without the military service do not even join the labour market after they complete their studies while 'they are waiting to be called for the military service' (T15 owner). This has been argued to be a major reason for the very high share of the young people 'not in education, employment, or training' (NEET) in Turkey: 13 per cent of men aged 15–19 years were in NEET, while the OECD average was 7 per cent in 2013, and Turkey has the highest share of men NEET for this age group (OECD, 2020e).

---

[19] For example, female labour force participation in Turkey was 31 per cent in 2015, when the OECD average was 52 per cent (World Bank, 2020b).

5.3 Conclusion and complementarities of the Turkish skill system

This chapter has examined the national institutions that influence the skilling strategies of firms in Turkey. Table 5.3 summarises the four main elements in this regard and shows that the state plays the major role in the Turkish skill system through its high involvement in all macro-level complementarities of the skill system. Firstly, the state shapes the public VET system in Turkey not only through its commitment to VET, but also by affecting both firms' and workers' involvement in the system. The state's commitment to public VET system has been high, and there are some mechanisms for firms to get involved in the public VET system, particularly the CVET system, although these are regulated by the state. The state in Turkey has also influenced both firms' and workers' involvement in the VET system. On the one hand, the corporatist structure and the governments' relations with the TOBB have made the TOBB the key representative of business interests in policy platforms, including VET policies, which has resulted in the high involvement of this organisation in providing, financing, and controlling VET, and particularly CVET. On the other hand, the state has restricted union activity in Turkey, which has weakened the unions' organisational and representational power and their involvement in the VET system. The state's high involvement in the public VET system together with its influence over the collective business and labour organisations have led to a *statist VET system with some collectivist elements* in Turkey.

Table 5.3 The role of national institutions in Turkey and the state's high involvement in them

	Institutions
High state involvement	**Statist VET system with some collectivist elements**
	High state commitment to providing, financing, and controlling VET
	Some firm involvement in the VET system, although regulated by the state
	Corporatist business organisations and the state's links with the TOBB
	Restrictions on union activity and limited union power
	Labour regulations and wage-setting institutions
	Regulations on work contracts, particularly subcontracting
	Limited unionisation
	High minimum wage
	Occupational certificate requirement and the rigorous implementation of the requirement
	Firms' location and transportation services
	Turkish AAI firms' placement in OIZs
	Affordable and accessible public transportation networks
	Military service requirement
	For all men at the age of 20

Secondly, the state shapes the skill system in Turkey through the regulations on contracts and wages, as well as the rigorous implementation of these regulations. Although the Labour Law in Turkey is 'strict' in terms of work contracts, there are several exemptions for smaller firms, and the Law provides the possibility of subcontracting to large firms, which affects the employment patterns of small and large firms. The state also shapes the minimum wage structure in Turkey, which has been a key institution for defining the wages in the country and has been used as a state strategy for providing welfare. The state in Turkey has maintained a 'high' level of minimum wage, and this has affected the competition for workers between firms in different industries, putting the AAI firms at a disadvantage in this regard. In addition to these, the statutory requirement of an occupational certificate for 'heavy and dangerous' jobs, and the rigorous implementation of this requirement, has increased the demand for workers with a VET certificate and thus will influence the Turkish AAI firms' skilling strategies.

Thirdly, the state affects the AAI firms' access to different types of workers, as well as these workers' mobility, through its promotion of OIZs and its investment in public transportation. The state's promotion of OIZs for Turkish companies has resulted in the establishment of many Turkish auto parts supplier firms within or nearby these zones, where these firms compete with similar firms for workers, and which increase workers' mobility and firms' risk of their workers being poached. Furthermore, although the OIZs and AAI firms are located in remote locations of large cities, these firms have access to a wider range of workers through transportation provided by the OIZ or public transportation that is accessible and affordable.

Fourthly, and lastly, the state in Turkey affects the labour market dynamics of young workers through the compulsory military service. The military service requirement for all young men at the age of 20 years creates a break in their employment. This, on the one hand, influences employers' skilling decisions for those who have and have not completed the military service. On the other hand, the military service requirement reduces the bargaining power of the workers who have not completed this service, usually resulting in their employment in more precarious conditions, lesser commitment to work and higher mobility, and sometimes their withdrawal from the labour market.

All four institutions that are shaped by the state's involvement in them influence the mechanisms of skill formation available to firms and the quality and quantity of skills existing in the labour market, as well as firms' demands for distinct skills, and consequently influence the hiring, training, and employee development practices of Turkish auto parts suppliers. Therefore, these four institutions constitute the complementarities of the multilevel skill system in Turkey because, even though they may not be directly related to one another, they together influence a third phenomenon, namely the firm-level skilling practices ([A&B]→C, where A, B, and C are complementary, see Chapter 2). Furthermore, these institutions are all shaped by the state's involvement in them, and they, together with the firm-level skilling practices, form parts of a whole, namely the (multilevel) skill system.

6
Institutions of skill formation in Mexico

the role of the (missing) state

Following Chapter 5 on the national institutions complementing the skill system in Turkey, this chapter investigates the institutional arrangements that complement the skill system in Mexico. It builds on the literature on comparative capitalisms and the comparative political economy of skill formation (CPEoSF) that discusses the complementarities of institutions that lead to distinct skill-formation systems, and examines the role of the state in these institutions. In this regard, it scrutinises the public vocational education and training (VET) systems and the other institutions that influence firms' skilling strategies.

The first part of the chapter focuses on the Mexican VET system. It elaborates on the public initial vocational education and training (IVET) and continuing vocational education and training (CVET) programmes, and the VET regulations in the Mexican Federal Labour Law (*Ley Federal del Trabajo*) (hereafter, the Labour Law), which give important responsibility to firms regarding VET. It evaluates the state's commitment to and firms' involvement in the VET system, and defines the Mexican VET system based on the neuralgic points suggested by Busemeyer and Trampusch (2012a). The second part of the chapter discusses the other institutions, which include the regulations on work contracts and the minimum wage, as well as the location of Mexican auto parts suppliers and the public transportation system around these locations. The last part summarises the findings and highlights the main arguments of the chapter.

6.1 The *de jure* statist and segmentalist, *de facto* liberal VET system in Mexico

The Mexican VET system can be described as *de jure* statist and segmentalist, *de facto* liberal. This is because of the *de jure* coexistence of multiple VET programmes that put different responsibilities on the state and firms, and the weak *de facto* implementation of those programmes. Before going into an in-depth discussion on each component of the VET system, it is important to give an outline and a historical background about the VET system in Mexico in order to familiarise the reader with its complex structure. The Mexican VET system is a decentralised system that is 'kind of a jungle' (MS7) with multiple and overlapping VET programmes that are

Global Production, National Institutions, and Skill Formation: The Political Economy of Training and Employment in Auto Parts Suppliers from Mexico And Turkey. Merve Sancak, Oxford University Press. © Merve Sancak 2022.
DOI: 10.1093/oso/9780198860655.003.0006

managed by different state bodies. Although the Mexican VET system was centrally managed by the Secretary of Public Education (*la Secretaría de Educación Publica*— SEP) until the 1980s, the system experienced substantial restructuring and decentralisation in the 1980s and 1990s, when the Mexican economy was opened to international trade and investment, and it went through substantial decentralisation and privatisation (Shapiro et al., 2009). With the decentralisation in the education system, the responsibility of the federal state for VET was reduced, and separate training programmes were created to address the needs of different states (Interview Notes). In the scope of the decentralisation and deregulation of the VET system, and the neo-liberalisation of the Mexican education system, the state shifted the main responsibility of VET from the state to firms through the Article 132 Section XV of the Labour Law, which obliges all firms to provide training to their employees. This obligation was further strengthened by Article 123 of the Constitution of Mexico, which grants skill training to all workers in the country and obliges all firms—independently of their activity—to provide training to their employees (*Constitución Política de Los Estados Unidos Mexicanos*, 2014).

As a result of the decentralisation, deregulation, and the lower state commitment, the public VET system in Mexico has remained weak and highly fragmented. Currently, the SEP and the Secretary of Work and Social Provision (*la Secretaría del Trabajo y Previsión Social*—STPS) are the main public bodies in charge of the Mexican VET system. Table 6.1 summarises the main institutions of the Mexican VET system that are relevant to the auto parts-automotive industry (AAI), as well as the characteristics of these institutions. For the sake of simplicity, the table and the discussion on the VET system in this chapter focus only on the VET programmes that concern the skilling strategies of Mexican auto parts suppliers, while the programmes that are not related to the AAI are briefly mentioned when relevant.

6.1.1 Initial VET programmes

IVET in Mexico takes place at the secondary level and is carried out through two main 'subsystems' (*subsistemas*) of Upper-Secondary Education System (*Educación Medio Superior*), including the Technological High School (THS) (*Bachillerato Tecnologico*) and Technical Professional High School (TPHS) (*Educación Profesional Tecnica*). The THS is a centralised system and is managed by the SEP at the federal level. It is divided into three other subsystems according to the sector of economic activity. The subsystems for each sector are managed by separate Directorate Generals that include the Directorate General for Industrial Technological Education (*Dirección General de Educación Tecnológica Industrial*—DGETI), Directorate General for Agriculture and Livestock Education (*Dirección de Educación Tecnológica Agropecuaria*—DGETA), and the Directorate General for Sea Science and Technology Education (*Dirección General de Educación en Ciencia y Tecnología del Mar*— DGECyTM).

Table 6.1 The VET system in Mexico[*]

	VET type	VET Programme	Main Components	Management and Funding	Training Content
Public VET programmes	IVET	THS	DGETI	SEP (federal level)	60% general, 40% technical Practical training not required
		TPHS	CONALEP	SEP (federal and state level)	35% general, 65% technical Practical training required
	CVET	Training for work	CECATI	SEP (federal and state level)	More craft-based training, for the unemployed
			ICAT	SEP and STPS (federal and state level)	Depends on the state, more industrial training
			BÉCATE	STPS	On-the-job training of the unemployed
		Skill standardisation	n.a.*	CONOCER	n.a.
Labour Law on VET		Firm-level training	Training obligation Characteristics of training Liaison Committees (implementation)	Managed by the state and firm; financed by firm	Not specified

n.a. Not applicable

[*] Including only those that concern the firms in AAI

DGETI is the main institution relevant to the AAI firms within the THS system, as the schools managed by the DGETI generate the skills for this industry. The DGETI was managing 168 Centres of Industrial Technology and Services Studies (*Centros de Estudios Tecnológicos Industrial y de Servicios*—CETIS) and 284 Centres of Industrial Technology and Services High School (*Centros de Bachillerato Tecnológico Industrial y de Servicios*—CBTIS) around the time when the research for this book was conducted (Ahumada, 2014). Education in DGETI schools focuses mostly on academic areas and the development of general skills, as 60 per cent of education in DGETI schools is on general subjects, while 40 per cent is on vocational ones (Kis et al., 2009). Students in DGETI schools begin specialising in technical subjects in their second semester, and total training takes 3 years. The students need to complete all course requirements to receive a DGETI diploma, and practical training in a firm is not compulsory for these students. There are no formal restrictions for DGETI students to continue to higher education after completing their studies, which facilitates permeability between DGETI schools and general education.

The other subsystem of VET at the upper-secondary level is the National College of Technical Professional Education (*El Colegio Nacional de Educación Profesional Técnica*—CONALEP), which is part of the TPHSs. The CONALEP system is more decentralised compared to DGETI, and is primarily managed by the states' governments (except in Mexico City and Oaxaca), although the federal government still sets the general outline for training in these schools. Education in CONALEP schools lasts 3 years, and the share of technical education is much higher in these schools compared to DGETI schools: 65 per cent of training in CONALEP schools comprises technical subjects, while 35 per cent is on general subjects (Kis et al., 2009). There are different types of CONALEP schools addressing the needs of different sectors, such as Production and Transformation, Technology and Transport, Health, and Tourism (CONALEP, 2012). Practical training in a firm is mandatory to receive a CONALEP certificate, and it takes 4 months, during which the SEP pays the students a daily allowance called *beca*.

Even though practical training is mandatory for CONALEP students, there are important problems with this training. Firstly, many students do not have practical training in their area of study, and many CONALEP students end up being hired in low-skill tasks as cheap workers rather than trainees for skill development because of the absence of regulations about the requirements of and firms' responsibility in the firm-level training (Interview Notes). Secondly, the dropout rate in the CONALEP system has been very high, and many CONALEP students leave these schools without any practical training. Dropping out indeed has constituted an important problem for the job prospects of the CONALEP participants, as these individuals would join the labour market with no qualifications and hence would be considered as unskilled workers. In order to reduce the number of dropouts and to improve the job prospects of those leaving the system before their training is finished, some measures were introduced to flexibilise the CONALEP system in 2007 through the Integral Upper-Secondary Education Reform (*la Reforma Integral de*

Educación Media Superior—RIEMS). One important measure in this regard is the introduction of a 'certificate of participation' for those who drop out of CONALEP schools. While this is not an occupational certificate or a diploma, the certificate shows the training attended by the individual until they leave the school, which was hoped to improve the job prospects of these individuals. The students do not need to complete the firm-level training in order to receive this certificate of participation, which has further reduced the occurrence of firm-level training of CONALEP students (MS5).

It is important to mention the Mexican Model of Dual Training (MMDT) (*Modelo Mexicano de Formación Dual*) programme, which was initiated in 2013 and started to have impact on the CONALEP system when the fieldwork for this book was taking place. The MMDT is a multipartner programme that aims to improve the quality of training in CONALEP schools and to increase the responsiveness of this training to firms' skill needs. It is a dual training programme, and is based on the German apprenticeship system but is 'adapted to Mexico's realities' (MS17). In this programme, the CONALEP students spend half of their time at a firm, while spending the other half for theoretical training at a school (instead of the 80 per cent at firm and 20 per cent at school division in the German system). The MMDT project is commissioned by the German Federal Ministry for Economic Cooperation and Development, and the main partners of the project include the SEP, the German-Mexican Chamber of Commerce (*Cámara Mexicano-Alemana de Comercio e Industria*—CAMEXA), the Employers' Confederation of Mexico (*la Confederación Patronal de la República Mexicana*—COPARMEX), and the German Federal Institute for Vocational Education and Training (*Bundesinstitut für Berufsbildung in der Bundes*stadt—BIBB). Despite this institutional setting, the MMDT has constituted only a marginal part in the CONALEP system and has been used mostly by German firms and some (very large) Mexican firms in Mexico (Interview Notes).

Who provides VET?

Both the state's commitment to and firms' involvement in VET provision is low in the Mexican IVET system. The main responsibility of providing VET is on either the individual states or the federal government for DGETI and CONALEP schools, as the main training takes place at schools in both the THS and TPHS systems. Firms can contribute to the provision of VET in these systems through employing the students as trainees and giving them firm-level practical training. The division of responsibility between the state and firms for providing VET is different in the DGETI and CONALEP systems: the firms' responsibility is much lower in the former compared to the latter since firm-level training is not a requirement but is voluntary in DGETI. Despite this setting, both the state's commitment to and firms' involvement in providing VET are low in the DGETI and CONALEP systems. On the one hand, the state's commitment is low because both THS and TPHS occupy a small part of the Upper-Secondary Education System. On the other hand, firms' involvement in providing VET is low since very few firms in Mexico actually employ trainees from public VET programmes mainly because such training is voluntary, and the requirement of firm-level training is not strict for both DGETI and CONALEP students (Interview Notes).

The MMDT is an important exception regarding firms' involvement in VET in the Mexican IVET system since the trainees of this programme are required to spend half of their time in a firm for practical training. However, given the limited participation of Mexican firms in MMDT and the domination of German firms in the programme, it can be argued that Mexican firms' involvement in the provision of VET in the MMDT has been low, and very few of the interviewed firms participated in this programme (Interview Notes).

Who pays for VET?

Both public commitment to and firms' involvement in financing IVET programmes is low in Mexico. Although the state has the main responsibility of paying for VET in both the THS and TPHS systems, the share of spending for IVET has been very low in the public budget. For example, the budget assigned to upper-secondary IVET institutions comprised only 8 per cent of SEP's budget in 2013, while the main share of this budget was dedicated to general education (SHCP, 2014).[1] Furthermore, spending per student has been much lower for vocational tracks compared to the spending per student in academic tracks, even though VET is more expensive than general education.[2] In fact, Mexico was one of the two OECD members that spent less for VET students at secondary level compared to the students in academic tracks in 2010 (OECD, 2013b).[3] In addition to these, the small public budget spared for VET in Mexico has been directed mostly to the THS system and DGETI schools, which focus more on the teaching of general subjects instead of vocational ones (MS5). As a result, the CONALEP schools, which provide more training in vocational and technical subjects, have had a marginal share of the public education spending in Mexico (Figure 6.1).

Similar to the state, firms' involvement in financing VET has been low in Mexico. While in theory firms in Mexico can get involved in financing the public IVET programmes through paying for the firm-level training of trainees from DGETIs and CONALEPs, firms' contribution to financing IVET is very low since very few firms actually train students from the public IVET programmes. Even when firms provide such training, the state pays for the main costs of this training, such as through paying a daily allowance to the students in training, while firms are only responsible for the costs related to the within-firm training. Therefore, and because of low participation of firms in training students of public IVET programmes, it can be argued that firms' involvement in financing of public VET programmes is very low.

---

[1] In contrast, the budget for VET at upper-secondary level (for VHSs) formed the 14 per cent of the Turkish MNE's budget the same year (Chapter 5).

[2] For instance, public spending per VET student in secondary education was 1,150 USD in 2010 in Mexico, while it was 2,914 USD for the students in general tracks (OECD, 2013b).

[3] The other one was Hungary.

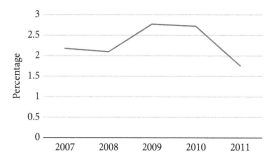

Figure 6.1 The share of spending for CONALEP in the budget of the SEP
Source: World Bank (2013)

Who controls VET?

De jure, the state is the main controller of VET in both the DGETI and CONALEP schools, as these schools are managed by the SEP and are part of the Mexican upper-secondary education system. Furthermore, the content, delivery, and education material in both CONALEP and DGETI schools are decided by the SEP at the state or federal level. However, *de facto*, the state control over the IVET system has been weak. The decentralisation and privatisation of the VET system throughout the neo-liberal era, and education system in general, have been the main reasons for the weak state control over VET, which have led to multiple and unstandardised VET programmes (Sancak, forthcoming-a). Additionally, the problems in the Mexican education system, including the problems related to the corrupt teachers' union, have been shown as important reasons for the lack of state control over the Mexican IVET system (Székely, 2013).

The main instruments for firms to have control over IVET include the Liaison Committees (*Comités de Vinculación*) in CONALEP schools, which aim to strengthen the linkages between the VET provided in these schools and the skills needed in the labour market, as well as the possibilities of firms to develop direct links with DGETI schools. Individual firms can also participate in the Liaison Committees at the state level, which make decisions about the content of training in different VET subsystems and include participants representing the state government. The Liaison Committees at both school and state levels are important platforms for firms to comment on the current training programmes and deliver recommendations for new programmes in the public IVET system.

Despite the institutional setting for firms' individual involvement in managing VET, the actual involvement of firms in this regard has been low. Most firms in Mexico do not participate in the Liaison Committees at either school or state level, and when they do, it is erratic, while many representatives of firms interviewed for this book mentioned they had never heard of these committees. The few firms that knew about such committees were reluctant to join them due to the vagueness of regulations about these committees, and the ambiguity surrounding their organisation and functioning (Interview Notes). Furthermore, firms' participation in and knowledge about the Liaison Committees vary across states, schools, and firms: firms are typically more involved in the Liaison Committees in states with higher public commitment to these committees, in schools with more interest from the school management in these committees, and in larger firms that require more technical workers (Hualde, 1999). In contrast to large firms, small firms rarely get involved in the Liaison Committees (Interview Notes).

Firms' collective involvement in the management of the IVET system is very low in Mexico, which is very different from the case in Turkey. The main business organisations that represent the large businesses in Mexico, such as the Coordination of Corporate Bodies of External Trade (*Coordinación de Organismos Empresariales de Comercio Exterior*—COECE), have not shown interest in VET policies or in getting involved in the IVET programmes, while rather focusing mostly on keeping the labour costs low. Although some regional branches of the National Chamber of the Industry of Transformation (*la Cámara Nacional de la Industria de la Transformación*—CANACINTRA), which is a major organisation that represents the small and medium-sized enterprise (SMEs), have developed VET programmes for their members, CANACINTRA does not have federal-level representational capacity or power and has not been an influential actor in the Mexican IVET system. Other regional business organisations, such as the Automotive Cluster of Nuevo León (*Cluster Automotriz de Nuevo León*—CLAUT) in north Mexico, also organise private VET programmes for their members, yet they do not get involved in the public IVET system.

Mexican Employers' Confederation (*Confederación Patronal de la República Mexicana*—COPARMEX) is an important institution for Mexican firms' collective involvement in the management of the IVET system, and it has been one of the main partners of the MMDT. The main reason for the inclusion of the COPARMEX in the MMDT was to ensure that the MMDT would be developed in line with the needs of Mexico and improve Mexican firms' access to and benefits from the programme (Interview Notes). However, the *de facto* involvement of the COPARMEX in the MMDT has been low. Even though the MMDT is different from the German dual apprenticeship system, the participation of Mexican firms in the programme has been very low (Interview Notes).

IVET as a viable alternative to general education?

The public IVET system has remained a weak part of the Mexican education system and has not been popular amongst either workers or employers. Therefore, IVET has not become a viable alternative to general education in Mexico. Despite the possibility for IVET students in both the THSs and TPHSs to continue to higher education after they complete their studies, a very small share of the upper-secondary school students have been participating in IVET programme, and they prefer rather the academic programmes that develop more general skills.

Even amongst those within the IVET tracks, participation in the programmes that concentrate on developing technical skills (i.e. TPHS) is much lower compared to those with more focus on general academic education (i.e. THS). For example,

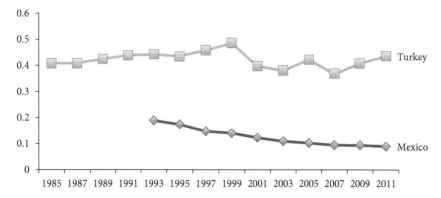

Figure 6.2 Share of VET students in secondary education
Source: OECD (2013b)

although 30 per cent of all upper-secondary students participated in technical education in 2011, more than half of these students were in the THSs (Ahumada, 2014).
In the same year, only about 9 per cent of the upper-secondary school students in
Mexico were in the CONALEP schools, and participation rates to CONALEP
schools has been decreasing over the years, widening the gap with Turkey regarding
the share of students in technical tracks in upper-secondary education programmes
(Figure 6.2). Understanding the differences between participation in DGETI
and CONALEP systems is important particularly when studying the implications
of these systems for the Mexican AAI firms' skilling practices, as the graduates of
the former have more general skills and do not typically join the labour market
after finishing their programme, while the latter includes more technical training
directly addressing the labour market and its graduates seek for employment after
graduating.

6.1.2 Continuing VET programmes

CVET constitutes a key part of the Mexican public VET system and includes multiple programmes run by different bodies of the federal and state governments.
Similar to the case of Turkey, the public retraining programmes for the unemployed
and the skill standardisation and certification system are the main CVET programmes in Mexico.

6.1.2.1 Retraining programmes for the unemployed

The retraining programmes for the unemployed are even more complex than the
IVET programmes in Mexico. While the STPS is the main body responsible for further training programmes, the SEP is in charge of managing some of these programmes. The public retraining programmes in Mexico are organised in two main
groups: 'training for work' (*capacitación para el trabajo*) and 'training at work'

(*capacitación en trabajo*). The former involves programmes for the unemployed and disadvantaged groups, while the latter concerns the training of workers who are currently employed. For the sake of simplicity, the rest of this section discusses the retraining programmes for the unemployed that concern the AAI, and does not explain training at work programmes in detail.[4]

The SEP runs two main programmes within the scope of 'training for work'. The first one is the Training for Work Centres (*Centros de Capacitacion para el Trabajo*— CECATI), which are financed and run by the federal government and aim to generate craft-based skills. The other VET programme is provided by the Work and Training Institutes (*Institutos de Capacitacion para el Trabajo*—ICAT), which are managed by state governments, while both the federal and state governments are responsible for their financing. The training offered in CECATIs and ICATs varies across the states in Mexico and depends on the priorities of the government in each state. None of the governments of the states where the interviewee firms are located, except the state of Guanajuato, offered VET programmes related to the AAI in their CECATI or ICAT institutes when the fieldwork for this book was conducted.

In addition to the programmes provided by the SEP, the STPS runs some 'training for work' programmes. The Scholarships Programme for Job Training (*Programa Becas para la Capacitación para el Trabajo*—BÉCATE) is the main one related to the AAI. In BÉCATE, an unemployed individual receives financial assistance from the state for attending training programmes or for developing some work experience. There are four subprogrammes of BÉCATE aimed at skill development through different measures and for different types of firms (see Ahumada, 2014 for more detail). Amongst the four, the 'mixed training' programme (*capacitación mixta*) is the main BÉCATE programme related to the AAI. In this programme, an allowance (*beca*) is provided to the unemployed to receive training in a firm. Firms that hire trainees within BÉCATE are obliged to provide both theoretical and practical training to these individuals, while the training can last from 1 to 3 months. Moreover, firms must offer permanent employment to at least 80 per cent of the successful trainees. Issues regarding the content and delivery of the training are completely decided by the firm, and there is no regulation in this regard. The trainees of BÉCATE do not go through any skill examination nor do they receive a standardised skill certificate when they complete their training.

De jure, the main responsibility for controlling, providing, and financing VET is on the state in all public retraining programmes that concern the Mexican AAI suppliers, while firms can get involved in these programmes at an individual level. However, the *de facto* commitment of both state and firms to public retraining programmes has typically been low, and it varies across the states depending on their priorities. As a result, the public retraining programmes for the unemployed have

---

[4] Some examples of training at work programmes include the Distance Training Programme for Workers (*Programa de Capacitación a Distancia para Trabajadores*—PROCADIST) or the Productivity Support Programme (*Programa de Apoyo a la Productividad*—PAP) (Ahumada, 2014).

not become an important method for skill development in Mexico. For example, while the state and firms share responsibility in providing VET in the ICAT and CECATI, only 1.6 per cent of the eligible population participated in one of these programmes in 2012 (Ahumada, 2014). Similarly, only 0.7 per cent of the unemployed participated in the 'mixed training programme' within the BÉCATE (Ahumada, 2014), whilst very large MNCs and their employees have formed the main beneficiaries of the public retraining programmes (MS11). States' commitment to and firms' involvement in financing the retraining programmes has also been low. For instance, the ICATs and CECATIs constituted a marginal share of the public budget, and only 180 million USD were dedicated to CECATI programmes in 2012, which barely made 1 per cent of the SEP's budget (SHCP, 2013). Similarly, firms' spending for training in ICAT was only 23 per cent of the total spending in these programmes in 2012 (Ahumada, 2014). Regarding 'who controls VET': firms have the main control over it in the public retraining programmes, as the training takes place in the firm, and firms make decisions about all aspects of the training. Although, in theory, the state could have some control over firm-level training through certification of skills, such control is very limited in practice due to the underdeveloped skill standardisation and certification system in Mexico, which is elaborated on in the next subsection.

The state of Guanajuato has been an important exception regarding the CVET programmes in Mexico, particularly with its ICAT centre. Promoting skill development has been the main strategy of the state government in Guanajuato to attract AAI investments to this state. In order to do this, the state has had high commitment to providing, financing, and controlling VET in the ICAT centre of Guanajuato, which is the State Institute of Training (*Instituto Estatal de Capacitación*—IECA). The IECA has specifically focused on generating skills for the AAI and has been offering training services to the AAI firms in the region, including both large MNCs and local supplier firms. The VET programmes provided by the IECA include training on both general subjects, such as quality management systems, and technical subjects such as welding techniques, which are complemented with practical training. The participants of IECA programmes receive a certificate at the end of their training, although this certificate is not always an occupational certificate but can be a 'certificate of participation' that shows the content of the training programme attended by the certificate holder. The high state commitment to the IECA has influenced the skilling practices of Mexican firms located in Guanajuato in distinct ways, resulting in their difference from the firms in other states, which is explained in Chapter 8.

6.1.2.2 The skill standardisation and certification system

Skill standardisation and certification constitutes a crucial part of national VET systems especially for countries like Mexico where numerous VET programmes coexist and create confusions about the skills developed in each VET programme. Since the 1990s, the government in Mexico has been working to develop a national skill standardisation and certification system and to form the National System of Competences (*Sistema Nacional de Competencias*—SNC). Within these efforts, the National Skill Standards Board (*El Consejo Nacional de Normalización y Certificación de Competencias Laborales*—CONOCER) was established in 1995 as an authority of the skill standardisation system. Initially, after their establishment, both the SNC and CONOCER had several problems due to the low commitment of the Mexican government to them in the 1990s, and the CONOCER was almost shut down in 2003. The SNC and CONOCER were revitalised in 2005 through the 'Multiphase Skills-Based Human Resources Development Program' and with the involvement of and financing from the Inter-American Development Bank (Sancak and Özel, 2018). Standards for several occupations have been developed since this revitalisation, although the skill standardisation and certification has not become an important part of the Mexican skill system (Sancak and Özel, 2018).

The CONOCER is the main authority for the standardised skill certification, and is under the management of the SEP. The skill standardisation and certification system in Mexico is regulated through the 'General Rules and Criteria for the Integration and Operation of the National Qualifications System', which was introduced in 2005 (Diario Oficial de la Federación, 2009). This Regulation outlines the Board and sector committees of CONOCER as tripartite bodies comprising the representatives of the state, businesses, and workers. The participants of CONOCER that represent the interests of the businesses involve the COPARMEX, Confederation of Industrial Chambers of the United States of Mexico (*Confederación de Cámaras Industriales de los Estados Unidos Mexicanos*—CONCAMIN), which are mainly the associations of large businesses, while the representatives of workers include the Revolutionary Confederation of Workers and Peasants (*Confederación Revolucionaria de Obreros y Campesinos*—CROC) and the Mexican Confederation of Workers (*Confederación de Trabajadores de México*—CTM) (Sancak and Özel, 2018). The state bodies within the CONOCER include, in addition to the SEP, the STPS, and the Secretaries of Economy, Agriculture, Finance, and the National Institution for the Education of Adults.

Despite this institutional setting, the state's commitment to and firms' involvement in both the SNC and CONOCER have remained low, while the participation of labour unions in these institutions has been minimal. As a result, the standards established by the CONOCER have remained disconnected from the country's needs, and particularly the needs of the AAI (Sancak and Özel, 2018). For example, the occupational standards related to the AAI comprised only 2 per cent of all standards in 2017, while the main focus has been on standardisation of more general skills that can be used in service industries (CONOCER, 2017). Furthermore, the standards developed by the CONOCER have become 'obsolete', as only 35 per cent of the CONOCER standards were actually used for skill certification in 2007–2011 (de Anda, 2011; Ricart et al., 2014).[5]

---

[5] See Sancak and Özel (2018) for more discussion on the skill certification system.

6.1.3 VET in the Mexican Federal Labour Law

The Federal Labour Law forms a crucial part of the Mexican VET system, as it is the key instrument for the state to become the 'driving force' of the VET system rather than its 'executor' (Casalet, 1994, p. 729). This law puts the responsibility of providing and financing VET on firms while giving the state a regulatory role and some control over VET. However, the functioning of the training requirement of the Labour Law has been problematic, which has led to limited and *ad hoc* firm involvement in VET.

According to Article 132 and Article 153 of the Mexican Federal Labour Law, employers in Mexico are obliged to provide training to all their workers and pay all expenses related to that training, which gives firms important responsibility for the provision and financing of VET. Furthermore, according to the Labour Law Article 153-E, all firms with more than 50 employees must have Joint Commissions of Learning and Training (*Comisiones Mixtas de Capacitación y Adiestramiento*; hereafter, Joint Commissions), and the decisions about the content and delivery of firm-level training need to be made within these commissions. The Joint Commissions are important platforms to discuss several issues related to firm-level industrial relations including wages and workers' health and safety. These Commissions are required to include an equal number of individuals representing the interests of employers and employees. The employer representatives typically include someone from the management departments, and mostly from the human resources (HR) department, while the union leaders represent the interests of employees. The Joint Commissions are also responsible for developing, implementing, monitoring, and improving the firm-level training. Therefore, these Commissions are important platforms for both firms and workers to influence the firm-level training.

While the Labour Law *de jure* puts the main responsibility of VET on firms and gives some control over VET to the state, firms' *de facto* involvement in VET has been low, and the state's control over VET has been weak. This is due to two main reasons: (i) the vagueness of the regulation about the firm-level training and (ii) the problems regarding the implementation of the mandatory firm-level training.

Although the Labour Law obliges firms to provide training to their employees, it does not have any requirements about the characteristics of the firm-level training. For instance, the Law states that the training can take place within or outside the firm, and can be delivered by internal personnel or an externally contracted specialist (Article 153-A). Furthermore, while the Law requires the training programmes to be based on 'occupational competence norms' (Article 153-H), these norms are not standardised norms, such as the occupational standards developed by the SNC, but are rather defined by individual firms, and are often based on the ISO/TS requirements (see Chapter 4). Therefore, firms have important control over the firm-level training, and are free to arrange the specifics of this training in accordance with their needs, which may not be skill-related needs.

The lack of regulation about the characteristics of the mandatory firm-level training has resulted in firms' minimal compliance with the training obligation, and has led to an important variation of firm-level training across firms. Most firms in Mexico provide only very short health and safety training to their employees instead of training on certain skills, and this has been sufficient to comply with the training requirement of the Labour Law (Interview Notes). The representatives of some firms mentioned that although they provide training on welding techniques or general training on personal attitudes, this is often because they need such workers, and not because it is required in the Labour Law. Furthermore, several firms are argued to record training activities even when they do not provide any training to their employees, and this does not often create problems due to the problems related to the implementation of the firm-level training requirement (MS5).

The main strategy adopted by the federal government in Mexico to ensure the implementation of firm-level training requirement has been the random firm inspections by the STPS, which has been very problematic in achieving its aim. Firms in Mexico are required to record information about firm-level training and show the training records to inspectors from the STPS during their visits to firms.[6] This method, nevertheless, has not been effective for ensuring the firm-level training. This is due to two interrelated reasons. Firstly, there are many areas to inspect in the STPS visits that are more important for the Secretariat, such as the formal registration of workers and health and safety at the workplace. Therefore, the inspection of the training requirement is not a priority in these visits and often gets omitted or overlooked. The representative from the STPS stated:

> There is a body in the STPS for inspection and supervision. The inspectors in this department check all aspects of the Labour Law when they visit a company, including informality, security, hygiene, work conditions and contracts. In addition to all of these, they also need to check if the firm has a plan for training and if they carry out training. This is too much work to do in one go.   (MS11)

The second reason for the ineffectiveness of the implementation of the training requirement through inspections is the limited personnel capacity of the STPS. The inspection and supervision body in the STPS has 'a very small number of staff in charge of millions of firms' (MS11), which increases the workload of each STPS inspector, and reduces the capacity of the STPS to carry out regular firm inspections. Indeed, very few of the interviewed firms mentioned that they had an inspection by the STPS in the last 3 years. Consequently, only about 30 per cent of the *registered* workforce received training from their employers in 2013 (Ahumada, 2014). When the vast size of the informal economy is also considered, the share of workers receiving training from their employers decreased to only 10 per cent for 2013 in Mexico (Ahumada, 2014).

---

[6] Before, firms were obliged to submit the training records to the STPS through an online platform (Article 153-V), this regulation was changed in 2012. (Interview Notes).

Another gap between the *de jure* regulations on firm-level training and their *de facto* implementation is related to the Joint Commissions. While the Labour Law requires firms to have these commissions, the existence and operations of Joint Commissions vary vastly across firms due to the problems in this regulation and its implementation. In fact, many of the smaller firms that were interviewed for this book did not have such Commissions. Even when such a commission exists in a firm, the training of employees constitutes a marginal issue, and the members typically focus on other aspects of industrial relations such as wage bargaining and workplace safety (Interview Notes). As a result, only 3 per cent of firm-level training in Mexico in 2012 was organised through the Joint Commissions (World Bank, 2013). Even when the Joint Commissions exist and have activities regarding firm-level training, the decisions are usually dominated by the interests of employers, while the workers' representatives do not have much power or influence. For instance, many interviewees from the HR departments did not know the name of the union representative within the Joint Commission (Interview Notes). Besides, the union leaders have been acting more as a 'contact point' between workers and administrative staff, and they 'get informed' (M18 HR) about the wage levels and firm's training strategy, which are unilaterally decided by the companies' managerial staff, rather than being equal members of these commissions.[7]

6.1.4 Defining the Mexican VET system and the role of the 'missing' state

It is challenging to describe the Mexican VET system using the typology of Busemeyer and Trampusch (2012) because of the complexity of the system, and the problems regarding the *de jure* institutions and regulations and their *de facto* functioning and implementation. Firstly, there are several public VET programmes in Mexico, which may give the Mexican VET system 'statist' characters. Secondly, the Mexican Labour Law puts the main responsibility of VET on firms, which makes it similar to segmentalist VET systems. Thirdly, the public VET programmes cover a marginal share of the labour force, and the state's commitment to these programmes is very low, while very few firms in Mexico follow the training requirement in the Labour Law and provide training to their employees, which makes the Mexican VET system liberal. Therefore, the Mexican VET system can be described as *de jure* statist and segmentatilst, *de facto* liberal.

The state plays the major role in the *de jure* statist and segmentalist, *de facto* liberal VET system in Mexico not only through the lack of its commitment to VET and enforcing the labour regulations, but also through shaping other actors' involvement

---

[7] It is important to note that the discussion here is based on the interviews with local auto parts suppliers. Other studies on large original equipment manufacturers have shown that the firm-level unions in these firms may have influence on the industrial relations, yet this also varies across firms (Cook, 2007; Roxborough, 1983).

in the VET system. As this chapter so far has shown, the state has had a low commitment to VET in the secondary education system, and has *de jure* put the responsibility of VET on firms. However, the limitations in the implementation of labour regulations by the state have led to a *de facto* liberal VET system with low level of VET.

The state in Mexico has influenced the Mexican VET system also through shaping the involvement of non-state actors in this system, particularly the businesses and workers. More specifically, and similar to the state in Turkey, the state in Mexico has affected the participation of businesses and workers in the Mexican VET system through influencing these actors' collective action capacity, and through endorsing these actors' individual involvement in the VET system rather than collective involvement (Sancak, forthcoming). A main reason for this is because the state in Mexico has shaped the businesses' collective action capacity and has promoted business representation that favours large firms instead of smaller ones. While Mexico had a corporatist business structure until the 1990s, this structure was changed within the scope of neoliberal transformation since the 1980s, which has resulted in the significant power loss of organisations representing the SMEs and the weak influence of these organisations over VET policies. In line with the liberalisation efforts, the compulsory membership to business chambers was abolished in 1994, which led to voluntary organisation of business associations. With these, CANACINTRA, which has been an important association representing the SMEs in Mexico, lost important power after the abolishment of the corporatist structure and consequently was pushed out of the policymaking platforms, which has substantially reduced the collective action capacity of the SMEs and their power to influence public policies (Shadlen, 2002, 2004). Resultantly, although the SMEs would have more interest in promoting VET (Culpepper, 2003, 2007), they have not had the power to promote VET policies in Mexico.

In contrast to the diminishing power of the SMEs, the voluntary membership in business associations has led to an '*Anglo-Saxon style*' of lobbying' in Mexico, which has empowered large conglomerates, as well as the exclusive business associations representing large companies, such as the Coordinating Council of Business (*Consejo Coordinador Empresarial*—CCE) (Özel, 2014, p. 10). Also through the clientelistic links of large firms and associations representing these firms with the governing political parties, the interests of large firms have dominated the policymaking in Mexico. These large firms, however, having the capacity to provide firm-level training, have not been interested in the public VET system but have focused on maintaining low labour costs to sustain their comparative advantage in labour-intensive sectors in the global economy (Bizberg, 2019). Therefore, business associations have not been important actors in shaping the VET system because of the structures for organising business interests in Mexico that give more power to large firms. Although the associations representing large firms have been members of some VET platforms, they have not sufficiently committed to these platforms, leading to the low firm involvement in the VET system. Instead of collective involvement, the state in Mexico has promoted firms' *individual involvement* in the VET system through the training requirement in the Labour Law, the Liaison Committees in CONALEP schools and at state level, as well as the firm-level Joint Commissions.

The state in Mexico has also shaped workers' involvement in the VET system by influencing their collective action capacity, and by promoting workers' individual involvement in VET at the level of the firm, instead of their industry- or country-level collective involvement. Although labour unions were powerful institutions before the economic liberalisation, the union movement in Mexico has been 'state dependent' (Kuş and Özel, 2010). During the state-led import substituting industrialisation period, the major unions such as the Confederation of Mexican Workers (*Confederación de Trabajadores de México*—CTM) formed clientelistic relationships with the governing Institutional Revolutionary Party (*Partido Revolucionario Institutcional*—PRI), which gave these major unions important powers to influence public policies (Bizberg, 1990; Collier and Collier, 1991; Murillo, 2001). Later, with the neoliberal transformations in the 1980s and 1990s, the state in Mexico aimed to reduce the union power and played an important role in the fragmentation of labour unions through 'new unionism' that curbed down the power of traditional unions and eventually reduced collective bargaining to company level (Kuş and Özel, 2010). The power or labour unions to collectively organise and influence public policy has decreased significantly during the neoliberal restructuring, as the share of unionised waged workers in Mexico fell from 21 per cent in 1992 to 12 per cent in 2016 (Herrera and Melgoza, 2003; ILO, 2020a). As a result, the labour unions in Mexico have not become influential actors in the organisation and management of the VET system. Although the unions are members of certain VET platforms, such as the sector committees of CONOCER, unions' *de facto* participation in these platforms has been very low. Instead of workers' collective involvement in the VET system, the state in Mexico has aimed to address workers' VET interests through their involvement via more individual means, such as the firm-level Joint Commissions and inclusion of the firm-level union representatives in these commissions. However, the *de facto* functioning of these commissions and inclusion of unions' interests has been very problematic, resulting in the minimal influence of workers in the Mexican VET system.

6.2 State regulations and the structure of the labour market in Mexico

While the VET system in Mexico sets out the training programmes available to workers and firms, and thus defines the characteristics of workers available in the labour market, there are other institutions and regulations that affect the labour market dynamics and become the complementarities of the skill system. The key other institutions that affect firms' skilling strategies in Mexico are similar to the ones in Turkey and include the labour regulations on work contracts and wages, as well as firms' location and transportation services (while the military service is not a key institution in Mexico).

6.2.1 Labour regulations and wage-setting institutions

The main labour market institutions that complement the Mexican skill system include the regulations in the Labour Law concerning work contracts and the institutions of wage setting, and particularly the minimum wage. These are important complementarities because they influence firms' hiring and training costs and thus shape their skilling strategies. Furthermore, all these regulations and institutions are shaped by the (lack) of state's involvement in regulating and the limited implementation of existing regulations in Mexico.

6.2.1.1 Work contracts

The regulations on work contracts in the Mexican Federal Labour Law constitute a key complementary of the Mexican skill system through its three main features: (i) strict regulations on hiring and firing, (ii) the limited implementation of the strict regulations, and (iii) the flexibilities within the Labour Law regarding the initial employment of new recruits. All these are shaped by the Mexican state and its focus on developing an 'international outsourcing capitalism' that is subordinate to external markets (Bizberg, 2019), for which the state has prioritised minimising labour costs. The state in Mexico is argued to have oppressed the labour costs and flexibilised the labour market dynamics through a 'backdoor institutional change', namely not through replacing the labour regulations with more flexible ones, but through relaxing the implementation of the existing, and out-dated, regulations (Bensusán, 2006; Bayón, 2009). As a result, the Mexican Federal Labour Law has not had major changes since the early 1980s, and the labour regulations in Mexico are considered as 'highly inflexible' (Figure 6.3), where firms are argued to 'face considerable barriers to hiring and layoff' (World Bank, 2013, p. 5). The limitations on hiring and firing have important implications for the labour market dynamics in the country. On the one hand, the inflexible labour regulations make it very costly for firms to dismiss workers once they are hired. This, together with the limited availability of workers with a standardised occupational certificate, would increase firms' hiring costs due to the higher risks when hiring skilled workers (see Chapter 2.1). On the other hand, such inflexibility in the labour market will potentially decrease the labour turnover and thus, reduce firms' costs for training unskilled workers.

While the regulations on work contracts in the Labour Law are strict, the implementation of these regulations has been low, which is similar to the case of the firm-level training requirement in the Labour Law explained in the previous section. Indeed, it has been argued that Mexico is the country with the biggest gap between the labour regulations and their implementation in Latin America (Bensusán, 2006). Consequently, the labour legislation of Mexico has been described as 'regulatory

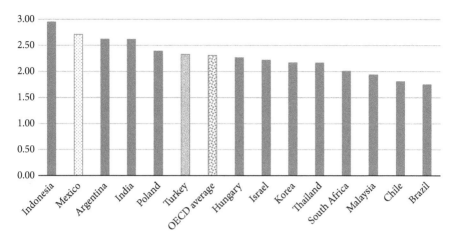

Figure 6.3 Strictness of employment protection in selected emerging market economies (2012)
Source: OECD (2020a)
Individual and collective dismissals (regular contracts). The data for Malaysia is from 2013.

with a high compliance cost (especially for smaller firms), but a very low non-compliance cost' (Bayón, 2009, p. 307). Large firms in Mexico have been avoiding certain requirements and responsibilities of the Labour Law also through using intermediaries and subcontracting firms (Bensusán and Alcalde, 2000). Therefore, while the large firms may comply with the labour regulations for the workers they directly employ, they create a secondary group of workers employed through the sub-contractors, which may not, and usually do not, comply with the labour regulations.

The weak implementation of the strict labour regulations leads to several types of employment and sizeable informal employment, resulting in a segmented labour market in Mexico. In fact, the strict labour regulations with limited implementation are shown as one of the major reasons for the large informal sector and the seg-mented labour market in this country, where 52 per cent of employment was in informal jobs in 2017 (ILO, 2020b).[8] Currently, in addition to the workers employed in large firms with relatively secure full-time jobs and the workers in informal jobs with precarious work arrangements, there are several other types of employment in Mexico including the workers in small (subcontracting) firms, workers with tem-porary contracts, and workers in part-time jobs.

Another key element in the Labour Law for the Mexican skill system is the sec-tion on a trial or training period for new employees, which gives firms the possibility to employ workers for a limited period of time and on more flexible terms. According to Article 39 of the Labour Law, there is a 'trial period' (*periodo de prueba*) for new entrants for 30 days, after which firms need to provide a permanent contract to a new entrant. However, if the person is going to carry out technical work and is going

---

[8] While the level was 23 per cent in Turkey in the same year.

to be trained in the firm for this, the initial period is called 'training period' (*capacitación inicial*), and it can last up to 3 months. The trial/training period can be extended up to 6 months if the worker will 'perform specific professional activities' or will carry out managerial tasks.[9]

The trial/training period influences the Mexican firms' skilling strategies through at least three main ways. Firstly, the up-to-6-month 'training period' gives firms sufficient amount of time to get to know the worker before offering them a permanent contract or making large investments in these workers' skill development, and thus, reduces their hiring costs that would occur due to information costs (Chapter 2: Section 1). Secondly, employers can dismiss the workers within the trial/training period with no repercussions, which then reduces the firing costs of employers. Thirdly, employers may pay less to the workers in the trial/training period compared the regular employees, which then decreases firms' training costs for these workers. In the end, the possibility of employment through trial/training period can encourage firms to employ unskilled workers and provide basic training within this period, when they get to know the worker better and can make more informed decisions about offering a permanent contract to these workers (see Chapter 2: Section 1 on hiring and training costs).

All in all, the strict labour regulations, the limited implementation of these regulations, and the flexibilities within the regulations constitute the key components of the Mexican Labour Law that will influence firms' skilling strategies. The state in Mexico has had an impact on all these elements through its adoption of 'outsourcing capitalism' (Bizberg, 2019), which has led to its low level of involvement in regulating the labour markets and implementing the existing regulations.

6.2.1.2 The role of the minimum wage

Similar to the case of Turkey, the minimum wage is an important institution for the Mexican skill system for two main reasons. Firstly, a large share of the workers in Mexico receive the minimum wage as their salary, while the earnings of all Mexican workers are defined based on the minimum wage. For example, in 2016, about 19 per cent of the employed population received the minimum wage or below in Mexico and more than half of the workers received the double of the minimum wage or below (INEGI, 2020). Figure 6.4 shows the share of the workers in Mexico based on their earnings in 2016. In addition to the earnings of workers, payments made to the trainees of public VET programmes, namely *beca*, as well as the pensions and severance pay for the laid-off workers, are defined through the minimum wage. Therefore, the minimum wage—and its level—is key for determining the labour costs in Mexico.

Secondly, the minimum wage is a key institution for the Mexican skill system because it has been extremely low, which has led to exceptionally low level of wages in the country in general and thus, low labour costs. Mexico has had the lowest

[9] http://www.stps.gob.mx/bp/secciones/junta_federal/secciones/consultas/ley_federal.html.

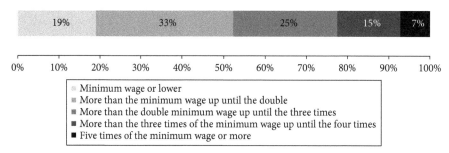

Figure 6.4 Share of (formal) employees based on their earnings in 2016 in Mexico
Source: INEGI (2020)

minimum wage amongst the OECD countries, and the hourly real minimum wage was 1 USD in 2016, when it was 6.4 USD in Turkey, namely more than the six times of the one in Mexico (OECD, 2020d) (see Figure 5.3).[10] When the gap between the minimum wage in Turkey and Mexico is considered together with Figure 6.4, it can be seen that more than 93 per cent of the workers in Mexico earn less than 5 USD hourly, which is by itself less than the minimum wage in Turkey.

The low wages are mentioned as the key advantage of the Mexican AAI and for remaining competitive in global auto parts-automotive value chains (AACs) by several interviewees, including the representatives of firms, industry associations, and state bureaucrats. The low wage paid to employees is particularly important for the AAI firms in Mexico, as these firms require workers with some skills but usually cannot find such workers in the labour market due to the weak public VET system. Therefore, many of these firms need to develop these skills within the firm, and the extremely low wages in Mexico reduce firms' labour costs, which makes firm-level training a feasible option for skill development. The low minimum wage in Mexico also gives the AAI firms an advantage in their competition for new workers with other industries: thanks to the already low minimum wage, the auto parts suppliers can offer a wage above the minimum wage to attract new workers to their company without undermining their competitiveness in global AACs, which is not the case in Turkey where the minimum wage is already very high (see Chapter 5).

Similar to the case of labour regulations, the state in Mexico has played the main role in maintaining the low minimum wage, and low wages in general, due to its promotion of 'international outsourcing capitalism' (Bizberg, 2019). Suppressing labour costs, the relaxed implementation of labour regulations, and dismantling of the labour unions have been the main tools adopted by the Mexican state to attract foreign direct investment to the country and to promote Mexican economy's integration to the global economy in low value-added production (Bensusán, 2006; Bizberg, 2019). The minimum wage in Mexico is decided by the National Minimum Wage Commission (*Comisión Nacional de Salarios Mínimos*—CONOSAMI). Although this

---

[10] In 2018, constant prices at 2018 USD purchasing power parity.

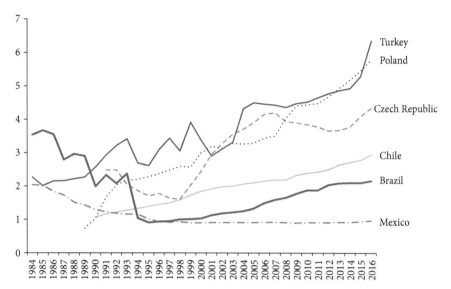

Figure 6.5 Hourly real minimum wage in selected emerging market economies (constant prices at 2018 USD purchasing power parity)
Source: OECD (2020d)

is a tripartite body, including the representatives of labour unions, business associations, and the state, the labour unions have not had much influence on this commission, resulting in the 'subordination of workers' representatives to government policies' (Bayón, 2009, p. 308). Through the state's links with large businesses, including the foreign and domestic ones, the interests of these firms have dominated the decisions about workers and wages in Mexico. As a result, the minimum wage in Mexico diminished substantially in the 1980s and early 1990s, when the neoliberal transformation happened, and since then, the rise of the minimum wage has remained below the inflation rate, increasing the gap between Mexico and other emerging market economies (Figure 6.5). The state has played an active role in maintaining the low wages in Mexico also through its influence over unions and collective bargaining structures. Due to the weak union organisation and power, as well as the clientelistic links between some union confederations and the state, the unions have not been effective players for increasing wages in Mexico (Kuş and Özel, 2010).

6.2.2 Firms' location and transportation services

In Mexico, the accessibility between workers and firms is limited by two main factors that are shaped by the lack of state's involvement in the economy: the location of Mexican auto parts suppliers in remote and isolated areas, and the limited public transportation facilities in the areas where the AAI firms are located.

Unlike their counterparts in Turkey, the Mexican firms are not located in organised industrial zones (OIZs) but are typically in remote and isolated areas that are not easily accessible via public transportation. Although there are industrial parks in Mexico, their historical development and the beneficiaries of these parks have been very different from the OIZs in Turkey (see Chapter 5). The industrial parks in Mexico facilitate the operations of firms located in these areas by providing several services such as access to energy, roadwork, and water, and by reducing the bureaucracy these firms have to deal with, which is similar to the OIZs in Turkey (Reforma, 2016). However, foreign MNCs and some very large Mexican firms have been the main beneficiaries of the industrial parks in Mexico, which is very different from the case of OIZs in Turkey, which have mainly benefited the domestic firms, including smaller ones. In contrast to the OIZs in Turkey, which have been used for promoting the development of the local industry, industrial parks were introduced in the 1960s in Mexico to resolve the unemployment problem in these years through attracting foreign investment and promoting the necessary infrastructure to foreign MNCs, namely *maquiladoras*. Resultantly, the majority of firms located in industrial parks have been foreign MNCs operating in Mexico, while most Mexican AAI companies are located outside the industrial parks and usually in isolated areas.

Another key institution that restricts Mexican firms' access to different workers, and Mexican workers' access to different firms, is the limited public transportation in the areas where the Mexican AAI firms are located. The investments made for public transportation within cities has been low in Mexico, and the main AAI regions studied for this book, including Puebla, Nuevo León, as well as the areas in the state of Guanajuato, do not have extensive public transportation networks, while the existing transportation services are not usually affordable for shop floor workers in AAI firms.[11] Because of the limitations to accessible and affordable public transportation, the Mexican auto parts suppliers typically employ individuals who reside near their firm, and within a walking or cycling distance from the company.[12] The HR representative from M5 explains workers' access to firms as follows:

> Our operators' transportation opportunities are very limited because of their low income. They cannot spend a lot for transportation and therefore an operator needs to be from around here so that they can walk or cycle here.

The location of the Mexican AAI firms in remote and isolated areas and the limited affordable transportation facilities, both of which are shaped by the state's (low) involvement in these structures, affect Mexican firms' access to workers with different skills and the labour turnover in these firms. On the one hand, the Mexican AAI firms can employ only the workers residing in these areas, which limits the skill profile they have access to and thus increases firms' costs of hiring skilled workers. On the other hand, the employees of the Mexican AAI firms cannot easily change jobs

---

[11] Firms located in the State of Mexico are more accessible via public transport, and one firm in Puebla offers free private transportation to its operative staff.

[12] Workers at higher positions, however, come from a wider area and access the firm by a personal car.

Table 6.2 The national institutions in Mexico and the state's involvement in them

Institutions

De jure **statist and segmentalist,** *de facto* **liberal VET system**

- Low state commitment to financing, providing and controlling VET
- *De jure* high, *de facto* low firm involvement
- Institutions for voluntary collective action of business and state's links with large firms
- Dismantled unions with limited influence

Labour regulations and wage setting institutions

- Strict regulations on work contracts with limited implementation
- The possibility for initially flexible employment for new workers
- Extremely low minimum wage, and low labour costs

Firms' location and transportation services

- Location of Mexican AAI firms in remote and isolated areas
- Limited and unaffordable public transportation

Low state involvement

due to the limited job opportunities in those remote areas and limited and/or unaffordable public transportation, which then reduces the labour turnover in firms and thus decreases Mexican firms' costs for training unskilled workers. These together have important influence on the Mexican AAI firms' skilling strategies, which are explained in Chapter 8.

6.3 Conclusion and complementarities of the Mexican skill system

This chapter has focused on the national institutional structures that complement the Mexican skill system and shown that the state's low involvement plays a main role in these institutions. The main institutions that complement the skill system in Mexico are similar to those in Turkey and include the public VET system, labour regulations on work contracts and minimum wage, and firms' location and transportation services (except the military service requirement of Turkey). However, these institutions have very different features in Mexico because of the low state involvement in them, and will influence the firm-level skilling practices in distinct ways.

Table 6.2 summarises the discussion and demonstrates how the low state involvement in national institutional arrangements shape the Mexican skill system. Firstly, the state plays a defining role in the Mexican VET system through its commitment to VET and shaping other actors' involvement in the VET system. Although the Mexican VET system looks like a statist and segmentalist VET system *de jure*, it is *de facto* liberal because of not only the limited overall state commitment to it, but also the low involvement of firms and workers in VET, which is affected by the state. The dismantling of the corporatist business structure and the weakening of labour unions have resulted in the limited involvement of both businesses and workers in the skill system. Instead of their collective involvement, the state in Mexico has promoted the individual involvement of workers and firms in the VET system. Nevertheless, *de facto* functioning of these structures has been problematic, and has resulted in low involvement of both firms and workers in the VET system.

Secondly, the state affects the Mexican skill system through labour regulations concerning employment contracts and the level of minimum wage. The state in Mexico has been promoting an international outsourcing capitalism that is subordinate to external markets, for which reducing labour costs constituted an important strategy. Therefore, the minimum wage—and wages in general—have been suppressed, and have remained stagnant throughout the neoliberal era. Furthermore, although the 'strict' labour regulations have been maintained, firms have important flexibilities in their employment practices due to certain flexibilities in regulations, such as the training/trial period and subcontracting, as well as substantial gaps between the regulations and their implementation. The active dismantling of labour unions, and the squeezing of the union activity to the firm level, have further contributed to the reduction of labour costs in Mexico.

Thirdly, the state's focus on industrial parks for foreign firms rather than for Mexican firms and limited investments in affordable public transportation have restricted the accessibility between workers and Mexican firms. Resultantly, the Mexican AAI firms are typically located in remote areas with limited public transportation facilities, which has important impact on the quantity and quality of skills available to firms, as well as on the labour turnover within these firms.

All three elements that are shaped by the state's involvement in them have major influence on Mexican auto parts producers' training and hiring practices. Therefore, these three elements constitute the complementarities of the multilevel skill system in Mexico, first because they together influence a third phenomenon (i.e. skilling practices) ([A&B]→C, where A, B, and C are complementary, see Chapter 2), and then because together they form parts of a whole. The implications of the institutional environment on the skilling practices of the Mexican firms and outcomes of these practices for workers and firms are explained in detail in Chapter 8.

PART 3

SKILLING PRACTICES AND DEVELOPMENT IMPLICATIONS

7

The skilling practices of Turkish firms and their outcomes for workers and firms

> To understand why we do what we do, you should look at state policies at first. Policies are very important for our activities. Today, accepting the Syrian refugees affects us. The changes in the education system affect us. Collective agreement regulations affect us.
>
> (T10 HR)

After explaining the macro- and meso-level dynamics that affect the auto parts suppliers in Mexico and Turkey in the previous three chapters, namely the governance structures in global auto parts-automotive value chains (AACs) and the institutional environment, this chapter and the following one focus on firm-level hiring, training, and employee development practices. These two chapters link macro-level dynamics with firm-level skilling practices and investigate the outcomes of these practices for workers, firms, and the development prospects of Turkey and Mexico.

The focus in these two chapters is on the hiring, training, and employee development practices of firms. According to the researchers of High-Performance Work Systems (HPWSs), these systems include several human resources management practices that improve the competitiveness of firms and the career progression opportunities for workers. The HPWSs require workers with general and polyvalent skills since such skills facilitate the shift of workers between different departments and thus, improve firms' ability to respond to changes in demand and technology. Additionally, workers with general and polyvalent skills are argued to have more opportunities for progressing to tasks that require higher skills, and that pay a better salary. The current and following chapters investigate the Turkish and Mexican skill systems in these aspects to examine the skilling practices in the auto parts suppliers and to evaluate the implications of these practices for workers' career progression and firms' competitiveness. This then helps to make inferences about the implications of the skill systems for these countries' high-road development prospects.

In the first part, the current chapter explains the implications of the national institutions in Turkey for firms' skilling practices. It shows that the national institutions influence firms' skilling practices through two main ways: (i) affecting the labour market dynamics, namely the labour supply, demand as well as the mobility of

Global Production, National Institutions, and Skill Formation: The Political Economy of Training and Employment in Auto Parts Suppliers from Mexico And Turkey. Merve Sancak, Oxford University Press. © Merve Sancak 2022.
DOI: 10.1093/oso/9780198860655.003.0007

workers, and (ii) defining the training mechanisms available to firms. The second part of the chapter focuses on firm-level training and hiring strategies, as well as firms' linkages with public vocational education and training (VET) programmes. The third part discusses the outcomes of the skilling strategies for workers and firms in the Turkish auto parts-automotive industry (AAI), and the wider implications of the skill system for the development experience of Turkey.

7.1　Skilling implications of the institutional arrangements in Turkey

The institutions that complement the skill system in Turkey—which include the VET system, labour regulations and wage-setting institutions, firms' location and public transportation facilities, and the military service—have important effects on the labour market dynamics in the country, and, thus, they influence the skilling practices of AAI firms in Turkey. Table 7.1 summarises the impact of the national institutions on labour market dynamics, as well as their implications for firms' skilling practices.

Table 7.1　Skilling implications of the institutions in Turkey

Institutions		Implications for Skilling
Statist VET system with some collectivist elements and some permeability	→	High(er) number of students in VHSs Low number of VHS graduates in the labour market Limited number of trainees in the apprenticeship system and UMEM Some mechanisms for firm involvement in the VET system that are regulated by the state
Labour regulations and wage-setting institutions	→	Employment possibility on fixed-term contracts with lower benefits Employment possibility on permanent contracts with higher benefits Employment of unionised and nonunionised workers High level of mobility among entry-level workers Low supply of entry-level VET graduates to AAI firms High demand for VET graduates by AAI firms
Firms' location and transportation services	→	High access of firms to more workers High access of workers to different jobs
Military service requirement	→	Interruption in male workers' career development Low supply of entry-level workers in the labour market Vulnerability to work in precarious conditions by those not completing the service

7.1.1 Implications of the Turkish VET system

The public VET system in Turkey has been an important resource to generate the necessary skills for the Turkish auto parts supplier firms, and all firms interviewed for this book mentioned that they generally prefer to utilise the public VET programmes to address their skill needs. The content of training in public VET programmes and the number of individuals graduating from these programmes and joining the labour market constitute the two main elements of the Turkish VET system that influence the Turkish AAI firms' skilling practices.

The content of public VET programmes in Turkey is key for firms' skilling strategies because it not only affects the *types of skills* available in the labour market, but also defines the *mechanisms for firms' involvement* in the public VET system. Firstly, the public VET system is an important institution in Turkey that shapes the types of skills available to AAI firms. For example, the VHSs in Turkey, which constitute the largest share of the public VET system, provide important technical and theoretical knowledge and some key general skills to their participants. Therefore, thanks to this training, the VHS graduates employed in the AAI possess key skills that give them the possibility to be shifted across different production departments and be promoted to positions requiring higher-level skills. In contrast to VHSs, the training offered in the apprenticeship system and in the retraining programmes for the unemployed (i.e. the Specialised Occupation Centres Programme, Turkey (UMEM), see Chapter 5) is specific and does not involve as much theoretical learning or the development of general skills. Therefore, the individuals participating in these programmes develop mostly specific technical skills, which creates challenges for these workers to be shifted to other production functions or to be promoted to higher-level positions. Secondly, the working of the VET programmes in Turkey defines the mechanisms for firms' involvement in the VET system and thus influences their skilling practices. For example, firms in Turkey can recruit VET students as trainees during their studies. This helps firms to develop links with these individuals, get to know them, provide training at low cost, and employ them as regular workers after their training is completed. There are other mechanisms for the Turkish firms to get involved in the public VET system, such as through establishing VET institutes, which then influences firms' training and hiring strategies.

In addition, the public VET system in Turkey affects the Turkish AAI firms' skilling strategies through shaping the number of individuals participating in public VET programmes, and the number of VET graduates joining the labour market. The influence of the VHS system is particularly complex in this regard. On the one hand, the high state commitment to the VHS system in Turkey leads to a high number of individuals participating in VHSs, which would reduce firms' costs for hiring skilled/certified workers. On the other hand, the possibility of continuing to higher education, and the preference for higher education amongst VHS students, restricts the availability of VHS graduates in the labour market for AAI firms. Many firms interviewed for this book complained that most of their trainees from VHSs do not continue to work in the company because they start studying in postsecondary-nontertiary

MYOs (*Meslek Yüksek Okulu*) thanks to the possibility of 'direct transition' (*dikey geçiş*), or because they prepare for the university entrance exam.[1] For instance, the HR representative from T10 stated:

> Before, we could easily find VHS graduates with a degree in metal works. We would have so many applications in our database that we would delete the applications older than 2 years. But now, we barely receive applications from these graduates. They want to study at a university rather than to work.

The Turkish AAI firms also face challenges when recruiting trainees and graduates from other public VET programmes, including the apprenticeship system and the UMEM. A very low number of individuals in Turkey have been attending apprenticeship training or UMEM courses mainly because of the better social status associated with general and higher education as opposed to the lower status associated with VET. The HR representative from T10 explains this as follows:

> Continuing to higher levels of education has become very easy now. Parents want their children to have higher education and all parents want their kids to become doctors. So, they want their kids to study in general schools instead of becoming apprentices. Not even the peasants' kids are apprentices anymore…Before, we would have 100 apprentices training in the company. Now, we barely find 20!

The limited availability of VET students and graduates in the labour market constitutes an important element that affects the skilling strategies of Turkish AAI firms, and because of this, many firms have been developing additional strategies to attract more trainees and graduates of public VET programmes. These strategies have been shaped by the state regulations about firms' involvement in the public VET programmes, which are elaborated in the next part of the chapter.

7.1.2 Implications of the other institutions

Similar to the case of the public VET system, the three other institutions that complement the skill system in Turkey—the labour regulations and wage-setting institutions, firms' location and public transportation facilities, and the military service requirement—have significant impact on the labour market dynamics in Turkey. Therefore, they influence the Turkish AAI firms' skilling practices.

The different Labour Law requirements for firms with different sizes, the regulations on work contracts with the possibility of subcontracting, and the low level of

---

[1] The 'direct transition problem' has been raised in several VET policy platforms by the Union of Chambers and Commodity Exchanges of Turkey. Later in 2017, the possibility of direct transition was lifted. However, this happened after the interviews for this book were conducted, and the effects of this change are not studied in the book.

unionisation have important impacts on the Turkish AAI firms' skilling practices and lead to a segmentation of worker groups in the Turkish AAI. For instance, the flexibilities provided to smaller firms about their employees together with the possibility of subcontracting often lead to different skilling practices for posts requiring lower and higher skills. Consequently, the AAI firms in Turkey can employ entry-level workers on fixed-term contracts as auxiliary workers/trainees while employing the more experienced workers as permanent employees.

The minimum wage is a key institution that affects both the labour market dynamics and labour costs in Turkey and thus influences AAI firms' skilling strategies in several ways. Because the minimum wage is 'too high' in Turkey, the supplier firms in the AAI have been facing serious challenges to attract new workers to the entry-level positions, particularly workers with a VET certificate. Even after receiving training in an area related to the AAI, most graduates of VET schools prefer working in the service or retail industries to working in the AAI because of the similar wages paid in entry-level posts but different work environments in these sectors. This reduces the number of VET graduates available to the Turkish auto parts suppliers, and for example, in 2017, less than half of the VHS graduates finishing VET programmes related to the AAI started working in a job in the area of their training (MEB, 2018). Because of this, many AAI suppliers in Turkey have developed additional strategies to address their skill needs, as explained in the rest of the chapter.

The mandatory occupational certificate is the other key institution that affects the labour market dynamics and skilling strategies of the AAI suppliers in Turkey. With the introduction of the occupational certificate requirement (see Chapter 5), the demand for workers with a VET certificate has rapidly escalated in Turkey. This requirement has impacted not only the Turkish firms' skilling strategies when recruiting new workers, but also their training practices regarding their current employees. Combined with the restricted availability of workers with a VET certificate in the labour market, the Turkish auto parts producers have developed several strategies to address their increased need for certified workers.

The Turkish AAI firms' location in organised industrial zones (OIZs) and the affordable public transportation networks available in the main cities for the AAI increase the mobility of workers in these cities and raise these firms' access to different types of workers. On the one hand, the higher mobility amongst workers increases firms' training costs, due to higher risks of poaching. On the other hand, the Turkish AAI firms can reach more workers residing in further distances, and can poach other firms' employees, which then reduces these firms' costs of hiring skilled workers. These factors then influence the Turkish auto parts suppliers' hiring, training, and employee development practices.

Last, the military service requirement creates two main groups of (male) workers in the AAI, namely those completing and those not completing this service, and it leads to different employment practices for these groups. While those without the military service have fixed-term contracts and receive the minimum wage, which helps firms to reduce their labour costs, those with the military service are more likely to be employed on permanent contracts and become unionised. These lead to distinct hiring, training, and employee development practices for workers who have and have not completed the military service.

7.2 Skilling strategies of Turkish AAI firms

Due to the high state commitment to providing and financing VET, as well as the state's high involvement in regulating the institutions that complement the skill system, the Turkish AAI firms have closely aligned their hiring, training, and employee development practices with the public VET programmes. The institutions in Turkey lead to three main types of skilling practices for the Turkish AAI firms when addressing their skill needs on the shop floor, which are shaped by the governance structures in global AACs as discussed in Chapter 4: (i) recruitment and temporary employment of inexperienced individuals without military service as auxiliary workers/trainees, (ii) recruitment and permanent employment of workers with military service and some experience as operators/team members, and (iii) firm-level training of current employees and their upgrading to foreman/team leader and shift supervisor/group leader positions (Figure 7.1).

Figure 7.1 Firm-level skilling practices in Turkey[2]

7.2.1 Hiring individuals with VET as auxiliary workers/trainees

Auxiliary workers/trainees constitute an important group of workers in Turkish supplier firms to reduce labour costs and, thus, to address the price expectations in the global AACs. In Turkish firms, a large group of auxiliary workers/trainees are employed with the prospect of their departure or dismissal after a few years of employment, when the firm starts making fewer mistakes in production and needs fewer workers (see Chapter 4), and when the entry-level workers need to pursue their military service. There are four main institutions that influence the employment of the auxiliary workers/trainees in Turkey including the statist public VET

---

[2] The 'dashed line' represents the temporary break in workers' career progression due to military service.

system, the minimum wage, the occupational certificate requirement, and the military service requirement.

All Turkish suppliers aim to employ individuals with a certificate from the public VET programmes and those who have not completed the compulsory military service as auxiliary workers/trainees. The AAI firms want to employ the students and graduates of public VET programmes and, particularly, the VHSs, because these individuals have theoretical training about production processes thanks to their training at a VET institute and learn quickly, even when they do not have any practical experience on the task. Another key reason for employing workers with a VET certificate is the statutory occupational certificate requirement, which obliges the AAI firms to employ certified workers in *all* positions on the shop floor, ranging from auxiliary workers/trainees to shift supervisors.

The AAI firms in Turkey hire individuals who have not completed the compulsory military service for the auxiliary worker/trainee positions because this helps firms to reduce their labour costs. Those who have not completed the military service, who are usually young workers aged around 17 or 18 years and who are from public VET programmes, are employed on short-term contracts, and receive the minimum wage. These individuals enter the company as inexperienced auxiliary workers/trainees with very limited on-the-job experience. Throughout their employment as auxiliary workers/trainees, these workers gain practical experience and learn about certain firm-specific issues, such as the production processes and the quality requirements. However, these workers leave the firm after a few years of employment to conduct the military service, which helps the firms to reduce their labour costs in the later years of a project with a lead firm in AACs (see Chapter 4). The HR department representative from T9 explains this as follows:

> [i]t is very difficult to dismiss unionised workers . . . employing workers without the military service helps us to create a group of non-unionised workers and it is not as problematic to dismiss them. Also, most of the workers without military service leave the company themselves to do this service, and then sometimes we don't need to dismiss that many workers.

Although the employment of future conscripts with a certificate from public VET programmes is the most preferred way of finding auxiliary workers/trainees for the Turkish firms, this does not always work in practice due to the low supply of and high demand for workers with a VET certificate, and the high level of mobility amongst entry-level workers in Turkey. As a result, firms in Turkey have developed additional strategies to access workers with a VET certificate for entry-level auxiliary worker/trainee posts. The main strategies in this regard include (i) developing links with public VET institutes and employing trainees from these institutes, (ii) employing uncertified workers and investing in their certification through external certification institutes, and (iii) establishing VET institutes that have links with the public VET system, which is the case only for large companies.

7.2.1.1 Hiring trainees of and developing links with public VET programmes

In order to reach the recent graduates of public VET programmes, a majority of firms in Turkey hire trainees from public VET institutes with the expectation of employing some of them as full-time auxiliary workers/trainees when they finish their traineeship. While hiring trainees from VHSs constitutes the most common method to employ workers with a VET certificate, some firms also hire trainees through the apprenticeship system or the UMEM.

Hiring trainees from VHSs

All firms studied for this book had trainees from VHSs at the time of the interviews and the interviewees mentioned that employing trainees from VHSs is a key component of their firm's skilling strategy. While the Labour Law requires firms to train VHS students, this has not been the main reason for training VHS students, and firms do this in order to increase their chances of employing workers with a VET certificate (which is required by the Labour Law). The required internship for VHS students gives the students a chance to familiarise themselves with the practical work and the industry, and to learn about the career opportunities in the industry, although it is too short to develop substantial skills or experience. The training of VHS students also gives the firms an opportunity to get to know these students and understand their suitability to the firm as full-time employees (Interview Notes).

Nevertheless, although firms provide practical training to numerous VHS students, very few of these students become full-time employees when they finish their traineeship. The firm representatives mention that the majority of their trainees from VHSs leave the firm to continue studying in a MYO, to prepare for the university entrance exam, or to wait for the military service. Therefore, the auto parts suppliers in Turkey mentioned that they have adopted certain strategies to attract more trainees from VHSs, and to increase the number of students remaining in the firm. A key strategy in this regard has been developing direct links with VHSs. There are several ways outlined in the VET Law and the Labour Law for firms in Turkey to develop links with VHSs and other public VET institutes (see Chapter 5). Some firms have developed channels for continuous communication with VHSs, especially with those located nearby their manufacturing plant, to increase the familiarity of VHS students with their firm and the opportunities of these students in the firm. Through these channels, such as direct links between the school principle and the HR department of the firm, the firms stay informed about the school curriculum and the internship requirements for students, and this information helps firms to organise the firm-level training programmes in accordance with schools' calendar and internship requirements and to advertise traineeship posts in those schools. Another strategy for the AAI suppliers in Turkey to develop links with VHSs has been through the teachers at these schools. For example, VHS teachers have been visiting some of the interviewed firms to monitor the practical training of their students and to observe their progress. Furthermore, a few firms mentioned that they have been involved in training the teachers in VHSs, while others hire VHS teachers in their firm as part-time instructors.

The interviewed firms have also used other measures to appeal to more VHS students. Activities to increase VHS students' familiarity with the firm and to improve their knowledge about career opportunities in the AAI constitute significant activities in this regard. As explained in Chapter 5, the main reason for the low supply of VHS graduates in the AAI is the unpopularity of manufacturing jobs amongst young people. However, the firm representatives mention that although the entry-level jobs in the AAI are not appealing for young workers, the AAI offers more opportunities for career development and income progression with experience, particularly when compared with the jobs i the retail and service industry. Nonetheless, the career opportunities and work conditions in the later years of employment in the AAI are not known amongst the students of VHSs or their families. In fact, many interviewees mentioned that it is highly likely for the children or friends of AAI workers to be employed in the AAI, as they know the opportunities in this industry, while it is more difficult to recruit the students with parents working in other industries (Interview Notes).

Some firms studied for this book have been organising several activities in order to improve the understanding about the career opportunities in the AAI, and to appeal to more VHS students to work in this industry and their company. For instance, T6, which is the largest firm interviewed for this book from Turkey, has dedicated resources to improve the company's visibility among the VHS students in Bursa—where the company is located. The company has been publicised in various VHSs through school visits, posters, and seminars about the company and the job opportunities it offers. The teachers, students, and parents from key VHSs have been invited to the company, where they have had the chance to see the shop floor and to get to know the company and possible career pathways. In the end, the HR representative from T6 mentioned that about 80 per cent of students participating in these activities have been applying for a job or traineeship in the company afterwards. Some of the smaller firms also have been following a similar strategy, although at a much smaller scale. For instance, some smaller firms have developed links with the parents of their trainees from VHSs and organised occasional parents' meetings, which helped to familiarise the parents with the company and to find out the concerns of both the students and their parents. Furthermore, a number of firms (both smaller and larger) have been participating in the programme initiated by the Association of Automotive Parts and Components Manufacturers (*Taşıt Araçları Tedarikçileri Sanayi Derneği*—TAYSAD) called 'Don't Throw Away; Recycle and Strengthen the Vocational Schools' (*Atma Değerlendir Meslek Okullarını Güçlendir*). In this regard, some firms have been donating their machinery to VHSs with the aim of improving their infrastructure, which also helps these firms to develop links with the schools and familiarise the students at these schools with the firm and their machinery (Interview Notes).

Hiring apprentices

The apprenticeship system has been another main strategy for finding workers for some auto parts suppliers, especially for those located near a Vocational Training Centre (MEM), although it is applied to a much lesser extent (Interview Notes). The firms utilising the apprenticeship system typically employ unskilled and inexperienced workers, who are mainly high school dropouts, and register them as apprentices in a MEM located nearby. Some firms also contact the MEMs to recruit their students as apprentices. While the apprentices spend most of their time in the firm, they receive theoretical training in the MEM one day a week (see Chapter 5).

The apprenticeship system has helped several AAI firms to comply with the certificate requirement while also developing the skills necessary for their firm. The apprenticeship system also gives the apprentices an opportunity to receive an occupational certificate and gain work experience before they conduct the military service. Despite these benefits of the apprenticeship system for both firms and workers, its use by firms has remained limited mainly because of the low number of apprentices available (Interview Notes). Representatives of some firms mentioned that although the apprenticeship system is a very useful tool for them to generate the necessary skills, and they would prefer to employ more workers through this system, they have faced significant challenges to find apprentices. Thus, they cannot use this system as much as they would like to.

Hiring trainees from the UMEM

The UMEM courses constitute another key mechanism to generate the necessary workforce for some suppliers in the AAI in Turkey. Within this programme, firms recruit inexperienced and uncertified workers from the unemployed pool of İŞKUR, and hire them as UMEM trainees. These workers develop practical experience within the firm, while they receive theoretical training organised by the MEB, which often takes place in a VHS or MEM. The training lasts about 4 months (depending on occupation), and the İŞKUR pays a daily allowance to workers (20 Turkish Liras per day[3]). A number of firms interviewed for this book were hiring trainees from the UMEM when the field research was conducted in Turkey, or had hired them before. The firms that participated in the UMEM stated that the programme was very useful for workers to become familiar with the firm and the job while developing some basic skills. At the same time, the programme helped firms to get to know the worker and to comply with the requirement to employ workers only with a valid occupational certificate. Despite its benefits, many firms stated that they struggled to find trainees within the UMEM and to maintain the trainees they recruited. The interviewees mentioned that this is because of the low daily allowance paid to the UMEM

---

[3] Approximately 12 USD.

trainees, which has been 'demotivating' for these trainees, as this is much lower than the minimum wage generally paid to entry-level workers. As a result, some firms have been topping up this payment up to the minimum wage in order to reduce the desertion rate amongst the UMEM trainees (Interview Notes).

7.2.1.2 Firm-level training and external certification

Many smaller firms in Turkey face important challenges to recruit workers who already hold a VET certificate or to attract trainees from VET institutes. Applying the strategies mentioned in the previous section (i.e. developing comprehensive programmes to attract VHS students) is also costlier for smaller firms as they lack the financial and human resources for it. Therefore, several smaller firms in the Turkish AAI have been hiring inexperienced and uncertified workers and supporting their certification. This is particularly the case for posts that require less complex skills, such as injection operators and press machine operators. While the new workers start learning in the firm first by observing other workers and then on the job, they are registered to a certification programme that is managed by an external institute and financed by their employer. Within the certification process, these uncertified workers receive some theoretical training provided by a MEM or another public VET institute, while also developing firm-level experience and knowledge. After a few months of theoretical and practical training, these workers go through an external examination and get certified on that particular occupation if they are successful. With their longer employment within the firm, these workers continue gaining experience, receive training in other tasks, and can update their occupational certificates with the new skills they develop.

The length and cost of the firm-level training and external certification vary across occupations, and there were several state subsidies provided to smaller firms for certifying their workers when the research for this book was conducted. The representatives of most firms mentioned that the external certification of workers is not that costly for them if the workers they certify stay with them. For example, training for a Level 3 press operator takes approximately 1 month, and the certification for this costs about 450 TL (MYK, 2020). Nonetheless, firm-level training and external certification can become costly due to the high labour turnover amongst entry-level workers. For instance, the owner of T2 mentioned:

> Training and certifying one worker is not expensive. But, when we employ unskilled workers, we give them the minimum wage at first. But when they see another firm (in this OIZ) that offers only 50 liras more [monthly][4], they leave and work in that firm. So, then we need to find someone else. And it becomes expensive to find a new person and start training them again.

---

[4] About 16 USD in September 2015.

It is important to remember that the main reasons for the high level of turnover amongst the entry-level workers are the temporary employment of those without the military service in these positions, the already high minimum wage that makes the service and retail industries important competitors for the AAI firms for entry-level workers, and the high accessibility between different firms and workers in the AAI regions in Turkey (see Chapter 5).

For posts that require more complex technical skills, such as welding operators, the smaller firms in Turkey often hire uncertified but experienced workers and initiate their certification process. This is because developing such skills within the firm takes more time and thus is costlier for firms compared to the posts requiring skills that are less complex. Therefore, when firms cannot find certified workers with experience for these posts, they recruit individuals who have worked in similar industries, such as domestic electrical devices or auto mechanic workshops, but do not possess an occupational certificate. Upon their recruitment, these workers are sent to an external institution for theoretical training, skill examination, and certification while they develop practical skills related to the auto parts production in the firm.

It is important to mention that the certificate requirement was introduced in 2009, shortly before the fieldwork for this book took place. Therefore, the certificate requirement, and the rigorous implementation of this requirement, was having an important influence on firms' recruitment and training activities when the field research for this book was conducted. When the regulation was first introduced, many firms in the sample had employees without an occupational certificate, and the new regulation required firms to get these workers certified. For this, many firms developed agreements with external training institutes that first carried out a skills assessment in the company and identified additional training needs for workers to get a certificate. Based on this assessment, the training institutes and firms developed training programmes to provide the necessary skills and knowledge for the certification of firms' employees. These employees then were examined by external certification bodies that are accredited by the MYK, and they received an occupational certificate if they were successful. The length and cost of additional training and certification expenses vary across occupations, and firms needed to pay for all related costs, although there were some state subsidies provided to firms to pay for the certification. While this certificate requirement has created additional costs for firms, and workers have been reluctant to take part in skill examination, the certification of these workers has been important for increasing their bargaining power in the job market, especially given the occupational certificate obligation of firms and the high demand amongst employers for certified workers (TS8).

7.2.1.3 Establishing VET institutes

Establishing VET institutes and linking these institutes with the public VET system has been an important skilling strategy adopted by the large AAI firms in Turkey. While firms including T6 and T10 established their own VET institutes, other firms got involved in setting up VET institutes through the business associations they are part of, or the OIZs they are located in. Although the main aim of these VET institutes has been to provide the workforce for the companies setting them, these institutes are linked to the public VET system and are open to the participation of the public. Therefore, these institutes have become key VET centres not only for the firms that established them and the employees of these firms, but also other firms and workers located in these areas.

T6, which is the largest firm in the firm sample, has had two important VET institutes, including a training institute with direct links with the company and a VHS with looser links. The training institute of T6 was established in 1988, a few years after the VET Law was introduced (see Chapter 5), to create the necessary workforce for this company. Due the VET Law, which aimed a standardised VET in the country under the central management of the MEB, T6 linked its training institute with the public VET system and was accredited to provide a VHS diploma to its graduates, even though this institute is not a VHS or a public institution. The links of the company's owner with the politicians and key bureaucrats at the time played an important role for the T6 to receive an accreditation to provide a VHS diploma, which has helped the training institute to gain recognition amongst the public, both employers and students, and has attracted many trainees to this institute (Interview Notes).

The VET institute of T6 currently has a foundation status, and its expenses are met by the conglomerate of T6. The institute provides technical and theoretical training to young unemployed individuals who already hold an upper-secondary education diploma. The theoretical training includes 12 months of learning in the institute, which is in line with the theoretical training in VHSs and is delivered by part-time teachers of VHSs, and, thus, by teachers who already know the MEB curriculum. The participants of the T6's VET institute spend 6 months in different production departments in T6, where they develop practical experience, have the opportunity to get to know different jobs and career paths, and decide in which areas of the company they are more suited to work. Those successfully completing the training receive a VHS diploma and are usually employed full-time in T6. While the trainees of this institute do not have any obligation to work in T6, most of them prefer to do so unless they continue their studies in a postsecondary institution.

In addition to the training institute, T6 had established a VHS that is entirely under the control of the MEB. The school was established in Bursa in the early 1990s with the aim of contributing to the public VET system in the city, rather than directly providing a workforce for the company. T6 does not have any direct control over the school or the content of training within the school. The graduates of the school hold a VHS diploma and thus can easily work in other companies in the city. In contrast to its low involvement in the *provision* of and *control* on VET in this VHS, T6 still continues to contribute to its *financing* through donations for improving its infrastructure. The company also regularly recruits trainees and employees from this school.

T10 is the other AAI firm in the sample which established a VET institute, although the characteristics of the T10's institute are very different from that of T6. T10 initially was organising structured and comprehensive training programmes to generate the skills necessary for the firm. However, most of the workers it was training were being poached by similar companies in the area. Therefore, the owner of T10 initiated cooperation with similar firms in the region to establish a VET institute, which was founded in 1992. Although the founding members of the institute aimed to provide a VHS diploma to the participants of VET programmes, the institute could not receive the permit from the MEB (in contrast to T6), which made the centre and its training programmes less appealing to individuals (Interview Notes). In order to give the institute an 'official status', and thus to increase its appeal amongst individuals, it was transferred to the local business chamber in Bursa and currently provides training within the scope of the public retraining programmes (Interview Notes). While the control of T10 on the institute has decreased since the institute's transfer to the local chamber, the company, and especially the owner, still has a considerable influence on the organisation and the management of courses in this institute.

The institute initiated by T10 at present offers training in several occupations for the AAI and other key industries in the region such as textile manufacturing. The training in this institute includes training on theoretical subjects, which takes place in the institute's dedicated building, and practical training in firms that are members of the local business chamber. The individuals successfully finishing the training programmes at this institute go through a standardised examination and receive an occupational certificate approved by the MYK when successful. Resultantly, these individuals can work in any firm, and although some of them are employed by T10, the majority of trainees work in other companies in Bursa.

In addition to the individual firms' initiatives for establishing VET institutes, as is the case for T6 and T10, some AAI firms in Turkey have been involved in projects for collectively establishing VET institutes, which has been taking place since the introduction of the regulation that promotes the establishment of VHSs in OIZs in 2012 (MEB, 2019). The VHS by the Automotive Industry Exporters' Association (*Otomotiv Endüstrisi İhracatçıları Birliği*—OİB), which was established in 2011, is a prominent example of this.[5] While the OİB VHS is managed by the MEB and its teachers are centrally appointed, the OİB has an important influence over the school, as the whole infrastructure and training equipment are provided by this organisation and its member firms, and the OİB makes a large contribution to the school's financing (Munyar, 2012). The VET provided in this school is 'top quality', according to the interviewees, and the graduates of this school 'do not really need to study at a university because they develop substantial skills at school and can start working in the automotive firms as highly skilled technicians' (TS2). While most of the graduates of the OİB VHS were employed by the large firms located in the area, the school was still very new when the fieldwork of this book took place (only 4 years after it

---

[5] The OİB is a collective association for the AAI firms located in and around Bursa. The majority of its members are Turkish firms, both smaller and larger firms, and two firms interviewed for this book were OİB members.

was established), and it is highly likely for it to also benefit the smaller firms located in the area, as it creates a trained labour force that is also available other firms (TS2). Other examples of VET institutes collectively established by firms include the ones located in OIZs, such as the ones in Ikitelli OIZ and Dudullu OIZ in Istanbul.

7.2.2 Hiring experienced workers with VET as permanent operators and their promotion to higher-level positions

The employment of workers who return to the labour market after completing the military service on permanent contracts is the main skilling strategy for the operator positions in Turkish AAI firms. These operators develop further knowledge, gain experience during their employment, and are promoted to higher-level positions that require multiple and more complex skills, such as team leaders and shift supervisors. The institutions in Turkey have important influence on these skilling practices for posts that require higher skills and more experience. The rest of this section provides a detailed discussion about the hiring, training, and employee development practices for the higher-level posts.

7.2.2.1 Employing the labour market re-entrants as permanent operators

The auxiliary workers/trainees who are typically employed on fixed-term contracts do not become permanent operators since they leave the company to conduct the military service or to continue studying in the case of trainees from public VET programmes. However, these individuals return to the labour market after they complete their military service, and they seek employment. They rejoin the labour market as workers with a VET certificate and with a few years of experience, and the AAI companies in Turkey aim to hire these individuals for permanent operator positions. In fact, a VET certificate, 1 to 2 years of work experience, and the completion of the military service constitute the minimum requirements for permanent operator positions in the Turkish AAI firms (Interview Notes).

The certified and experienced workers who have completed the military service are offered permanent contracts with a higher wage and better social and employment protection compared to auxiliary workers, and they can become unionised if there is a union representation in their workplace. While the previous employees or trainees of a firm who have left the company for the military service may come back for permanent employment, this does not always happen. Even when the previous employees come back, they are not automatically offered employment and they need to go through the whole recruitment process, although they are advantaged and the firms prefer employing these workers since both parties are familiar with each other, which decreases firms' information costs (see Chapter 2).

When the Turkish auto parts suppliers recruit certified workers with some experience as operators with permanent contracts, they do not need to carry out comprehensive skill training since the person has substantial theoretical knowledge thanks to their training in VET institutes and the experience they would have gained before conducting the military service. Therefore, new recruits for the permanent operator posts first go through a company induction, health and safety training, and training about the firm's processes and machinery. All these are completed in a short period (about 5 days), and after this, the worker can get directly involved in production, although the level of their involvement at this stage depends on the task and the worker's previous experience.

The operators who are hired on permanent contracts and hold a VET certificate continue gaining experience in different functions in the firm, while the skill development of these operators is recorded on their 'skills matrix' (see Chapter 4). As these workers gain more experience, they can become senior operators, and their earnings increase. This whole process provides important opportunities for career progression and salary increase to the shop floor workers in the AAI firms in Turkey. For example, a graduate of the Metal Works department of a VHS can enter a firm at the minimum wage before they conduct the military service. However, after completing the military service, this person can re-enter the labour market and earn a salary that is about 1.8 times the minimum wage.[6] Moreover, this worker can become a senior operator as they gain more experience, and their salary can increase up to five times the minimum wage (Interview Notes).

7.2.2.2 Promotion of operators to high-level positions

While hiring is the main skilling strategy for operator positions in the Turkish AAI firms, employee development and the promotion of current employees constitute the key skilling strategies for the 'higher-level positions' that require experience and multiple skills (i.e. the foreman/team leader and shift supervisor/group leader positions). During their employment, the permanent operators work in different production functions within the firm, which provides them skills and knowledge about these functions. With experience, and if they have the necessary general and analytical skills, they can become a foreman/team leader. These positions may require additional skills that the operators may not possess, such as team-management and leadership skills. In these cases, their employer provides such training to the experienced operators within the firm or through external training institutes. The time required for shifting from an operator to a foreman/team leader position varies across production departments and firms, and depends on the operators' previous training.

After becoming a team leader/foreman, these employees have the opportunity to be promoted to group leader, shift supervisor, and even plant manager positions in the Turkish AAI firms. During their work as a foreman/team leader, these employees learn the processes in the other production departments and develop knowledge about the functions in the maintenance departments. Furthermore, these employees

---

[6] For instance, in 2014, entry-level workers of *Türk-Metal* received 1,350 TL a month (approximately 450 USD), while the monthly wage of nonunionised entry-level workers was the minimum wage, which was 890 TL (approximately 296 USD) (BizBize, 2014).

get to know the firm and its production functions better, develop substantial knowledge about the clients of the firm and the expectations of these clients throughout their employment years, and improve their leadership and team-management skills. With this experience, the foremen/team leaders can be promoted to shift supervisor/group leader positions if they have the required theoretical knowledge about production processes and if the possess the key skills for these positions, such as problem-solving and communication skills.

The requirements concerning the additional general skills and theoretical knowledge for the group leader/shift supervisor positions create complexities about the ability of different workers' progression to shift supervisor/group leader positions. More precisely, while all operators in the Turkish AAI firms have the opportunity to become foremen/team leaders, their progression to shift supervisor/group leader positions is less straightforward and differs between workers with a certificate from VHSs and other VET programmes. The graduates of VHSs are by default employable for the shift supervisor/group leader positions since they have important theoretical knowledge about production functions in the area of their training, as well as analytical skills thanks to the general training in VHSs, in addition to the vocational ones. For instance, students attending to the Metal Technologies Department at an Industrial VHS (*Endüstri Meslek Lisesi Metal Teknolojileri Departmanı*) receive training only on general subjects in their first year, such as Maths, Literature, and English. In their second year, they continue their learning in general subjects while also starting theoretical training about metal manufacturing. By the time they graduate, they have knowledge about four areas of metal production, including welding, heat treatment, steel construction, and metal cutting. Building on this basis, the shop floor workers from VHSs can more easily understand the different production processes of a firm and improve their learning about new technologies. Therefore, the training in VHSs equips the students of these schools with important theoretical knowledge about production and important general skills that are key for the group leader/shift supervisor positions, and, thus, facilitate the promotion of operators with a VHS diploma (Interview Notes).

In contrast to the VHS graduates, the promotion to shift supervisor/group leader positions is challenging for those holding an apprenticeship certificate or a certificate after and UMEM course. As the shift to supervisor/group leader positions require certain general skills and theoretical knowledge, the Turkish AAI firms employ individuals with at least an upper-secondary school diploma for these positions, which is usually a VHS diploma. Such requirements restrict the possibility of upgrading for many operators with an apprenticeship certificate or those from continuing vocational education and training (CVET) programmes, as these workers have on average a secondary school diploma. Therefore, many workers from the apprenticeship system and CVET programmes do not comply with the requirements of shift supervisor/group leader positions unless they gain a postsecondary certificate. Although it is possible to complete the upper-secondary education through distance learning (*akşam lisesi*), very few employees do so (Interview Notes).

In addition to the promotion of operators to foremen and supervisor positions, it is possible for the Turkish AAI firms to hire skilled workers externally for these posts, although this happens very rarely. For example, some firms may prefer hiring to firm-level promotion when the firm does not have any operators with the necessary experience or general skills to promote at that moment. Nevertheless, the Turkish AAI firms still prefer upgrading the current employees, rather than hiring new employees.

The AAI firms in Turkey mention three main reasons for preferring firm-level skill development and promotion to hiring new workers for the foremen and supervisor positions. The first reason the employers mention is productivity. The firm representatives maintain that the employment of workers first as trainees and operators helps them to see the 'muddy parts of the job' (*işin çamurunu görüyor*)[7] (T7 HR), and gain technical and practical experience on certain tasks. As they continue working, these operators, and particularly those from VHSs, are shifted across different departments on the shop floor, which helps them to develop multiple skills and get to know the production processes and understand the expectations in AACs better, and thus provides them the key skills that facilitate their promotion to higher-level positions. Having employees with multiple skills and experience in different departments creates important advantages for the Turkish auto parts suppliers to make adjustments in their workforce when it becomes necessary, and thus they have more possibilities of applying flexible employment and employee development, which are key components of HPWSs.

The second reason is the lower skilling costs of shifting the current employees to positions requiring higher skills. Firm-level promotion is less costly because of the lower information costs, as firms already know the skill profile of their employees and can make better assessments about these workers' suitability with the post and the skill gaps to be addressed. Furthermore, the firm-level skill development and promotion can help firms to directly generate the skills that they need within the firm, while hiring such workers can take time and hence be very costly. For instance, the HR manager from T5 stated:

> Lately we have struggled a lot to find workers for this position called 'tool grinding' (*takım bileme*). Workers for this position need to know certain processes and have certain specific skills. We looked everywhere; we asked the İŞKUR office and industry chamber . . . We couldn't find any workers. Then we realised that one of our apprentices had some manual skills that could be used for this post. So, we shifted him to this post and complemented his training. Now, he works as our 'tool-grinding technician' and trains new workers for this post.

---

[7] It is an idiom meaning that the workers develop core knowledge via understanding the more basic production processes and pursuing more manual tasks.

The third main reason for the firm-level skill development and promotion is to reduce labour turnover and increase motivation amongst operators and auxiliary workers/trainees. Many representatives of Turkish AAI firms stated that the promotion of operators to higher-level posts helps firms to address the challenges related to the lack of information about the career prospects in the AAI amongst new entrants, and, thus, to attract and retain more workers with a VET certificate. For instance, the HR representative from T3 mentioned:

> We want our shift supervisors to be someone coming from below. So, when our operators ask 'what are we going to be in the future', we can show the shift supervisors. It is a good example for them and increases their motivation to work and stay [in the company].

7.3 Implications of the Turkish skill system for workers and firms

The skill system in Turkey, in which firms closely align their skilling practices with the public VET programmes, provides important general and specific skills to its participants, and is accessible to both workers and firms. The content of the skills generated in the Turkish skill system and this system's accessibility to workers and firms, moreover, give important opportunities to workers for career development and firms for contentious growth. Resultantly, the skill system in Turkey creates important opportunities for a high-road development.

7.3.1 Outcomes for workers

The Turkish skill system is likely to promote inclusive development because of the opportunities it gives shop floor workers, and particularly those from disadvantaged backgrounds. Firstly, the skill system in Turkey increases workers' *horizontal mobility*, namely their mobility across different workplaces, and thus raises their bargaining power against employers, which will be important to improve their employment conditions. Secondly, this skill system improves workers' *vertical mobility*, namely their career development and their progression to higher paying jobs. These together help to reduce the segmentation amongst the shop floor workers in the Turkish AAI firms, which leads to lower labour market segmentation and inequality between workers in this industry when compared to Mexico.

A major benefit of the Turkish skill system for workers is increasing workers' horizontal mobility, which happens due to the high state involvement in not only the public VET system, but also the other institutions that complement the skill system. Because the AAI firms link their skilling strategies with the public VET programmes, the workers who develop skills for the AAI in Turkey typically hold an occupational certificate that shows the skills possessed by that worker. The development of (general and specific) skills via public VET programmes and the possession of skill certificates improve the job opportunities of AAI workers and facilitate these workers' ability to move between jobs. This gives an important advantage to workers over the employers who compete with each other to recruit workers with a public VET certificate, and can result in pay raises for workers in the AAI. For example, the HR representative from T3 stated:

> There are many qualified workers in Bursa [a key AAI city] thanks to the VHSs here, and these workers have experience in [manufacturing] firms. And these workers also possess occupational certificates. However, there are also many firms in Bursa and they try to employ these workers. So, to attract and retain the qualified workers, we need to offer higher wages.

Another factor that increases the workers' mobility across firms is related to the structures that affect workers' geographical mobility: the employees in the AAI in Turkey can access several jobs thanks to the transportation links of OIZs and the public transportation facilities in the key cities for the AAI (see Chapter 5). Consequently, the operators in the interviewed firms 'are very confident that they can find a job in the company next door if they leave [their current employer]' (T19), which then raises these workers' bargaining power against employers.

In addition to the horizontal mobility across firms, the skill system in Turkey creates important benefits for the AAI workers through creating opportunities for their vertical mobility. The workers employed in the Turkish AAI firms in general possess both general and specific skills because the main skills for the AAI are developed through the public VET programmes, and particularly the VHS system, which facilitates the promotion of the AAI workers to posts that require higher-level skills. In fact, as elaborated in the previous section, the auxiliary workers/trainees, who are initially employed at the minimum wage and in insecure contracts, re-enter the labour market as permanent operators at a higher wage after they complete their military service. With experience, these operators have the opportunity to promote to the senior operator, foreman/team leader, and shift supervisor/group leader positions (Figure 7.1). Such career progression then helps the shop floor workers to increase their income. Based on this and the fact that those participating in VET programmes are often from more disadvantaged backgrounds (see Chapter 5), it can be concluded that the skill system in Turkey gives important opportunities to individuals with such backgrounds and may facilitate *inclusive development*, which involves those from disadvantaged groups. Furthermore, the possibilities of career and income progression for the individuals from disadvantaged groups can help to reduce the shop floor segmentation and income inequality between workers with different backgrounds. Indeed, it is important to remember that Turkey was one of the very few OECD countries that had lower income inequality in the 2010s compared to 1980s, and the skill system would have had an important role in this (see

Chapter 1). The impact of the Turkish skill system on labour segmentation and income inequality can be understood better when it is compared with the Mexican skill system, which is explained in Chapter 8.

Despite its benefits, the Turkish skill system is far from perfect and has important issues that will hinder inclusive development. An important challenge is related to the precarious employment of the entry-level workers in the AAI. Although the skill system gives an opportunity to entry-level workers for improving their skills and gaining experience prior to the military service, the employment of these workers in precarious terms and at the minimum wage creates challenges for these workers, and produces inequalities between workers from different socio-economic groups. Although the minimum wage in Turkey is higher than in many middle-income country (MICs) (Chapter 5), it is not sufficient for many families in Turkey for a decent living, as most families have single male breadwinner. For example, according to Türk-İş, the 'poverty' line for a family of four was 4,364 Turkish Liras in 2015,[8] when the minimum wage was 1,000 Turkish Liras[9] (Türk-İş, 2018). Therefore, a family of four with one worker earning the minimum wage would be living in poverty in Turkey in 2015, which would create important inequalities between different households with single or multiple breadwinners. In fact, representatives of several firms mentioned that turnover is very high amongst the recent graduates of VET programmes who live with their parents 'because they have their parents to pay the bills and they don't need this job' (T15 Owner). While most of these individuals end not in education, employment, or training (NEET) (see Chapter 5), those who are from lower-income families or who are the single breadwinner in the family are more likely to continue working at minimum wage and in precarious conditions.

Another shortcoming of the Turkish skill system is related to the segmentation it creates on the shop floor between workers with different types of VET, although the segmentation is lower compared to Mexico (see Chapter 8). While the AAI workers in Turkey have opportunities for career progression for the workers holding a VHS diploma, such opportunities are limited for the individuals from the apprenticeship system and CVET programmes. Because of the type of skills generated in apprenticeship and CVET programmes, the participants of these programmes can at best become senior operators or foremen/team leaders, and cannot be promoted to higher-level posts. Still, given that the VHS system constitutes the main part of the Turkish VET system, and the share of the apprenticeship and CVET programmes is small, it can be argued that the Turkish skill system gives important opportunities for the skill and career development to individuals from disadvantaged backgrounds through the VHS system.

---

[8] Approximately 1,604 USD. According to the Oxford English Dictionary, the *poverty line* is 'the official level of income that is necessary to be able to buy the basic things you need such as food and clothes and to pay for somewhere to live'.
[9] Approximately 368 USD according to the 2015 average exchange rate.

7.3.2 Outcomes for firms

In addition to employees of the AAI, the skill system in Turkey has important implications for the firms in the AAI with regards to responding to the price, quality, and in-time delivery expectations of their clients in AACs, which will affect these firms' competitiveness in global AACs and thus, their prospects of continuous economic growth. Additionally, the accessibility of the skill-formation system—and workers with VET—to different firms will reduce the inequalities between smaller and larger firms and the employees of these firms, which will then affect the inclusivity of development in Turkey.

The skill system in Turkey has important implications for the AAI firms to address the price expectations of their clients in global AACs, which is critical for the modular AACs (Chapter 4). On the one hand, there is the possibility of employing auxiliary workers/trainees in precarious contracts and at the minimum wage, and the ability to dismiss these workers in the later years of a project, which give employers important flexibilities (see section one in this chapter). On the other hand, the high minimum wage in Turkey limits the ability of Turkish AAI firms to compete with firms in other industries for entry-level workers, and restricts their price competitiveness in global AACs, where these firms are competing with firms from countries with lower labour costs (Interview Notes). Resultantly, the interviews with AAI firms and experts reveal that many Turkish auto parts suppliers have experienced downgrading when trying to comply with the price expectations in global AACs, and have shifted their activities to sectors with lower value-added such as the furniture industry (Interview Notes).

Similar to the price expectations, there are several elements in the Turkish skill system that help the Turkish AAI suppliers to address their clients' quality expectations. Because the Turkish skill system provides key general skills and theoretical knowledge to the AAI workers, the supplier firms in Turkey can shift their shop floor employees across different posts and promote them to higher-level posts as they develop new skills, which are key elements of HPWSs (Appelbaum, 2000; Jürgens and Krzywdzinski, 2016). This can help the Turkish AAI firms to respond to the quality expectations of their clients in AACs, adapt to the changes in the demands of their clients more easily, and address the problems in production more quickly, as also elaborated by the supplier firms themselves (see Chapter 4). Consequently, it can be argued that the skill system in Turkey facilitates the Turkish AAI firms' competitiveness in captive AACs, which then can promote these firms' upgrading in global AACs. In fact, it is highly possible that the Turkish skill system has played a key role in the growth and improvement of the Turkish AAI and particularly the auto parts industry, whose competitiveness increased by four times in 1990–2010.[10]

---

[10] Based on the RCA index tables in Simoes and Hidalgo (2011). The index includes both the domestic and foreign firms' exports, and there is no separate data based on firm nationality.

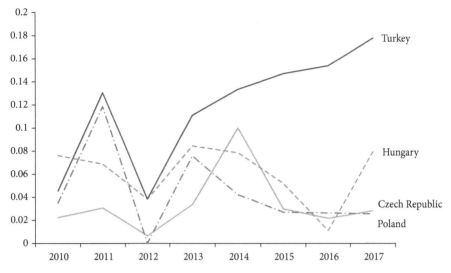

Figure 7.2 Growth in labour productivity for SMEs in manufacturing[11]
Source: OECD (2020f)

A key implication of the Turkish skill system for high-road development is related to the inequalities between larger and smaller firms. In addition to large firms, smaller firms in Turkey have access to experienced workers with a VET certificate, since there are several skilled and experienced workers in the labour market who are looking for a job after completing their military service. Furthermore, because of the high mobility of operators in the cities where the AAI is located, smaller firms can 'poach' operators and experienced workers for higher-level posts from the other, and sometimes larger, AAI firms. Indeed, the interviewees from smaller firms mentioned that they usually hire experienced workers with a VET certificate in key positions within the production departments via offering them a higher salary and better benefits compared to their competitors (Interview Notes). Although the smaller firms may be at a disadvantage in attracting skilled workers when compared with larger firms, they can still access trained and certified workers relatively easily, particularly when compared to the smaller firms in Mexico, which is explained in the next chapter.

The skill system in Turkey is thought to have played a critical role in the economic growth for the Small and medium-sized enterprises (SMEs) in this country in the last 2 decades, which has been much higher than the Mexican SMEs, and which has been pointed out on several occasions by the representatives of the Union of Chambers and Commodity Exchanges of Turkey (TOBB) (Interview Notes). For example, the productivity of the workers employed in SMEs has been growing much faster in the Turkish manufacturing industry compared to Mexico (Figure 7.2).

---

[11] Labour productivity is measured as value-added per person employed.

Similarly, a much smaller share of Turkish SMEs has pointed the 'inadequately educated workforce' as a major challenge compared to the SMEs in Mexico (Chapter 8). Resultantly, SMEs in Turkey have had a key role in the Turkish economy: in 2009–2013, 46 per cent of the growth in manufacturing industry value-added was generated by the SMEs in Turkey, while only 17 per cent of such growth was created by SMEs in Mexico (OECD, 2020f).[12]

7.4 Conclusion

This chapter has discussed the firm-level skilling practices in Turkey, and explained the outcomes of the Turkish skill system for workers and firms, which will then affect the country's prospects for high-road development. It demonstrates that the institutional environment that complements the skill system in Turkey results in three main types of skilling activities by the Turkish auto parts suppliers when addressing their skill needs that are defined by the governance structures in global AACs: recruiting the trainees and recent graduates of public VET programmes as auxiliary workers/trainees, hiring labour market re-entrants (after the military service) as permanent operators, and promoting current operators to positions requiring higher-level skills. Within each type of skilling activity, however, there are further variations that are shaped by the institutional environment surrounding firms, which particularly affect the skilling practices for entry-level positions. The AAI firms usually face difficulties to find workers for entry-level positions, and this leads them to adopt additional strategies for finding auxiliary workers/trainees. The 'additional strategies' include hiring trainees from and developing links with public VET institutes, firm-level training of inexperienced workers and their certification by external institutes (for smaller firms), and establishing VET institutes (for larger firms).

The chapter also shows that the skill system in Turkey contains important elements that can facilitate high-road development. On the one hand, the skill system facilitates *continuous* development by increasing the opportunities of Turkish firms to remain competitive in AACs and to upgrade higher value-added activities in these chains. On the other hand, the Turkish skill system is likely to lead to an *inclusive* development because (i) it gives important opportunities for job mobility, career development and income progression to workers from disadvantaged backgrounds, and (ii) it provides access to skilled workers for smaller firms, which reduces the differences between the skill profiles of small and large firms. The implications of the skill system in Turkey becomes clearer when they are compared with the implications of the Mexican skill system, which are explained in the following chapter.

---

[12] *SMEs* are defined as firms with 1–249 employees. Value-added calculated as factor costs in Turkey and basic prices in Mexico.

8

The skilling practices of the Mexican firms and their outcomes for workers and firms

In parallel to the analysis in the previous chapter, this chapter focuses on the hiring, training, and employee development practices in the Mexican auto parts suppliers, and the implications of these practices for firms and workers in the auto parts-automotive industry (AAI) of Mexico. It investigates the linkages between the national institutions, pressures in global auto parts-automotive value chains (AACs), and firm-level skilling practices. In the first part, the chapter summarises how the national institutions in Mexico (elaborated in Chapter 6) define the labour supply and demand in the country and shape the training mechanisms available to firms. The second part demonstrates the skilling practices of Mexican auto parts suppliers, and analyses the links between these practices and institutional structures and pressures in global AACs. The third part of the chapter turns to the outcomes of skilling practices for workers and firms, and it explains the implications of the skill-systems for the development prospects of the country.

Table 8.1 Skilling implications of the institutions in Mexico

Institutions		Implications for Skilling
De jure statist and segmentalist, *de facto* liberal VET system	→	- Limited capacity of the public VET system to address Mexican firms' skill needs - Low number of workers with a VET in the labour market - Limited and sporadic firm involvement in VET
Labour regulations and wage-setting institutions	→	- Segmented labour market - Lower labour costs in the trial/training period - Limited influence of unions on industrial relations - Low labour costs
Firms' location and transportation services	→	- Low labour mobility - Firms' limited access to skilled workers

Global Production, National Institutions, and Skill Formation: The Political Economy of Training and Employment in Auto Parts Suppliers from Mexico And Turkey. Merve Sancak, Oxford University Press. © Merve Sancak 2022.
DOI: 10.1093/oso/9780198860655.003.0008

8.1 Skilling implications of the institutional arrangements in Mexico

The main institutions in Mexico include the *de jure* statist and segmentalist *de facto* liberal vocational education and training (VET) system, the regulations on work contracts, and the institutions of wage setting, as well as firms' location and public transportation services (Chapter 6). All of these institutions influence the labour market dynamics and training mechanisms available to firms in Mexico, and together, they shape the skilling strategies of Mexican AAI firms. Table 8.1 summarises the implications of national institutions in Mexico for skilling.

8.1.1 Implications of the Mexican VET system

The *de jure* statist and segmentalist *de facto* liberal VET system in Mexico has two main implications for the Mexican auto parts suppliers' skilling strategies. Firstly, the public VET programmes do not constitute a key mechanism for Mexican firms to find workers with the skills necessary for them because they are very limited in their scope (i.e. cannot address the skill needs of the AAI suppliers), and very few people participate in public VET programmes. Consequently, there are very few students in public VET schools and very few workers in the labour market who hold a VET certificate. These increase the Mexican AAI firms' costs for hiring workers through the public VET programmes, and because there are no regulations about the Mexican firms' responsibilities in the public VET system, skilling through the public VET programmes is very rare for Mexican firms. The second main implication of the Mexican VET system is related to the mandatory firm-level training, particularly the vagueness of the regulations around this and the limited implementation of the firm-level training requirement. As firms are not 'constrained' by regulations on firm-level training, their commitment to skill training has been very limited. Furthermore, even if firms provide some training, this training focuses solely on addressing firms' very specific needs, which leads to different types of training practices across firms in Mexico.

8.1.2 Implications of the other institutions

The other institutions that complement the Mexican skill system, which include the labour regulations, the wage-setting institutions, and the limited public transportation system (see Chapter 6), affect the supply of and demand for different types of workers, and, thus, influence the Mexican AAI firms' skilling practices. The strict labour regulations and their flexible implementation have an important impact on the labour market dynamics in Mexico, leading to important segmentation in the labour market (Table 8.1). *De jure*, the 'strict' regulations on employment contracts increase firms' hiring costs while reducing their labour turnover and, thus, decreasing training costs. Furthermore, the possibility of flexible employment during the trial/training period gives firms an important amount of time to employ unskilled workers temporarily and to provide some basic training to these workers, which then helps these firms to reduce their training costs. These dynamics take place mainly in very large firms, which are more likely to follow the labour regulations. However, many of the interviewed firms do not follow all requirements in the Federal Labour Law: the weak implementation of labour regulations in Mexico gives the Mexican AAI firms substantial flexibilities in their hiring, training, and dismissal practices, while reducing their costs in these three aspects. Furthermore, such flexibilities in hiring and training create several types of employment arrangements in the Mexican labour market, and lead to segmentation amongst workers, with the ones in secure employment contracts in large firms being the most advantageous ones and the ones in the informal sector being the ones with lowest benefits.

The extremely low minimum wage, which is often paid to inexperienced workers in entry-level positions, and the weak labour unions in Mexico significantly reduce Mexican firms' labour costs and thus their costs for firm-level training. Thanks to the low wages they pay to unskilled workers, the firms in Mexico can easily hire these workers in entry-level positions on the shop floor, and provide them some training to carry out the activities. The training of unskilled workers becomes much cheaper than hiring skilled workers, given the absence of such workers in the Mexican labour market, due to the limited public VET programmes.

The factors that affect the accessibility between firms and workers in Mexico, including the remote location of AAI firms and the limited availability of affordable public transportation, affect the labour supply and workers' mobility and thus influence Mexican firms' skilling strategies. On one hand, the location of Mexican AAI firms in remote areas without transport facilities limits the workforce they have access to, which then increases their costs of hiring skilled workers. On the other hand, because the workers in the remote areas do not have many employment options, both due to the limited public transportation and the absence of other job opportunities in those areas, their mobility and the risk of getting poached are low. Therefore, the workers residing near the Mexican suppliers become dependent on these firms for not only training but also employment. This substantially reduces the costs of training for the Mexican AAI firms. In fact, the Mexican firms interviewed for this book have in general a much lower labour turnover amongst their shop floor workers (around 1–3 per cent) compared to their counterparts in Turkey (around 10 per cent).[1]

8.2 Skilling strategies of Mexican AAI firms

The institutional environment surrounding the Mexican firms and the implications of this environment for the Mexican labour market lead to two distinct skilling

---

[1] Although the labour turnover may change between firms depending on firms' capacity.

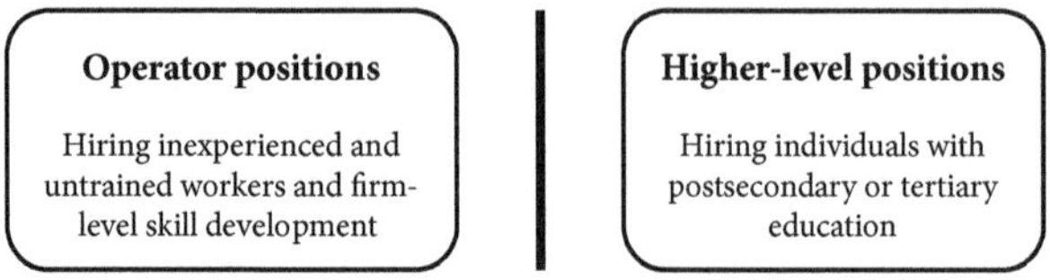

Figure 8.1 Skilling practices in Mexico

strategies for the two main groups of shop floor workers, and create more possibilities for the lead firms to directly influence suppliers' skilling practices. The first skilling practice for the Mexican AAI firms is the recruitment of unskilled workers with secondary education and their firm-level training for operator positions. The second skilling practice is the recruitment of workers with postsecondary education for posts that require higher and multiple skills. Figure 8.1 demonstrates the two types of skilling practices in the Mexican AAI firms. The solid line between the two positions signifies the impossibility of progression from operator level to higher-level positions in the Mexican firms, which is elaborated in the rest of this chapter.[2]

8.2.1 Firm-level training by employers for operator positions

Due to the absence of public VET programmes and the availability of low-cost labour, firm-level training is the main skilling strategy for the Mexican AAI firms: Many Mexican firms hire untrained and inexperienced individuals as auxiliary workers/trainees, develop skills in accordance with their needs, and shift the auxiliary workers/trainees to permanent operator positions when they satisfy the requirements. Nonetheless, the content of the firm-level training shows significant variation across firms depending on their characteristics, particularly their capacity and region. Within-firm training and on-the-job leaning constitute the main skilling strategies applied by all Mexican AAI firms while some firms complement the within-firm training with external training programmes for some of their workers. The rest of this section explains the details of firm-level training and its variation across the Mexican AAI firms.

8.2.1.1 Training within the firm
The majority of the Mexican AAI suppliers develop the necessary skills for the shop floor operator posts within the firm and on-the-job. The generation of the necessary skills for the shop floor operator posts happens in two main steps: (i) the recruitment of inexperienced and untrained individuals as auxiliary workers/trainers and

---

[2] The difference between the operator positions in Mexico and Turkey becomes clearer when this figure is compared with Figure 7.1 on the skilling skilling practices of the AAI suppliers in Turkey.

their within-firm skill development for operator posts, and (ii) further skill development for operators and their promotion to more senior operator posts.

Recruitment and within-firm training for operator posts

The main requirements for the auxiliary worker/trainee posts for the Mexican AAI firms include at least a secondary level of education and certain basic skills such as mathematics, reading and writing while no previous experience or training is expected.[3] When the new recruits enter the company, they first go through a health and safety training as well as basic induction about the firm and the job. After this, their skill training starts with learning by observation and by helping more experienced operators. After about one month of their recruitment, the new workers can start getting involved directly in less complex operations on the shop floor. The total 'initial training' lasts about 3 months, which is also the maximum length for the training/trial period according to the Mexican Federal Labour Law (Chapter 6).[4] The new recruits are expected to learn a few elements of the production process in the training/trial period and most of the training is delivered by a more experienced operator on-the-job. Although some basic theoretical training may be provided about issues, such as health and safety, theoretical training on production or management is not common.

The firms interviewed for this book mentioned that the training/trial period imposed by the Federal Labour Law has important influence on their skilling strategies. On the one hand, this period reduces firms' information costs for hiring new workers, as it gives firms the chance to get to know the new recruits and their fit with the company better before offering them a permanent contract. On the other hand, the training/trial period provides firms an opportunity to give some basic training to the new recruits at a very low cost, as these workers do not have the rights of permanent employees during the training/trial period. This gives an opportunity to the Mexican firms to employ these workers at a salary that is lower than regular workers' salary while the workers in the training/trial period can be dismissed with no compensation. In addition to these, in the training/trial period the AAI firms in Mexico sometimes provide the new recruits certain skills that are essential to minimise disruptions in production and to avoid workplace accidents.

At the end of the training/trial period, the auxiliary workers/trainees go through an evaluation carried out by their trainer, the shift supervisor, and/or someone from the HR department. This evaluation includes an assessment of workers' personal traits and general skills such as teamwork, their progress up to that point, and their capacity to learn further. If the new recruits are successful in the evaluation, they are offered a permanent contract and start working as Level-1 operators. The training of these operators continues on-the-job and they may receive also some theoretical

---

[3] Although many of the interviewed firms in Mexico had employees with below secondary-level education at the time of interviews.

[4] For some positions, the trial/training period lasts up to 6 months (see Chapter 6).

training, although this varies across firms. Similar to initial training, the training of new operators is delivered by senior operators while the shop floor workers in higher skill positions and those in management posts may provide training on certain issues, such as quality management principles. Although the firm representatives state that the firm-level training is delivered by 'certified' trainers, this 'certification' means that the trainer is certified by the firm itself, rather than an external certification in teaching or training. Therefore, the term 'certified trainers' refers to the experienced staff with important level of knowledge about the firm who can deliver training.

The length, content and delivery of training vary across the AAI firms in Mexico. The within-firm training in smaller firms is typically ad hoc, takes place as the need for training arises, and is on-the-job and short. In contrast, large firms often have comprehensive training plans for their shop floor workers, which include both theoretical training on production processes and on-the-job learning.[5] Similarly, although most firms spend on average one month for the initial training of auxiliary workers, small firms mentioned that they spend about 2 weeks while large firms spend 3–6 months for such training.

The nature of the task to be carried out by an operator is another factor that leads to differences in the firm-level training. For example, the training for Level-1 press machine operators in metal parts providers can take from 1 to 2 months. In contrast, it takes about 3 years for an inexperienced and untrained auxiliary worker to become a "real welder" (M14 Shift Supervisor).

Further training and career progression of operators

As the operators continue working in the company, they gain experience on-the-job and learn new skills, which facilitates their career development and possibility of promotion to more senior operator positions. Indeed, firms in Mexico mention that they prefer upgrading their current employees to the senior operator posts to hiring new workers because of the lower skilling costs associated with training than hiring, as finding trained and experienced operators is very difficult. For instance, the representative from the Human Resources (HR) department of M1 mentioned:

> "The problem is that we can almost never find a welding operator. Most workers who apply to welding positions are people who have been working in construction. They have some experience in working with electrical machines, but not necessarily in welding. When they come, we assess their manual skills and develop new skills accordingly. But we cannot find welding operators directly. We have to train them ourselves."

Another reason for firm-level skill development for senior operator posts is the lower information costs of training compared to hiring. The interviewed firms mention that as employers, they already know their current employees' skills, strengths,

---

[5] The within-firm training is sometimes complemented with external training in some firms, and this is explained in the next sub-section.

weaknesses, and their fit with the company. Therefore, these firms have the opportunity to complement the skills of their existing employees in accordance with firms' needs (Interview Notes). Furthermore, the current employees of firms already have substantial knowledge about these firms, their principles, products and the machinery, as well as the expectations of their clients. This helps the firms to address the expectations in AACs more easily. In contrast to the substantial information about their existing employees, firms do not have sufficient information about the new workers they may hire, and there may be mismatches between firms' skill needs and the new workers' skill profile. The information costs associated with hiring new workers increase further due to the absence of a standardised skill certification amongst AAI workers, which makes it even more challenging for firms to understand the skill profile of the workers in the labour market. The representative of M3 explains this as follows:

"When recruiting externally for such positions [senior operator positions], we need to conduct various interviews and then get to know the workers during the trial period. After that, we need to do an evaluation...all these require our personnel and are costly. And the trial period is too short to really get to know the new workers [for the experienced operator positions]. But we already know our internal personnel and their skills, competences and behavioural patterns. So, we prefer promoting them rather than finding someone new."   (M3 Quality)

As a result, the AAI supplier firms in Mexico prefer developing the skills of their existing operators and promoting these workers to senior operator posts that require experience and higher skills. Firms mention that they may hire an experienced worker for the senior operator pots only when the firm "*need(s) an operator urgently and when the training an existing worker would take too long*" (M5 Owner).

The promotion of junior operators to more senior posts typically happens within one production department. For example, injection operators can become mouldfitters when they gain sufficient experience and develop knowledge about different moulds, although they may need to go through some additional training. Similarly, an auxiliary worker being trained as a press operator can become a senior press operator after years of experience. Nevertheless, shifting or progressing to posts across production departments does not usually take place in the Mexican AAI firms. This is because the firm-level training of operators is specific to one department, and does not typically provide the skills necessary for other departments. Furthermore, the focus on the on-the-job learning without adequate training on general skills or theoretical knowledge limits operators' learning and thus, their trainability for and employability in other departments. As a result, auxiliary workers/trainees employed for one department typically stay in the same department until they leave the firm or more often, until they retire (Interview Notes).

The skill matrices (Chapter 4) constitute an important tool for managing the firm-level skill development for operator posts in the Mexican AAI firms. The representatives from the Mexican AAI suppliers mentioned that the skill requirements for each level of operator post are organised through the skill matrices and in line with the requirements of the ISO/TS system. All information about each worker is recorded in their skill matrix, which is updated as the worker gains experience, receives training, and/or develops new skills. The skill matrices are then used to evaluate the auxiliary workers/trainees after the initial training/trial period, and to decide if they should be employed as permanent operators. Furthermore, the skill matrices help the firms to observe the progress of each worker and define the skill gaps in the firm, which they then can address through providing additional training to fill those skill gaps. The skill matrices are also important sources of information for decisions about job appraisals, career development, the promotion of junior operators to more senior posts, as well as the decisions about salary increases (Interview Notes).

8.2.1.2 Training by external institutes

While the within firm training is the main strategy for skill development in all Mexican AAI firms interviewed for this book, representatives of a few firms mentioned that they also utilise certain external training programmes for skill development, and to complement the within-firm training. The VET programmes offered by public IVET and CVET institutes, private training companies, and business associations are the main external training programmes used by the Mexican AAI firms. The usage of external training varies across firms depending on their capacity and region: while large firms utilise the external training programmes often, firms with low or medium capacity use these programmes when their clients in AACs require external training. Furthermore, firms are more likely to utilise external training programmes if such programmes exist in the geographical area where they are located, which reinforces the argument that the Mexican AAI firms are not utilising the public VET programmes because of the limited availability of those programmes in the country.

Training by public VET institutes

Because the public VET programmes are very limited in their scope and the share of the population they cover, the public VET system has not become a key institution for skill development for the AAI suppliers in Mexico. Only a few firms in the study mentioned that they benefit from the public VET programmes when generating the skills necessary for them. The Mexican AAI firms utilise public VET programmes through three main ways: (1) hiring workers who already hold a VET certificate, (2) hiring students of public VET programmes as trainees (although this is extremely rare), and (3) training their workers through public CVET programmes.

Hiring workers with a public VET certificate: The firms interviewed for this book maintain that they prefer hiring workers who have training from public VET programmes for all shop floor positions. Nevertheless, they cannot do this because of two main reasons. Firstly, there are very few public VET programmes that address the skill needs of AAI firms. For instance, pointing the importance of availability of public VET programmes that respond to firms' skill needs, as well as the accessibility of firms and the role of transportation, the HR representative from M13 stated:

> "This CONALEP [near where the firm is located] has only a few programmes that interest us. However, we also need workers with mechatronics training but this programme does not exist here. So, we have to organise that training our-selves...There is another CONALEP by the airport [far from the company]. They may provide training on mechatronics but that wouldn't work for us. That school is too far. Maybe students [from that school] would come to us for their training but then they wouldn't stay afterwards. They would work somewhere nearer to where they live. So, we don't hire students from there."

The lack of suitable public VET programmes has been an important problem for the plastic parts producers in Mexico, resulting in the lack of employment of workers with vocational training in these firms. The representative from the Quality depart-ment of M3 explains this as follows:

> "Here in this company, we do plastic injection...Maybe a CONALEP graduate could be employed in 'technical processes' or 'moulding' positions. But still, their education does not fully fit into these areas, and we would need to give them more training. So, we don't hire CONALEP graduates."

The second reason for the low number of employees with a VET certificate is the limited availability of such workers in the labour market. The very few workers from CONALEP or DGETI schools are hired by the very large AAI firms while firms with low and medium capacity can rarely recruit such workers. Indeed, the two largest firms in the study sample, namely M12 and M13, stated that they regularly employ production workers from CONALEP schools. Both firms mentioned that these workers usually come from the programmes on electro mechanics (*electromecanico*) and machine tools *(maquinas herramientas)*, and are hired as operators in direct production functions. In contrast to large firms, the representatives of smaller firms mentioned that they did not have any employees with a CONALEP or DGETI cer-tificate in direct production functions. As it is hard to find such workers, the smaller firms focus on employing those from public VET programmes in key positions in *indirect production*, such as the positions related to quality and maintenance of machinery (Interview Notes).

Training students of public IVET programmes: The training of students from pub-lic IVET institutes is not a regular skilling strategy for Mexican firms, although some firms mentioned that they hired trainees from these institutes in the past. Interviewees from most firms mentioned that they hired trainees from CONALEP or DGETI schools once or twice and for a particular project. However, these trainees left the firm after they completed the traineeship. Other firms, and particularly the smaller ones, mentioned that they never had trainees from public IVET programmes and did not know about several public VET programmes such as the ICATs or BECATE (see Chapter 6 for public VET programmes in Mexico).

Some large firms, including M12 and M13, have been employing the students of public VET programmes on a more regular basis and they utilise these programmes for generating the skills necessary for their company. However, the firm-level training of these students varies significantly across firms because of the lack of regulation and standardisation regarding the firm-level training. For instance, M13, which is the largest firm in the study, has developed an organised training programme for CONALEP students that comprises three hours of theoretical training followed by practical training every day. However, M13 was the only firm in the sample with such organised training programme for the students of IVET programmes. In fact, the firm-level training of IVET students varies significantly across firms and its content depends on firms' 'good will'. The HR representative of M13 explains this as follows:

> "This [training method for CONALEP students] is only specific to us, but there is no state requirement or regulation to make it this way. And this is a risk. I talked to an employer in another firm. He told me that he employed four CONALEP students and put them directly in operations [on the shop floor]. He didn't provide any training. These students are not treated as students in learning, but as cheap employees. These students don't even know about basic health and safety. This is very risky."

It is important to note that some of the interviewee firms, namely M13, M14 and M16, had initiated the process to hire trainees within the Mexican Model of Dual Training (MMDT) programme for direct production functions (see Chapter 6). These firms' participation in the MMDT is an important exception for this programme since most of the beneficiaries of this programme were German companies when the fieldwork for this book took place. Although the reasons for these three firms to participate in the MMDT programme are very different, it can be argued that firms' familiarity with the dual training concept and links with the public VET system constitute important factors for firms' participation in the MMDT programme. For example, the representative from M14 mentioned that they decided to utilise the MMDT programme for skilling because the firm was familiar with the programme and the concept of dual training through its close relations with its German client. M16, similarly, had sent its workers in the past to a private dual training programme organised by a German training institute, and was satisfied with the programme and thus decided to hire trainees through the MMDT. Different from M14 and M16, M13 knew about the programme because of its links with the Secretary of Education (SEP) in Nuevo León, and then pushed the local chamber for promoting the MMDT in the region.

Use of CVET programmes: Similar to the public IVET programmes, the CVET programmes in Mexico are mostly used by large firms. Training for Work programmes have been the main CVET programme used by the large firms interviewed for this book. Still, these programmes are usually used ad hoc rather than being a systematic method to address skill needs of AAI firms. Furthermore, the methods and reasons for using the public CVET programmes vary across firms with different capacity and in different regions.

Large firms located in the north of the country constitute the main group of firms in the study sample which mentioned that they have been using Training for Work programmes for skilling. The representative from the HR department of M12 mentioned that they have used the Training for Work programmes offered by a CONALEP school to train welding operators for the company. The representative from M13, moreover, explained that they carried out the initial training of their newly recruited workers through a CONALEP school located nearby. The representatives from both firms stated that they used these programmes because they "knew someone" in the state government, which helped these firms to become familiar with the public training programmes offered in that region. Other than these two large firms, the interviewee firms located in the north did not utilise the CVET programmes for skill training, and did not have any information about the CVET programmes they could benefit from.

The firms in the state of Guanajuato constitute an important group of firms that have used CVET programmes for their shop floor operator positions. In contrast to the case of the north, both small and large firms in Guanajuato have been utilising these programmes for skill development. This is mainly because of the efforts of the government in this state. The VET investments of the state government of Guanajuato, namely the IECA (see Chapter 6), have been welcome by the Mexican AAI firms in this region. Although the IECA centres have been more beneficial to larger firms in general, many small firms in this region also have had the opportunity to train their workers through IECA (ME8). For instance, M1 and M8 used the IECA training programmes specifically focusing on the needs of smaller firms to train some of their workers (Interview Notes). The representatives of these firms also mentioned the local IECA centre has been very useful for their firm for employing externally trained and certified workers, which was required by their client. In contrast to the AAI firms in the north and the state of Guanajuato, firms in other AAI clusters, including the State of Mexico and Puebla, have not been utilising any CVET programmes and have not had any information about the public VET programmes mainly due to the absence of such programmes in these regions (see Chapter 6).

Similar to the case of Training for Work programmes, very few Mexican AAI firms have been utilising the BÉCATE of skill standardisation and certification system, and it has been the larger firms who have had a better access to the BÉCATE and used it on a more regular basis (ME11). While some firms mentioned that they employed auxiliary workers/trainees through the BÉCATE programme in the past, it was a one-off situation for these firms and BÉCATE has not become a regular skilling strategy. The HR representatives of some interviewee firms did not even know about BÉCATE while the others stated that they did not participate in the programme because it was not suitable to address their needs.

Although the skill standardisation and certification system is a key component of the Mexican public VET system *de jure*, it has not had any *de facto* influence on Mexican AAI firms' skilling strategies. None of the firms in the study had workers with a CONOCER certificate, and firms do not consider these certificates an important element of their skilling strategy. Firms mentioned that they prefer 'certifying' their workers internally unless their clients require an external certification (see Chapter 3 about the meaning of 'internal certification'). This is due to two main reasons. Firstly, there are not many skill standards developed within the National System of Competences (SNC) that are related to the jobs in the AAI and thus, the skill standardisation and certification system has been irrelevant for the supplier firms in Mexico (Sancak and Özel, 2018). Secondly, external certification is expensive and firms are reluctant to have additional labour costs, given that the low labour costs is the key advantage of the Mexican AAI in global markets (see Chapter 6). As a result, the use of CONOCER and standardised certification by the Mexican AAI firms has been extremely rare.

Training by business associations and private institutes

Training programmes provided by industrial and regional business associations and private VET institutes constitute another common way for providing external training for the Mexican AAI firms. Similar to the case of the public VET system, the use of these programmes depends on their availability in the area where firms are located, and firms' capacity to access and afford these programmes.

Many firms interviewed for this book, although not all, were a member of regional or industrial business associations when the research for this book was carried out, such as the CANACINTRA and the National Auto parts Industry (*Industria Nacional de Autopartes*—INA). The main benefit of these associations for the Mexican AAI firms has been receiving information about the latest developments in the industry, new regulations that concern the supplier firms, and the economic situation of the country. In addition to these, a few of those associations, particularly the ones in the state of Nuevo León, have been providing training programmes for the employees of their members and a few of the interviewed firms from Nuevo León benefited from these training programmes. An important example in this regard is the Automotive Cluster of Nuevo León (*el Cluster Automotriz de Nuevo León*—CLAUT), which is a regional association bringing together the Mexican AAI firms in the state of Nuevo León. The CLAUT offers a number of training programmes for the employees of its member firms, in addition to its other activities. The training programmes offered by the CLAUT are developed collectively through the involvement of key HR staff from member firms and the members are expected to pay certain fees to get their employees trained through these programmes. Although some of the training programmes of the CLAUT may include training on more general skills and theoretical subjects, they do not offer an occupational certificate to its participants. The interviewees from most firms located in Nuevo León, including M4, M5, M6 and M13, mentioned that they have utilised the training programmes organised by the CLAUT in the past, and would like to participate in the future. Still, this is usually a one-off thing and is not a regular skilling strategy adopted by these firms.

In addition to the CLAUT, the sectoral committees in the Industrial Chamber of Nuevo León (*Cámara de la Industria de Transformación de Nuevo León*—CAINTRA), which is the regional office of the CANACINTRA in Nuevo León, has been offering sector-specific training to its members. Although some of the interviewed firms participated in the training offered by the CAINTRA in the past, these courses are not regular and firms' use of these programmes is sporadic. Other firms in the sample did not utilise any training provided by business associations.

A small number of Mexican AAI firms mentioned that they have utilised VET programmes provided by private institutes to develop the necessary skills for their employees on the shop floor. Firms pay the costs of this training and workers do not receive any certificate after such training, except for their firm-level skill matrix getting updated. The representatives from firms that have used the private VET institutes mention that they train their workers through these programmes when they cannot generate the necessary skills within the firm, when it is required by their buyers, and/or when other VET programmes are not available in the area where the firms are located, such as public VET institutes or VET programmes offered by business associations. The interviewee from M16 explains this situation as follows:

> "We needed well-trained operators for die-casting because our client asked it. But there is no training programme on this. It is nowhere…In no school…We looked for it and we looked a lot…Here [around the company area], there is no institute that offers training for die-casting. Not at an operator level. Yes, there are programmes at engineering level, but not at lower levels. So, we were looking for a programme to generate skills for die-casters for our firm, and we found this programme provided by [Training Company-X], and we started training our workers through them." (M16 Quality)

8.2.2 Hiring for foreman and supervisor positions

The Mexican auto parts producers recruit new workers who hold a postsecondary or even tertiary education diploma and have some experience for the foreman/team leader and shift supervisor/group leader posts, which require better technical skills, general skills and theoretical knowledge. The training and promotion of operators to the high-level positions happens very rarely because the operators do not possess the general skills and theoretical knowledge necessary for these positions.

At the time of interviews, the majority of Mexican AAI firms were requiring a minimum postsecondary education certificate for the foreman/team leader positions. While such educational threshold did not exist in the past, the Mexican AAI firms mentioned that they have been increasingly applying this as a requirement because of the higher competition in AACs, and the need for more skilled workers on the shop floor for producing products with zero defects. Therefore, the possibilities of operators in the Mexican auto parts suppliers to be promoted to the team leader/foreman posts are limited since the operators have secondary level education. Although the firm-level training provides substantial amount of skills to the operators, these skills are mostly task-specific and operators cannot develop the necessary general and analytical skills through the firm-level training. The representative from M9 explains the possibility of operators' career progression as follows:

> "[t]hese workers [operators] have on average secondary education and they cannot improve further after some level, because they cannot understand the processes or the technology. They [the operators with secondary education or below] have a limited capacity to understand the training for higher-level positions. But, the ones with more theoretical training in technical subjects, like those from CONALEP, can improve much more easily. But we can't find CONALEP graduates for operator positions. So, there is a limit to our operators' promotion because they don't have the background or the basic theoretical knowledge."   (M9 HR)

Although it may be possible for operators to take on additional education and training to become team leaders/foremen, this happens very rarely. Very few firms in the sample provide the flexibility to operators to allow them to participate in distance learning to complete the required level of education, such as arranging their shifts in accordance with the school schedule. Even when an operator takes the academic education necessary for higher-level posts, firms do not make any contributions to this and workers are expected to complete the necessary education in their own time and with their own financing. Only M13, which is the largest firm in the study and belongs to one of the largest conglomerates in Mexico, has been helping its operators to complete the formal education that is required for higher-level positions. The HR representative from M13 stated that they have been doing this because needed more team leaders but they did not have workers with the necessary general skills in the company, nor could they find them in the labour market. Therefore, the firm developed a programme for their existing operators to complete the necessary academic education and to improve their general skills, after which they could be employed as team leaders (M13 HR).

Interviewees from some firms stated that it may be possible for a few workers to be shifted to other technical functions in the company that require higher technical skills in the event that these workers develop the necessary skills. For instance, in suppliers producing plastic parts, the mould fitters have the possibility to become process technicians because they are familiar with the machinery, and gain knowledge about the processes when pursuing the tasks such as placing the mould in the machine and adjusting the moulds. Nonetheless, this knowledge is not sufficient to understand the whole process or the machinery. Therefore, the mould fitters need to have some theoretical training to become process technicians and firms ask them to complete a postsecondary programme at an external training institute, such as in a Technical University (*Universidad Technológico*). Workers can continue working while attending this education programme and some firms organise the shifts according to the employees' schedules in the *Universidad Technológico*. However, very few workers participate in such additional training, as they do not have the motivation or any financial support for this.

Similar to the foreman/team leader positions, hiring has been the main skilling strategy for the shift supervisor/group leader posts. At least postsecondary certificate, and for some firms a higher education degree, is required for these posts in the Mexican AAI firms. While firms prefer to upgrade their existing employees, such as team leaders/foremen, to these posts, the majority of firms mentioned that they hire new workers with engineering degrees. The reasons for this are similar to the case for the foreman/team leader posts, and is the lack of the general skills and knowledge necessary for the shift supervisor/group leader posts amongst firms' existing employees. As a result, most firms recruit engineers with a postsecondary or tertiary degree for the shift supervisor/group leader positions. The representatives from Mexican AAI firms mentioned that their hiring costs for these positions are not high because there are "plenty of engineers" in the job market (M10 Owner). Therefore, even though the mobility is high amongst these workers, the Mexican firms mentioned that this does not constitute a significant problem for them, as they can easily find new engineers.

8.3 Implications of the Mexican skill system for workers and firms

The skill system in Mexico, which leads two distinct skilling practices for operator posts on the one hand and for the posts that require higher skills on the other, influences the career progression of workers and different firms' access to skilled workers. With this, the skill system in Mexico creates important challenges for both continuous and inclusive growth, and makes it unlikely for the country to attain high-road development.

8.3.1 Outcomes for workers

The skill system in Mexico is likely to lead to noninclusive development because of its impact on the career and income progression of workers from different backgrounds, as well as its influence on the segmentation and inequality amongst workers in the labour market. In Mexico, individuals from disadvantaged groups, such as those from low-income families and/or with low academic scores, typically have a secondary or lower level of education. These people join the labour market as untrained and inexperienced workers and are employed as auxiliary workers/

trainees in Mexican AAI firms, after which they can become operators and senior operators. However, the skill system in Mexico limits the horizontal and vertical mobility of these workers, and leads to substantial segmentation between workers with different levels of education, in different posts, and in different companies.

8.3.1.1 Horizontal and vertical mobility of workers

The firm-level skill development for operator posts limits both the horizontal and vertical mobility of these workers in the Mexican AAI. The AAI workers' horizontal mobility is limited (especially when compared to the AAI workers in Turkey—see Chapter 7) because the skills of operators cannot be applied in other similar firms due to the specificity of firm-level training and lack of skill certification. The HR representative from M13 explains this as follows:

> These workers [who receive training from M13] become M13 technicians. You cannot start working in [Company-X] with this training because they won't recognise your skills because they won't really know your skills and experience.

Therefore, through firm-level skill development, the operators in Mexican firms become dependent on their employer for both skill development and employment. The remote location of firms, the absence of alternative job opportunities, and the restricted (and unaffordable) transportation facilities in the areas where firms are located and operators reside exacerbate the dependence of the AAI workers to their employer for work and skill development. All these, together with the weak union power within companies, restrict the bargaining power of operators in the Mexican AAI firms, and will have an impact on the substantially low wages in the Mexican AAI (Chapter 6).

In addition to workers' horizontal mobility, the skill system in Mexico limits workers' 'vertical' mobility, namely their opportunities for career development and income progression. The operators in Mexico have on average a secondary education, which limits their opportunities for promoting to higher-level posts, as elaborated in the previous section. The limited opportunities for career progression then restrict workers' likelihood to increase their income or have better employment conditions, which is different from the case in Turkey (see Chapter 7). For example, the salary of entry-level technicians in the Mexican AAI firms is about six times that of the entry-level operators (Interview Notes). However, those from disadvantaged backgrounds are unlikely to be employed in technician posts due to their education level which becomes an obstacle to their vertical mobility.

8.3.1.2 Segmentation amongst AAI workers

The second main influence of the Mexican skill system on workers concern the segmentation and inequality amongst workers with different levels of education and workers employed in different firms. Figure 8.2 summarises the segmentation amongst AAI workers in Mexico. The firm-level skill development, and adoption of different skilling strategies for operator and higher-level posts creates segmentation on the shop floor and generates inequalities between workers with different levels of education, (i.e. secondary and post-secondary education; between points 1 and 2 in Figure 8.2): While those with secondary education can only be employed as auxiliary workers or operators, those with post-secondary and tertiary education are recruited for higher-level posts with better conditions. The distinct skilling strategies for the two types of posts and the limited transition opportunities between them create hierarchy and segmentation between workers employed in different positions within the same firm.

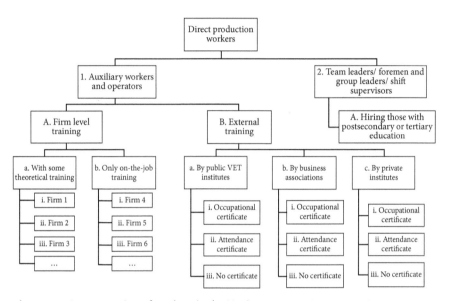

Figure 8.2 Segmentation of workers in the Mexican AAI

The skill system in Mexico creates segmentation also across workers employed in different firms. As the previous sections in this chapter have demonstrated, the supplier firms in the Mexican AAI adopt a variety of skilling practices for generating the skills necessary for them, and their skilling strategy depends on their region and capacity, while some firms do not provide any organised training at all. This creates important variation regarding the skill profile of workers in each firm. As shown in Figure 8.2, an important variation happens between firms that offer firm-level training only and those that train their employees through external training institutes (between points A and B). Furthermore, the firm-level training varies across firms since some firms offer theoretical training while others do not (between A. a and A. b), and because the firm-level theoretical training and on-the-job learning have different patterns across the firms in Mexico due to the lack of regulation or standardisation in this regard (between A. a. i; A. a. ii; and A. a. iii; and between A. b. i; A. b. ii; and A. b. iii). The skills developed through external training programmes are also different because firms utilise a variety of external training institutes including public and private institutes as well as the training programmes offered by business associations (B. a; B. b; and B. c). Some of these external training programmes provide an occupational certificate or certificate of attendance, while others provide no certification (such as B. a. i; B. a. ii.; and B. a. iii.). In addition to these variations across firms, the skill system in Mexico puts the employees of larger firms in a more advantaged position compared to those in smaller firms since the large firms offer more comprehensive skill training, which often includes training also on general skills, and they utilise the external training programmes more compared to smaller firms.

Figure 8.2 shows the segmentation only amongst the AAI workers, and does not reflect the further segmentation between the workers employed in the AAI and other industries, or the segmentation between the formally employed, informally employed, and unemployed individuals regarding the type of training they receive—or do not receive. The segmentation in the Mexican labour market will be even higher when certain facts are considered. For example, the probability of AAI firms providing some training to their workers is higher due to the higher skill requirements in this industry compared to other industries that carry out labour-intensive work, such as textile manufacturing or agriculture. Furthermore, the skill system in Mexico restricts skill formation to only those employed workers, while there not many opportunities of skill development for the unemployed.

In summary, the discussion here shows that the Mexican skill system does not create opportunities for individuals from disadvantaged backgrounds, and it creates important segmentation in the labour market. Therefore, it is likely to lead to development that is non-inclusive for all workers.

8.3.2 Outcomes for firms

The skill system in Mexico creates important challenges for the Mexican AAI firms' competitiveness in global AACs, and generates important inequalities between smaller and larger firms regarding the skill profile of their employees, which then hinders the country's prospects for attaining both continuous and inclusive development.

Before explaining its challenges, it is important to mention some of the 'benefits' of the Mexican skill system for the AAI firms in Mexico, which can be summarised in two main points. Firstly, the skill system in Mexico helps the AAI firms to minimise their labour costs, which then facilitates these firms' ability to address their clients' expectations regarding low-priced products, which is very different from the case in Turkey (see Chapter 7). The ability of Mexican firms to maintain low-cost products then helps these firms to remain competitive in AACs governed by modular relations (Chapter 4). The second 'benefit' of the Mexican skill system for firms is related to the flexibility given to firms regarding their skilling practices: by putting the responsibility of VET on firms and keeping the regulation on firm-level training at minimum, the firms in Mexico organise their skilling practices and firm-level training in accordance with their needs. This is then argued to have helped the Mexican firms to have more control over their employees and the skills of these employees (Interview Notes).

Despite its 'benefits', the skill system poses important challenges to the continuous growth of Mexican auto parts suppliers and, particularly, of smaller firms. Due to the firm-level skill development for operators in Mexican AAI firms, operators become very specialised in the task they carry out, lack general skills, and often do not know about the other production functions or the general principles of their firm. This limits Mexican AAI firms' abilities to implement High-Performance Work Systems (HPWSs), and particularly the practices regarding training and employee development. As demonstrated throughout this chapter, the narrow skill base of shop floor workers in Mexico limits the possibilities for employee development and career progression, and restricts the Mexican AAI firms' ability to shift operators across different production functions when necessary. This then can create important problems for the Mexican AAI firms to address their clients' expectations regarding the quality of products and timely response to changes and new demands, which are key for several lead firms in global AACs (Chapter 4). As a result, it can be argued that the skill system in Mexico creates important obstacles for the Mexican auto parts suppliers to remain competitive in global AACs that require quality production and in-time delivery (Chapter 4). This may then 'lock' the Mexican AAI suppliers into AACs led by modular relations, in which opportunities for upgrading and continuous growth are much more limited, particularly when compared with captive chains (Sancak, forthcoming-b). Based on this, it may be possible to argue that the skill system has played a role in the limited upgrading of the Mexican AAI since the 1990s: The competitiveness of the Mexican AAI to produce medium-technology-intensive products has not changed much since the early 1990s while the Turkish AAI firms' competitiveness quadrupled, and Turkish AAI upgraded from low value-added to medium value-added auto parts production in this period.[6]

The Mexican skill system creates difficulties particularly for smaller firms, and exacerbates inequalities between smaller and larger firms in the country (and consequently, between the employees of these firms), which further hinders the country's inclusive development prospects. Staying competitive in AACs is difficult, particularly, for smaller firms, since these firms have much more limited access to the public VET programmes and to the workers with a VET certificate when compared with large firms. Because of their limited access to public VET programmes, the small firms rely on firm-level skill development, which provides only specific skills. Smaller firms are more disadvantaged in the Mexican skill system also because they have limited resources to organise comprehensive firm-level training, while large firms can do this more easily. In fact, the main skilling strategy for the small AAI firms in Mexico, namely those with 'low capacity' and medium capacity (see Chapter 3), has been on-the-job training, while large firms, namely those with 'high capacity', make use of external training programmes and, particularly, public VET programmes, and they have more structured and more comprehensive training packages for shop floor operators. Similarly, according to the World Bank Enterprise Surveys in 2010, the majority of small and medium-sized enterprises (SMEs) in Mexico did not

---

[6] For 1990–2010, calculations were based on Pavlínek et al. (2009) and Simoes and Hidalgo (2011). Also, see to the RCA index tables of auto parts exports in Simoes and Hidalgo (2011).

provide training to their workers because they 'cannot afford the optimal level of training' or they do not 'have enough information about training programs' (World Bank, 2010). Consequently, while large firms in Mexico can have some workers with more general skills and theoretical training, which are key for HPWSs, the employees of smaller firms usually possess only specific skills, which restrict the human resource management (HRM) strategies of these firms and limit their ability to respond to changes in demand and problems in production.

The different skilling practices applied by smaller and larger firms create important inequalities regarding the skill profiles of employees in these firms, which leads to differences in their HRM strategies and, particularly, their ability to move employees across production functions and deliver employee development. Consequently, the skill system creates significant disparities between small and large firms' ability to remain competitive in global AACs and in the types of AACs they participate in. In fact, many of the Mexican suppliers in the AAI were shut down or bought by foreign companies in the last 3 decades (Interview Notes). The inequality between the smaller and larger firms in Mexico and the problems faced by smaller firms become more evident when the Mexican SMEs are compared with those in Turkey: while only 17 per cent of the growth in the value-added of manufacturing industry was generated by the SMEs in 2009–2013 in Mexico, the share of Turkish SMEs was 46 per cent (OECD, 2020f).[7] The low contribution of SMEs to the value added becomes even more problematic for this country's high-road development prospects when it is considered that 99.8 per cent of the firms in Mexico are SMEs (OECD, 2016).

8.4 Conclusion

This chapter has discussed the firm-level skilling practices of Mexican auto parts suppliers and the outcomes of these practices for the workers and firms in this industry. It shows that although the Mexican and Turkish firms need similar types of workers, and this need is shaped by the governance structures in global AACs, Mexican firms adopt very different skilling strategies to address those needs. This is because of the institutional structures that mediate the pressures in global AACs and result in distinct skilling practices. The institutions in Mexico result in two distinct skilling practices for shop floor positions: (i) hiring inexperienced and untrained individuals and training them for permanent operator positions, and (ii) hiring workers with a postsecondary education for higher-level posts that require general and multiple skills. Furthermore, although the firm-level training is the main commonality amongst the Mexican AAI firms for the operator posts, the features of this training vary significantly across firms because of the loose institutional arrangements and regulations, which gives firms more room and flexibility in their practices. The

---

[7] *SMEs* defined as firms with 1–249 employees. Value added calculated as factor costs in Turkey and basic prices in Mexico.

loose institutional arrangements in Mexico then create some space for the AAC lead firms to directly influence the skilling practices of Mexican suppliers, such as through the ISO/TS requirements and requirement of employing operators with external certification.

Based on this discussion, the chapter argues that the Mexican skill system creates important challenges for the high-road development prospects of the country. On the one hand, the development in Mexico is unlikely to be inclusive because it limits the opportunities of workers from disadvantaged backgrounds and exacerbates the segmentation in the labour market, while also restricting smaller firms' access to skilled workers. On the other hand, it is difficult to attain continuous development in Mexico because the skill system hinders Mexican AAI firms' ability to adopt certain key practices of HPWSs, which then will create challenges for these firms to address the quality and in-time delivery expectations in AACs.

PART 4

MEXICO AND TURKEY IN COMPARISON

9

Concluding remarks

The book's main aim has been to understand the political economy of skill systems that can lead to high-road development in middle-income countries (MICs). For this, it has studied the skill systems of Mexico and Turkey, two key MICs with similar initial development trajectories and linkages with the global economy, but diverging political economic structures and development experiences in the neoliberal era (particularly since the early 2000s). For a comprehensive discussion on the skill systems, the book cross-fertilises the research on comparative capitalisms (CCs), global value chains (GVCs), and employment systems (ESs) and human resource management (HRM), and it adopts a multilevel understanding of 'skill systems' which comprises the micro-level skilling practices, and macro/meso-level governance mechanisms in GVCs and the macro-level national institutions that influence firm-level skilling practices. For the empirical analysis, the book focuses on the local auto parts producers operating in the auto parts-automotive value chains (AACs) from the two countries, and it examines the impact of global competition and national intuitions on the skilling practices of auto parts producers. The book poses three interrelated questions that are addressed through three main lines of inquiry:

1. How are the governance structures in global AACs affecting the skilling strategies of the Mexican and Turkish auto parts suppliers? Are the pressures in the AACs leading to a convergence of skilling practices towards High-Performance Work Systems (HPWSs) or a race to the bottom for workers?
2. How are the national institutional structures affecting firms' skilling strategies? Which institutions are important for skilling practices and why?
3. What are the implications of skill systems for workers, firms, and the prospects of high-road development in Mexico and Turkey?

The book's main argument is *skill systems in countries with higher state involvement are more likely to facilitate high-road development, namely a development that is more inclusive and continuous*. This main argument is based on three subarguments that are elaborated in the chapter. The book rejects the arguments on the convergence of skilling practices in the context of globalisation, and emphasises the importance of institutions and the state for the skill systems and development experiences of MICs. With its multilevel analysis and arguments that draw from in-depth data on the skill systems of Mexico and Turkey, the book makes key contributions to the scholarly debate on the political economy of skill formation, convergence versus divergence of economic activity due to

TGlobal Production, National Institutions, and Skill Formation: The Political Economy of Training and Employment in Auto Parts Suppliers from Mexico And Turkey. Merve Sancak, Oxford University Press. © Merve Sancak 2022.
DOI: 10.1093/oso/9780198860655.003.0009

globalisation and/or national institutions, institutional complementarities and capitalist systems in MICs, and the political economy of development.

9.1 Subargument 1: national institutions matter even in the context of globalisation

The book suggests that although there is some evidence supporting the claims about the convergence of firm behaviour due to the pressures in the global economy, this convergence is limited because of the different institutional environments surrounding firms. The discussion on AACs and their impact on supplier firms support the arguments on the influence of governance structures and lead firms in AACs on the activities of supplier firms participating in these chains. Although there are different governance mechanisms in global AACs, namely the modular and captive AACs, the Turkish and Mexican auto parts suppliers participate in both types of AACs simultaneously, which then jointly influence their activities. Furthermore, the expectations from suppliers in these AACs and the strategies of lead firms to ensure that those expectations are met affect the activities of supplier firms both directly, through lead firms' supply chain management systems that include elements related to suppliers' employees, and indirectly through lead firms' expectations on price, quality and in-time delivery. Consequently, the Turkish and Mexican auto parts producers, which are located about 7000 miles apart from each other, have significant similarities regarding their skill needs and organisation of their shop floor workers.

Despite the similarities in the skill needs of suppliers, the pressures in the global economy do not create a convergence in skilling practices (i.e. they do not automatically lead to HPWSs or a race to the bottom in employment). Instead, the pressures in the global economy are mediated by the national institutions that shape *how firms respond to their skill needs*, and the different national institutions in Mexico and Turkey result in distinct skilling practices to address similar skill needs. When the institutions are *tightly coupled*, like in Turkey, they tend to 'constrain' and regulate firm activity and result in similar types of skilling practices across firms within these institutional settings. The tightly coupled institutions then leave a small room for the pressures in GVCs to influence suppliers' practices. In fact, Chapter 7 shows that the Turkish auto parts-automotive industry (AAI) firms adopt very similar skilling strategies despite their differences, and these are linked to the public vocational education and training (VET) programmes, while the direct influence of lead firms on suppliers' skilling practices is limited. In contrast, when the institutions are *loose*, like in Mexico, there are fewer institutions and regulations that 'constrain' firms' activities, which results in substantial variation of skilling practices across firms depending on their capacity and location, as explained in Chapter 8. The loose institutional arrangements, moreover, provide more room for GVC governance structures and lead firms to influence supplier firms' activities. Indeed, the governance structures in AACs have had important influence on the skilling practices of

Mexican suppliers, such as the use of ISO/TS 16949 system for managing the shop floor workers and the use of external skill certification due to client requests in Mexican suppliers (Chapters 4 and 8). Therefore, the book suggests that the GVC governance structures have much higher influence on suppliers in countries with loose institutional environment compared to countries with tighter institutional arrangements.

With its findings about the importance of national institutions, the book supports the claims in the comparative capitalisms literature about the continuing importance of national institutions despite globalisation. Different from the studies in this literature, the book makes this argument through its multilevel approach to understanding skill systems, which links the macro-level analysis on institutions with the macro/meso-level research on GVC governance and the micro-level study of firms. Therefore, the book addresses the important gap in the literature on comparative capitalisms, about them being overly concerned with national institutions and not paying sufficient attention to what really goes on in the firm or in the global economy.

With such multilevel understanding of skill systems and their complementarities, as well as its focus on two non-ideal types of capitalist societies, the book contributes to the discussions about complementarity and capitalist varieties. The findings about the institutions that complement the skill systems in Mexico and Turkey show that the different elements of skill systems, such as the VET system and minimum wage structure, complement each other not because they are functional (i.e. they increase the returns to one another) (Hall and Soskice, 2001). Rather, they are complementary because these different domains together affect a third phenomenon, namely firms' skilling practices (A&B → C makes A and B complementary, as also argued by Jackson [2005]). Furthermore, these different domains are complementary because they form a 'whole' together: the institutions that influence the skilling practices of firms, such as labour regulations and firms' location, do not directly affect each other but they are complementarities because, together, they form the (Turkish or Mexican) skill system (Crouch, 2005b).

Based on its understanding of complementarity, the book also proposes an approach that will help to better understand the institutions in countries that do not conform to the ideal types of capitalism. The book shows that the institutions in countries that do not conform to the ideal 'types of capitalism' are not 'fluid' or 'incomplete', as it was claimed in the studies of the CCs literature. They still matter and create complementarities, which influence economic behaviour in distinct ways, even though they may not be functional.

9.2 Subargument 2: the state plays the main role in skill systems

The book argues that that the state plays the main role in skill systems in both Turkey and Mexico. The state shapes all of the national institutions that complement the skill systems in both countries. The institutions that complement the skill systems include the public VET system, labour regulations and wage-setting institutions, firms' location and transportation services, and the military service requirement for Turkey. Furthermore, the state's influence over the collective action capacity of businesses and workers, and its relations with non-state actors (i.e. the business associations and labour unions) affect the involvement in and influence of these non-state actors on the skill systems in both countries. Through its study on Mexico and Turkey, two countries with different levels of state involvement in national institutions and regulation, the book suggests that high state involvement, like in Turkey, creates tightly coupled institutions that constrain firms' activities and consequently lead to similar skilling practices. For instance, in Turkey, the state's high involvement in the public VET system, policies about firms' involvement in VET, and regulations on the labour market limit Turkish firms' flexibility and lead to skilling practices that are linked with the public VET system. In contrast, lower state involvement in institutions and regulations, and the lower commitment to the implementation of these regulations, like in Mexico, result in looser institutional environment, which then leads to different skilling practices that vary across firms depending on their capacity and location.

The discussion about the role of the state in skill systems in the book supports the arguments of the studies on the comparative political economy of skill formation, but in a more nuanced way: The book's argument about the importance of state commitment to VET systems for the characteristics of these systems is in line with the discussion of Busemeyer and Trampusch (2012b). However, different from the authors, the book suggests that the state shapes skill systems not only through its commitment to the VET system, but also through its involvement in other institutions that complement the skill system, such as the minimum wage and the location of the AAI suppliers in industrial zones. Furthermore, the state also influences the collective organisations that represent businesses and workers and thus these organisations' involvement in skill systems and their influence on the institutions that complement those systems. For instance, the different types of organising business' interests in Mexico and Turkey, in both of which the state has played a key role, has been one of the main factors that has led to the divergence of the skill systems between the two countries (Chapters 5 and 6). Similarly, the oppression of the labour unions by the state in both countries has been a major reason for the low influence of these unions on the wage-setting institutions in Turkey and Mexico. The arguments about the state's wider impact on skill systems and their complementarities support the earlier work of Richard Whitley and Vivien Schmidt, who have argued that the type and depth of state's involvement play the main role in shaping the capitalist systems of advanced capitalist economies. The book provides empirical evidence that the state is still key in shaping national institutions, their complementarities, and the capitalist systems that result from these.

9.3 Subargument 3: skill systems with higher state involvement are more likely to promote high-road development

In skill systems with higher state involvement, like in Turkey, skill formation is usually linked to the public VET programmes, which facilitate the generation of some general skills and theoretical knowledge, in addition to specific skills. Relatedly, the state's involvement in the skill system limits workers' dependence on firms for skill generation and employment. Through these, skill systems with higher state involvement can facilitate inclusive and continuous development, and thus more likely to promote high-road development.

Firstly, the skill systems with high state involvement are more inclusive because they create better opportunities for career development and income progression for individuals from disadvantaged backgrounds compared the skill systems with low state involvement. The study on Turkey shows that, in a skill system with high state involvement, the individuals from disadvantaged backgrounds have important opportunities to develop both general and specific skills that are certified through the public VET system. In such skill systems, on the one hand, the skill certification and high accessibility between firms and workers (through affordable public transportation) increase the mobility of workers across jobs and raise their bargaining power against employers. On the other hand, possessing general skills and theoretical knowledge, in addition to the specific ones, gives important opportunities to these individuals to be promoted to positions that require higher skills and pay better salaries (Chapter 7). Consequently, the higher bargaining power against employers and the possibilities for career development and income progression increase the inclusion of disadvantaged groups in development and contribute to reducing the income inequality between different socio-economic groups. In contrast, individuals in skill systems with low state involvement, like in Mexico, are dependent on firms for both skill formation and employment, which limits workers' bargaining power against employers. Furthermore, the skill systems with low state involvement generate mostly specific skills where workers lack key general skills and theoretical knowledge, which limits their career and income progression (Chapter 8).

Secondly, the skill systems with higher state involvement are more likely to promote continuous growth as they create better outcomes also for firms. The labour costs may be high in the skill systems with high state involvement in the short-run due to the 'strict' regulations and the institutions that 'constrain' firms' activities. Nevertheless, these 'constraints' can become 'beneficial constraints' in the long run (Streeck, 1997) since they help to generating a workforce with some general skills and theoretical training. On the one hand, Having workers with such skills can help supplier firms to address the quality and in-time delivery expectations in global AACs and thus, to remain competitive in these chains. On the other hand, employing workers with general skills and theoretical knowledge may facilitate firms' adaptability to the changes in technology and clients' demands, because these workers can be shifted to new activities more easily when firms need to adapt their operations to such changes. This then can facilitate firms' competitiveness and consequently the continuity of their growth. In contrast, skill systems with low state involvement may be beneficial for firms in the short-run and in modular AACs because they reduce firms' labour costs. However, the lack of general skills and theoretical training will limit the possibilities of these firms for remaining competitive in the global economy, and are likely to restrict firms' adaptability to change. Consequently, skill systems with low state involvement can hinder the continuity of economic growth.

Thirdly, higher state involvement in skill systems will facilitate development that is more inclusive for small firms. This is because the workers with more general and certified skills are mobile, and, thus, are accessible to both small and large firms in skill systems with higher state involvement. Both smaller and larger firms can hire these skilled workers, which helps to reduce the differences between the skill profiles of small and large firms (Chapter 7).[1] In contrast, in skill systems with low state involvement, only the very large firms have workers with higher and more general skills in production functions, while the smaller firms employ workers mostly with very specific skills since the large firms snap up the very few graduates of public VET programmes and small firms do not have the capacity to provide comprehensive training (Chapter 8). The difference in skill profiles then will create substantial segmentation between the large and small firms' workforce, and generate inequalities regarding the chances of smaller and larger firms to stay competitive in the global economy.

The findings of the book regarding the development prospects of MICs contribute to the debates on the political economy of development. The book's argument about the role of state involvement for more inclusive development is in line with the arguments of Marius Busemeyer (2015a), who shows the impact of skill systems on the varying levels of socioeconomic inequalities in advanced industrialised countries. The book adds to the work of Busemeyer through its empirical focus on two cases of MICs, and through showing the importance of state involvement in skill systems not only for individuals from disadvantaged backgrounds, but also for the small and medium-sized enterprise (SMEs) and their growth prospects.

Additionally, the book contributes to the debates on development in the studies adopting both an international and a comparative political economy approach. It shows that neither the national institutions nor the global economy constitutes the only factor shaping the development experiences of MICs. Instead, the book shows that it is an intersection of both global and national dynamics that affects the development experiences of MICs. While the global economy defines the pressures on

---

[1] Although large firms are still more advantageous, the difference is much smaller in this system compared to the systems with low state involvement.

MIC firms, it is the national institutions of these countries and the depth and breadth of the state's involvement in those institutions that mediate the impact of the global economy. With this finding, the book challenges the arguments on development and work practices in the GVC literature, and adds to the discussions in the institution-alist literature about development, which has often overlooked the role of the state for development. With its emphasis on the role of the state for development, the book connects with the 'developmental state' literature (Wade, 1990; Amsden, 1992; Chang, 2009; Woo-Cumings, 2019).

9.4 Future research

The book leads to some questions that may create new avenues for future research. The first two of these are related to the static view of the book: as stated at the start, the arguments of the book are 'historically relative' (Sorge and Streeck, 2018, p. 587), and reflect the situation '*at a given period*, namely when the fieldwork for the book was conducted' (p. 34). Therefore, while the book shows that national institutions and the state's involvement in those institutions play the main role in skill systems, it does not explain why these institutions and the state's involvement in them are dif-ferent in Mexico and Turkey, and if, or how, they have been changing since the field-work was completed. To understand why Mexico and Turkey have ended up with different skill systems, the book could profitably be followed by a study on the his-torical development of the skill systems in Mexico and Turkey. One reason for such divergence between Turkey and Mexico can be related to the changing domestic political alliances in the two countries after the 1980s. In fact, in two recent studies on the recent changes in the skill systems of Turkey and Mexico, I argue that the Justice and Development Party (AKP) governments, and their coalitions with the 'outsiders', namely the SMEs and workers from disadvantaged backgrounds, have played a key role in the VET policies in the 2000s in Turkey, while such coalitions do not exist in Mexico (Sancak and Özel, 2018; Sancak, 2020). Another reason of the variation between the Mexican and Turkish skill systems could be about these coun-tries' (different) integration with the global economy: The United States, which is a prominent example of a 'liberal market economy' (Hall and Soskice, 2001), has been Mexico's main trade partner, and most of the inward foreign direct investment (FDI) to Mexico has been from the United States. In contrast, Turkey has developed eco-nomic and political relations with European countries and mostly with Germany and France, the main examples of 'coordinated market economies' and 'state-led capitalism' (Hall and Soskice, 2001; Schmidt, 2003). Similarly, Mexico's and Turkey's links with regional trade organisations, namely with the North American Free Trade Agreement and EU, and the different institutional capacities of these organisations may have influenced the varying state involvement in the skill systems of Mexico and Turkey.

A second avenue for new research concerns the changes in skill systems and the influence of global dynamics on these systems. The skill systems and their complementarities may change in the future because of both endogenous and exogenous pressures on the national institutions and firms. Indeed, the dynamics of globalisation have been shifting after the 2008 financial crisis, and there have been several global dynamics that may influence national institutions and firms' behaviour in Mexico and Turkey. For instance, international immigration has become an important phenomenon affecting the MICs like Turkey in the 2010s. Currently, Turkey is the country with the highest refugee population in the world, accepting the population displaced due to the civil war in Syria since 2011. By March 2020, there were 3.5 million Syrian refugees in Turkey, whose average age was 22.7 years (Mülteciler Derneği, 2020). The increasing numbers of Syrian refugees in Turkey has been changing the dynamics in Turkish society, including the labour market—particularly regarding the cost, mobility, and skill profile of workers. A higher availability of refugee workers in the labour market will influence competition for workers in different sectors and affect labour costs. Furthermore, the employment of refugees, who are typically employed in more precarious conditions and informal jobs, can undermine the inclusivity of the Turkish skill system and may lead to segmentation in the labour market. Therefore, the book can be followed by a study on the impact of other global pressures, such as international immigration, on national institutions and skill systems in Turkey, Mexico, or other MICs.

Thirdly, it will be important to understand the role of gender within the discussions on the skill systems of Mexico and Turkey. The book has focused on the auto parts-automotive industry, in which the majority of workers are male. Therefore, the book overlooks the case of female workers, whose employment and skilling will be shaped by very different institutional arrangements—and for example, not by the military service requirement. For instance, while the skill system and the tight institutional environment in Turkey may be more inclusive regarding the individuals from lower income groups compared to Mexico, its implications of the skill system may be different for women, especially given the substantially low labour force participation of women and the skill system's focus on generating manufacturing-related skills in Turkey. For this reason, the findings of this study can be complemented by, or challenged by, future research on other industries with high female employment such as the tourism and hospitality industry, which are also key sectors for both countries and employ more female workers.

All in all, this book on the skill systems and the AAI in Mexico and Turkey has critical implications for the debates on skill formation in multiple research fields, and it reveals new questions to be addressed in the future. As such, the book hopes to be an important step towards understanding the multilevel skill systems in MICs, and their implications for high-road development.

Major themes and subthemes in the qualitative analysis

Major themes

	Firm Characteristics	Customers	Workers Information	Skilling	VET Institutions	AAI Characteristics	State Involvement	Collective Activity
Subthemes	Annual earnings	Auditing by customers	Age of operators	ALMP training	Apprenticeship	Proximity to the United States	External funding for R&D	Benefits of BAs
	Departments in production	Company certificate; quality indicator	Company level union activity	Apprenticeship	BECATE	Competition with CEE	External funding for training	Membership to BAs
	Establishment year	Competitors	Education level	Certificate requirement	Certification requirement	Price	State subsidies	Relation with other Firms
	Exports	Customer expectations-quality/time/price	Gender	Certification of skills	CONALEP	History	Cooperation with a state institute	Training by BAs
	Export location	Customer's skill requirements	Level of technical skills needed	Company's own training institution	CONOCER	Main OEMs	Employment policy	Type of BA
	Firm's competitive advantage	Customers	Location of workers	Cost of training	Difference between MYO and VHS	Local AAI	Industrial policy	Compulsory
	Inside OIZ	Different relations with different customers	Number of workers	Department Difficult to find workers for	Firms' collective involvement	Foreign AAI	Development programme	Voluntary
	Location of the company	Frequency of contact with customers	Number of administrative workers	Ease and or difficulty to find workers with VET degree	Firms' involvement in public VET		EU relations	

Continued

Firm Characteristics	Customers	Workers Information	Skilling	VET Institutions	AAI Characteristics	State Involvement	Collective Activity
Management	Means of contact with customers	Number of production workers	Education requirement for upgrading	Intuitions and firm behaviour		IADB relations	
Organisation scheme	Meetings with customers	Skill requirements in production	Education support to operators	Labour contracts		Spending	
Other companies in other sectors	Reasons for contacting customers	Turnover	Finding skilled workers	Location of the school and relations		VET regulation	
Ownership	Support from customers	Unionised workers	Finding unskilled workers	MMDT			
Owners' involvement in management	Training by customers	Wages for high skill	Health and safety training	Military service			
Part of a group	When a problem occurs in production or delivery	Wages for low-to-medium skill	Initial training	Minimum wage			
Production method	Years of seniority	İŞKUR işbaşı eğitim		Obligation for training VHS Students'			
Products		İŞKUR-UMEM		Opinions about VHS graduates			
Relation between sister companies		military service		Relations with VET schools			
		New generation workers		SMEs Demand for workers			
		Reason for not finding workers for apprenticeship		Training requirement			
		Reason for not finding workers for VHSs/CONALEP		UMEM			

Reason for not
paying higher
wages in the
industry

Reason for
short tenure

Recruiting
higher-skilled staff

Recruiting
low-to-medium
skilled workers

Trainees from
VHSs that remain
at work afterwards

Trainees from
VHSs/CONALEP

Trainers

Training period for
VET students

Upgrading for
operators

VET graduates in
the company

Within-firm
training

AAI, Auto parts–automotive industry; BA, Business association; BECATE, *Programa Becas para la Capacitación para el Trabajo* (Scholarships Programme for Job Training, Mexico); CEE, Central and Eastern Europe; CONALEP *El Colegio Nacional de Educación Profesional Técnica* (National College of Technical Professional Education, Mexico); CONOCER, *El Consejo Nacional de Normalización y Certificación de Competencias Laborales* (National Skills Standards Board, Mexico); EU, European Union; IADB, Inter-American Development Bank; ISKUR, *Türkiye İş Kurumu* (Turkish Employment Agency); MMDT, *Modelo Mexicano de Formación Dual* (Mexican Model of Dual Training); MYO, *Meslek Yüksek Okulu* (Postsecondary Vocational Education Institute, Turkey); OEM, Original equipment manufacturer; OIZ, Organized industrial zone; R&D, Research and development; SME, Small and medium-sized enterprise; UMEM, *Uzmanlaşmış Meslek Edindirme Merkezleri* (Specialised Occupation Centres Programme, Turkey); VET, Vocational education and training; VHS, Vocational high school.

Interview list

Turkey stakeholder interviews

Code	Role	Date
TS1	UMEM Project Officer	15/10/2014
TS2	School Principle in a VHS	21/10/2015
TS3	Director General of Education in an employers' association	09/10/2015
TS4	HR Department representative in an OEM	22/10/2015
TS5	Expert at İŞKUR	15/09/2015
TS6	Expert at İŞKUR	15/09/2015
TS7	Secretary General in a trade union	16/12/2014
TS8	Director General in a training institute of an employers' association	24/10/2014
TS9	Academic	08/10/2014
TS10	Expert in VET in an employers' association	15/12/2014
TS11	Director General of Education in a trade union	26/08/2014
TS12	Policy Analyst in an education research institute	16/09/2014
TS13	Coordinator in a VET institute	15/12/2014
TS14	Director of Administrative Services in an OIZ	09/10/2014
TS15	Representative from Education Policies Department, the General Directorate of VET, MEB	16/09/2015
TS16	Representative from Social Partners and Projects Department, the General Directorate of VET, MEB	16/09/2015
TS17	Expert in the General Directorate of VET, MEB	16/09/2015
TS18	Education expert at a VET Institute	21/10/2015
TS19	School Director at a VET Institute	21/10/2015
TS20	Supply Chain Department representative at an OEM	21/10/2014
TS21	Vice Chairman of the Board of Directors at a VET Institute	21/08/2014
TS22	Technical expert at an international organisation	21/11/2014
TS23	Expert at TAYSAD	28/08/2014
TS24	VET expert at TOBB	12/10/2017

Mexico stakeholder interviews

Code	Role	Date
MS1	Director General in a state-level VET institute	17/08/2015
MS2	Academic	02/07/2015
MS3	Expert in AMIA	16/03/2015
MS4	Head of the Economic Studies Department in an employers' association	04/05/2015
MS5	Academic	19/06/2015
MS6	Assessor in an employers' association	19/03/2015
MS7	Productivity expert and consultant of VET in an international organisation	30/03/2015
MS8	Academic Coordinator for the Automotive Sector in a state-level VET institute	17/08/2015

Code	Role	Date
MS9	School Teacher and Manager in a VET institute	18/08/2015
MS10	Coordinator for the Liaison with the Private Sector in a public VET system	08/05/2015
MS11	Director of Programming, Evaluation and Information in a public VET system	10/07/2015
MS12	Regional Chairman in an employers' association	16/11/2016
MS13	Director General in a regional employers' association	15/07/2015
MS14	General Coordinator in a public VET programme	20/07/2015
MS15	Senior Associate of Corporate Communication in an OEM	24/02/2015
MS16	Academic	28/05/2015
MS17	Local technical expert in CAMEXA	19/03/2015
MS18	Academic	04/05/2015

Turkish firm interviews

Firm Code	Date	Number of Interviewees and Their Department
T1	09/09/2014	1 (Plant Manager)
T2	09/09/2014	1 (Owner)
T3	21/10/2015	2 (HR, Sales)
T4	15/10/2014	2 (HR, Sales)
T5	08/10/2015	2 (HR, Sales)
T6	21/10/2015	2 (HR, Sales)
T7	16/10/2014	2 (HR, Sales)
T8	01/12/2014	2 (HR, Sales)
T9	27/11/2014	2 (HR, Sales)
T10	22/10/2015	3 (Owner, HR [2])
T11	15/10/2014	3 (HR, Sales, training expert)
T12	16/10/2015	3 (HR, Sales, Quality)
T13	20/10/2015	1 (Plant Manager)
T14	08/10/2015	2 (HR, Quality)
T15	09/09/2014	3 (Owner, HR, Sales)
T16	29/08/2014	2 (Owner, Plant Manager)
T17	16/10/2014	2 (HR, Sales)
T18	20/11/2014	1 (Quality)
T19	26/08/2014	1 (Plant Manager)
T20	08/10/2015	1 (Quality)
Total number of interviews		38

Mexican firm interviews

Firm Code	Date	Number of Interviewees and Their Department
M1	17/08/2015	2 (HR, Sales)
M2	02/07/2015	3 (Owner, Sales, Shift Supervisor)
M3	25/06/2015	1 (Quality)
M4	17/07/2015	3 (HR, Sales, training expert)
M5	15/07/2015	2 (Owner, HR)
M6	15/07/2015	3 (Sales, HR [2])
M7	17/07/2015	2 (HR, Quality)
M8	19/08/2015	2 (Production Engineer, Quality)
M9	29/07/2015	2 (HR, Sales)
M10	30/04/2015	3 (Owner, HR, Sales)
M11	27/05/2015	2 (HR, Sales)
M12	16/07/2015	2 (HR, Sales)
M13	14/07/2015	2 (HR, Sales)
M14	27/06/2015	4 (Company Owner, HR, Sales, Shift Supervisor)
M15	19/06/2015	3 (HR, Sales, Quality)
M16	09/07/2015	3 (HR, Sales, Quality)
M17	03/07/2015	4 (Owner, HR, Sales, Shift Supervisor)
M18	18/06/2015	2 (HR, Sales)
M19	15/07/2015	3 (Sales, HR [2])
Total number of interviews	48	

AMIA, *Asociación Mexicana de la Industria Automotriz* (Mexican Automotive Industry Association); CAMEXA, *Cámara Mexicano-Alemana de Comercio e Industria* (German-Mexican Chamber of Commerce); İŞKUR, *Türkiye İş Kurumu* (Turkish Employment Agency); MEB, *Milli Eğitim Bakanlığı* (Ministry of Education Turkey); OEM, Original equipment manufacturer; OIZ, Organized industrial zone; TAYSAD, *Taşıt Araçları Tedarik Sanayicileri Derneği* (Association of Automotive Parts and Components Manufacturers, Turkey); TOBB, *Türkiye Odalar ve Borsalar Birliği* (Union of Chambers and Commodity Exchanges of Turkey); UMEM, *Uzmanlaşmış Meslek Edindirme Merkezleri* (Specialised Occupation Centres Programme, Turkey); VET, Vocational education and training; VHS, Vocational high school.

Bibliography

Acemoglu, D. (1996) 'Credit constraints, investment externalities and growth', in Booth, A. L. and Snower, D. J. (eds.) *Acquiring Skills: Market Failures, Their Symptoms and Policy Responses*. Cambridge: Cambridge University Press, pp. 41–62.

Acemoglu, D. and Pischke, J.-S. (1998) 'Why do firms train? Theory and evidence', *The Quarterly Journal of Economics*, 113(1), pp. 79–119. https://doi.org/10.1162/003355398555531.

Acemoglu, D. and Pischke, J.-S. (1999) 'Beyond Becker: training in imperfect labour markets', *The Economic Journal*, 109(453), pp. 112–42. https://doi.org/10.1111/1468-0297.00405.

Ahumada, I. (2014) *Formación profesional y capacitación en México*. CEPAL. Available at: http://www.cepal.org/es/publicaciones/36950-formacion-profesional-capacitacion-mexico (Accessed: 12 February 2020).

Alami, I. and Dixon, Adam D (2020) 'State capitalism(s) redux? Theories, tensions, controversies', *Competition & Change*, 24(1), pp. 70–94. https://doi.org/10.1177/1024529419881949.

Allen, M. (2004) 'The varieties of capitalism paradigm: not enough variety?', *Socio-Economic Review*, 2(1), pp. 87–108. https://doi.org/10.1093/soceco/2.1.87.

Allen, M. (2013) 'Comparative capitalisms and the institutional embeddedness of innovative capabilities', *Socio-Economic Review*, 11(4), pp. 771–94. https://doi.org/10.1093/ser/mwt018.

Allen, M. (2014) 'Business systems theory and employment relations', in Wilkinson, A., Wood, G., and Deeg, R. (eds.) *The Oxford Handbook of Employment Relations: Comparative Employment Systems*. Oxford, New York: Oxford University Press (Oxford Handbooks), pp. 86–113.

Allen, M. M. C., et al. (2021) 'State-permeated capitalism and the solar PV industry in China and India', *New Political Economy*, 26(4), pp. 527–39. https://doi.org/10.1080/13563467.2020.1807486.

Almond, P., et al. (2005) 'Unraveling home and host country effects: an investigation of the HR policies of an American multinational in four European countries', *Industrial Relations: A Journal of Economy and Society*, 44(2), pp. 276–306. https://doi.org/10.1111/j.0019-8676.2005.00384.x.

Alonso, J. A. and Ocampo, J. A. (eds.) (2020) *Trapped in the Middle?: Developmental Challenges for Middle-Income Countries*. Oxford, New York: Oxford University Press (Initiative for Policy Dialogue).

Althaus, D. and Boston, W. (2015) 'Why auto makers are building new factories in Mexico, not the U.S.', *The Wall Street Journal*, 17 March. Available at: http://www.wsj.com/articles/why-auto-makers-are-building-new-factories-in-mexico-not-the-u-s-1426645802 (Accessed: 22 August 2016).

Amable, B. (2003) *The Diversity of Modern Capitalism*. Oxford: Oxford University Press.

Amsden, A. H. (1992) *Asia's Next Giant: South Korea and Late Industrialization, Asia's Next Giant*. Oxford: Oxford University Press. Available at: https://oxford.universitypressscholarship.com/view/10.1093/0195076036.001.0001/acprof-9780195076035 (Accessed: 5 April 2021).

Appelbaum, E. (2000) *Manufacturing Advantage: Why High-performance Work Systems Pay Off*. Ithaca, NY: Cornell University Press.

Azevedo, J. P. and Atamanov, A. (2014) *Pathways to the Middle Class in Turkey—How Have Reducing Poverty and Boosting Shared Prosperity Helped?* Policy Research Working Paper 6834.

World Bank. Available at: http://documents.worldbank.org/curated/en/561801468310468845/pdf/WPS6834.pdf (Accessed: 15 May 2018).

Baccaro, L. and Pontusson, J. (2016) 'Rethinking comparative political economy: the growth model perspective', *Politics & Society*, 44(2), pp. 175–207. https://doi.org/10.1177/0032329216638053.

Barrientos, S., Dolan, C., and Tallontire, A. (2003) 'A gendered value chain approach to codes of conduct in African horticulture', *World Development*, 31(9), pp. 1511–26. https://doi.org/10.1016/S0305-750X(03)00110-4.

Barrientos, S. and Kritzinger, A. (2004) 'Squaring the circle: global production and the informalization of work in South African fruit exports', *Journal of International Development*, 16(1), pp. 81–92. https://doi.org/10.1002/jid.1064.

Barrientos, S. W. (2013) '"Labour chains": analysing the role of labour contractors in global production networks', *The Journal of Development Studies*, 49(8), pp. 1058–71. https://doi.org/10.1080/00220388.2013.780040.

Bayón, M. C. (2009) Persistence of an exclusionary model: inequality and segmentation in Mexican society. *International Labour Review*, 148(3), pp. 301–15. https://doi.org/10.1111/j.1564-913X.2009.00064.x.

Becker, G. S. (1993) *Human Capital: A Theoretical and Empirical Analysis, with Special Reference to Education*. 2nd ed. Chicago: University of Chicago Press.

Becker, U. (ed.) (2013) *The BRICs and Emerging Economies in Comparative Perspective: Political Economy, Liberalisation and Institutional Change*. 1st ed. London; New York: Routledge.

Becker, U. and Vasileva, A. (2017) 'Russia's political economy re-conceptualized: a changing hybrid of liberalism, statism and patrimonialism', *Journal of Eurasian Studies*, 8(1), pp. 83–96. https://doi.org/10.1016/j.euras.2016.11.003.

Bellmann, L., et al. (2014) 'Make or buy: train in-company or recruit from the labour market?', *Empirical Research in Vocational Education and Training*, 6, p. 9. https://doi.org/10.1186/s40461-014-0009-x.

Bensusán, G. (ed.) (2006) Diseño Legal y Desempeño Real: Instituciones Laborales En América Latina. Cámara de Diputados/Universidad Autónoma Metropolitana—Unidad Xochimilco/Miguel Ángel Porrúa.

Bensusán, G. and Alcalde, A. (2000) 'El régimen jurídico del trabajo asalariado', in Bensusán, G. and Rendón, T. (eds.) *Trabajo y Trabajadores en el México Contemporáneo*. Mexico, D.F.: Miguel Angel Porrúa, pp. 127–61.

Bensusán, G. (2015) 'Los Sistemas de Relaciones Laborales y las Políticas Públicas en Cuatro Países de América Latina: rupturas, continuidades, contradicciones', in Bizberg, I. (ed.) *Variedades de Capitalismo en América Latina. Los casos de México, Brasil, Argentina y Chile*. Mexico, D.F.: El Colegio de Mexico, pp. 11–40.

Bensusán, G. (2016) 'Organizing workers in Argentina, Brazil, Chile and Mexico: the authoritarian-corporatist legacy and old institutional designs in a new context', *Theoretical Inquiries in Law*, 17(1), pp. 131–62. Available at: http://www7.tau.ac.il/ojs/index.php/til/article/view/1375 (Accessed: 18 May 2018).

Bernstein, J. Z. and Alper, A. (2015) 'Toyota to invest $1 billion on new Mexico plant, create 2,400 jobs: source'. Available at: http://www.reuters.com/article/us-toyota-mexico-idUSKBN0N502X20150414 (Accessed: 23 August 2016).

Bhagwati, J. (1995) 'Trade liberalisation and "fair trade" demands: addressing the environmental and labour standards issues', *The World Economy*, 18(6), pp. 745–59. https://doi.org/10.1111/j.1467-9701.1995.tb00329.x.

Biesebroeck, J. V. and Sturgeon, T. (2010) 'Effects of the 2008-09 crisis on the automotive industry in developing countries: a global value chain perspective', in Cattaneo, O., Gereffi, G., and Staritz, C. (eds.) *Global Value Chains in a Postcrisis World: A Development Perspective.* Washington, DC:World Bank, pp. 209–44.

Bizberg, I. (1990) *Estado y Sindicalismo en Mexico.* Mexico, D.F.: El Colegio de Mexico.

Bizberg, I. (2015a) 'Tipos de capitalismo en América Latina', in Bizberg, I. (ed.) *Variedades del Capitalismo en América Latina: Los Casos de México, Brasil, Argentina y Chile.* Mexico, D.F.: El Colegio de Mexico, pp. 41–94.

Bizberg, I. (2015b) 'Tipos de capitalismo y sistemas de proteccion social', in Bizberg, I. (ed.) *Variedades del Capitalismo en América Latina: Los Casos de México, Brasil, Argentina y Chile.* Mexico, D.F.: El Colegio de Mexico, pp. 473–544.

Bizberg, I. (2019) *Diversity of Capitalisms in Latin America.* London: Palgrave. https://doi.org/10.1007/978-3-319-95537-7.

Bizberg, I. and Théret, B. (2015) 'Introducción', in Bizberg, I. (ed.) *Variedades del Capitalismo en América Latina: Los Casos de México, Brasil, Argentina y Chile.* México, D.F.: El Colegio de México.

BizBize (2014) 'MESS, Türk Metal Sendikası ve Çelik-İş Sendikası ile yeni döneme ilişkin Grup Toplu İş Sözleşmesi'ni imzaladı', *MESS.* Available at: https://www.mess.org.tr/media/files/82_XSJ6CS544Lbizbize150.pdf (Accessed: 27 February 2020).

Blatter, M., et al. (2016) 'Hiring costs for skilled workers and the supply of firm-provided training', *Oxford Economic Papers*, 68(1), pp. 238–57. https://doi.org/10.1093/oep/gpv050.

Blatter, M., Muehlemann, S., and Schenker, S. (2012) 'The costs of hiring skilled workers', *European Economic Review*, 56(1), pp. 20–35. https://doi.org/10.1016/j.euroecorev.2011.08.001.

Bohle, D. and Greskovits, B. (2009) 'Varieties of capitalism and capitalism « tout court »', *European Journal of Sociology/Archives Européennes de Sociologie*, 50(3), pp. 355–86. https://doi.org/10.1017/S0003975609990178.

Bohle, D. and Greskovits, B. (2012) *Capitalist Diversity on Europe's Periphery.* Ithaca, NY: Cornell University Press. Available at: https://cadmus.eui.eu//handle/1814/24382 (Accessed: 24 March 2021).

Boyer, R. (2005) 'How and why capitalisms differ', *Economy and Society*, 34(4), pp. 509–57. https://doi.org/10.1080/03085140500277070.

Boyer, R. and Saillard, Y. (2005) *Regulation Theory: The State of the Art.* London: Routledge.

Bozkurt-Güngen, S. (2018) 'Labour and authoritarian neoliberalism: changes and continuities under the AKP governments in Turkey', *South European Society and Politics*, 23(2), pp. 219–38. https://doi.org/10.1080/13608746.2018.1471834.

Brewster, C. (1999) 'Strategic human resource management: the value of different paradigms', *Management International Review*, 39(3), pp. 45–64. https://doi.org/10.1007/978-3-322-90993-0_5.

Brewster, C. (2004) 'European perspectives on human resource management', *Human Resource Management Review*, 14(4), pp. 365–82. https://doi.org/10.1016/j.hrmr.2004.10.001.

Brewster, C., et al. (2007) 'Collective and individual voice: convergence in Europe?', *The International Journal of Human Resource Management*, 18(7), pp. 1246–62. https://doi.org/10.1080/09585190701393582.

Brewster, C. and Mayrhofer, W. (2009) 'Comparative HRM: the debates and the evidence', in Collings, D. G. and Wood, G. T. (eds.) *Human Resource Management: A Critical Approach.* London: Routledge, pp. 278–95.

Brewster, C., Mayrhofer, W., and Cooke, F. L. (2015) 'Convergence, divergence and diffusion of HRM in emerging markets', in Horwitz, F. and Budhwar, P. S. (eds.) *Handbook of Human Resource Management in Emerging Markets.* Cheltenham, UK: Edward Elgar Publishing Ltd, pp. 451–69.

Brewster, C., Mayrhofer, W., and Morley, M. (2004) *Human Resource Management in Europe: Evidence of Convergence?* Oxford: Elsevier/Butterworth-Heinemann.

Brumana, M. and Delmestri, G. (2012) 'Divergent glocalization in a multinational enterprise: Institutional-bound strategic change in European and US subsidiaries facing the late-2000 recession', *Journal of Strategy and Management*. Edited by M. G. Heijltjes, A. Saka-Hemhout, and A. van Witteloostuijn, 5(2), pp. 124–53. https://doi.org/10.1108/17554251211222875.

Buğra, A. and Savaşkan, O. (2014) *New Capitalism in Turkey: The Relationship Between Politics, Religion and Business.* Cheltenham, UK; Northampton, MA: Edward Elgar.

Buhr, D. and Frankenberger, R. (2014) 'Emerging varieties of incorporated capitalism. Theoretical considerations and empirical evidence', *Business and Politics*, 16(3), pp. 393–427. https://doi.org/10.1515/bap-2013-0020.

Busemeyer, M. R. (2014) *Skills and Inequality: Partisan Politics and the Political Economy of Education Reforms in Western Welfare States.* Cambridge: Cambridge University Press. https://doi.org/10.1017/CBO9781107477650.

Busemeyer, M. R. (2015a) 'Educational institutions and socio-economic inequality', in Busemeyer, M. R., *Skills and Inequality: Partisan Politics and the Political Economy of Education Reforms in Western Welfare States.* Cambridge: Cambridge University Press, pp. 177–214.

Busemeyer, M. R. (2015b) *Skills and Inequality: Partisan Politics and the Political Economy of Education Reforms in Western Welfare States.* Cambridge: Cambridge University Press.

Busemeyer, M. R. and Iversen, T. (2014) 'The political economy of skills and inequality', *Socio-Economic Review*, 12(2), pp. 241–3. https://doi.org/10.1093/ser/mwu013.

Busemeyer, M. R. and Trampusch, C. (2011) 'Review article: comparative political science and the study of education', *British Journal of Political Science*, 41(2), pp. 413–43. https://doi.org/10.1017/S0007123410000517.

Busemeyer, M. R. and Trampusch, C. (2012a) 'Introduction: the comparative political economy of collective skill formation', in Busemeyer, M. R. and Trampusch, C. (eds.) *The Political Economy of Collective Skill Formation.* Oxford: Oxford University Press, pp. 3–38.

Busemeyer, M. R. and Trampusch, C. (2012b) *The Political Economy of Collective Skill Formation.* Oxford: Oxford University Press.

Campbell, J. L. and Pedersen, O. K. (2001) *The Rise of Neoliberalism and Institutional Analysis.* Princeton, NJ: Princeton University Press.

Carney, M., Gedajlovic, E., and Yang, X. (2009) 'Varieties of Asian capitalism: toward an institutional theory of Asian enterprise', *Asia Pacific Journal of Management*, 26(3), pp. 361–80. https://doi.org/10.1007/s10490-009-9139-2.

Carney, R. W. and Witt, M. A. (2014) 'The role of the state in Asian business systems', in Witt, M. A. and Redding, G. (eds.) *The Oxford Handbook of Asian Business Systems.* Oxford: Oxford University Press, pp. 538–60.

Casalet, M. (1994) 'La formación profesional y técnica en México', *Comercio Exterior Revistas Bancomext*, August, pp. 725–33.

Cattaneo, O., et al. (2013) *Joining, Upgrading and Being Competitive in Global Value Chains: A Strategic Framework.* WPS6406. The World Bank, pp. 1–52. Available at: http://documents. worldbank.org/curated/en/254001468336685890/Joining-upgrading-and-being-competitive-in-global-value-chains-a-strategic-framework (Accessed: 25 June 2017).

Çelik, A. (2013) 'Trade unions and deunionization during ten years of AKP rule', *Perspectives Turkey*, (3), pp. 44–9. Available at: https://www.boell.de/sites/default/files/perspectives_turkey_3_eng.pdf (Accessed: 30 July 2021).

Çelik, A. (2015) 'Turkey's new labour regime under the justice and development party in the first decade of the twenty-first century: authoritarian flexibilization', *Middle Eastern Studies*, 51(4), pp. 618–35. https://doi.org/10.1080/00263206.2014.987665.

Chang, D. (2009) *Capitalist Development in Korea: Labour, Capital and the Myth of the Developmental State.* London: Routledge.

Coe, N. M., et al. (2004) '"Globalizing" regional development: a global production networks perspective', *Transactions of the Institute of British Geographers*, 29(4), pp. 468–84. https://doi.org/10.1111/j.0020-2754.2004.00142.x.

Coe, N. M., Dicken, P., and Hess, M. (2008) 'Global production networks: realizing the potential', *Journal of Economic Geography*, 8(3), pp. 271–95. https://doi.org/10.1093/jeg/lbn002.

Collier, R. B. and Collier, D. (1991) *Shaping the Political Arena: Critical Junctures, the Labor Movement, and Regime Dynamics in Latin America*. Princeton, NJ: Princeton University Press.

CONALEP. (2012) *Modelo Académico de Calidad para la Competitividad 2007–2012*. SEP/CONALEP.

CONOCER. (2017) *National Council for Standardization and Certification of Labor Competencies: Towards a National Competence (Skills) Standards System, That Contributes to Economic Competitiveness, Educational Development and Social Progress*. Available at: https://conocer.gob.mx/wp-content/uploads/2017/05/Presentation_CONOCER_Junio_2017_INGLES.pdf

Constitución Política de los Estados Unidos Mexicanos (2014). Secretaría de Gobernación. Available at: http://www.dof.gob.mx/constitucion/marzo_2014_constitucion.pdf (Accessed: 30 March 2016).

Contreras, O. F., Carrillo, J., and Alonso, J. (2012) 'Local entrepreneurship within global value chains: a case study in the Mexican automotive industry', *World Development*, 40(5), pp. 1013–23. https://doi.org/10.1016/j.worlddev.2011.11.012.

Cook, M. L. (2007) *The Politics of Labor Reform in Latin America: Between Flexibility and Rights*. University Park: Pennsylvania State University Press.

Cooke, F. L., et al. (2019) 'How far has international HRM travelled? A systematic review of literature on multinational corporations (2000–2014)', *Human Resource Management Review*, 29(1), pp. 59–75. https://doi.org/10.1016/j.hrmr.2018.05.001.

Cooney, R. (2002) 'Is "lean" a universal production system?: Batch production in the automotive industry', *International Journal of Operations & Production Management*, 22(10), pp. 1130–47. https://doi.org/10.1108/01443570210446342.

Crane, A., et al. (2019) 'Governance gaps in eradicating forced labor: from global to domestic supply chains', *Regulation & Governance*, 13(1), pp. 86–106. https://doi.org/10.1111/rego.12162.

Crouch, C. (2005a) *Capitalist Diversity and Change: Recombinant Governance and Institutional Entrepreneurs*. Oxford: Oxford University Press.

Crouch, C., et al. (2005) 'Dialogue on "Institutional Complementarity and Political Economy"', *Socio-Economic Review*, 3(2), pp. 359–82. https://doi.org/10.1093/SER/mwi015.

Crouch, C. (2005b) 'Three meanings of complementarity', *Socio-Economic Review*, 3(2), pp. 359–63. https://doi.org/10.1093/SER/mwi015.

Crouch, C., Finegold, D., and Sako, M. (1999) *Are Skills the Answer?: The Political Economy of Skill Creation in Advanced Industrial Countries*. Oxford: Oxford University Press.

ÇSGB (2015) *İşçi ve Sendika Üye Sayıları- 2015 Temmuz Ayı İstatistiği*. Available at: http://www3.csgb.gov.tr/csgbPortal/ShowProperty/WLP%20Repository/sgb/dosyalar/sgb2016Sunum (Accessed: 12 July 2016).

ÇSGB (2016) *2016 Bütçe Sunumu TBMM Plan ve Bütçe Komisyonu*. Available at: http://www3.csgb.gov.tr/csgbPortal/ShowProperty/WLP%20Repository/sgb/dosyalar/sgb2016Sunum (Accessed: 12 July 2016).

Culpepper, P. D. (2003) *Creating Cooperation: How States Develop Human Capital in Europe*. Ithaca, NY: Cornell University Press.

Culpepper, P. D. (2007) 'Small states and skill specificity: Austria, Switzerland, and interemployer cleavages in coordinated capitalism', *Comparative Political Studies*, 40(6), pp. 611–37. https://doi.org/10.1177/0010414006295927.

de Anda, M. L. (2011) Implementing competence frameworks in Mexico. *Journal of Education and Work*, 24(3–4), pp. 375–91. https://doi.org/10.1080/13639080.2011.584698

De Backer, K. and Miroudot, S. (2013) 'Mapping global value chains', *OECD Trade Policy Papers*, No. 159. Paris: OECD Publishing. Available at: https://doi.org/10.1787/5k3v1trgnbr4-en.

Deeg, R. and Jackson, G. (2007) 'Towards a more dynamic theory of capitalist variety', *Socio-Economic Review*, 5(1), pp. 149–79. https://doi.org/10.1093/ser/mwl021.

Demirbag, M., et al. (2014) 'High-performance work systems and organizational performance in emerging economies: evidence from MNEs in Turkey', *Management International Review*, 54(3), pp. 325–59. https://doi.org/10.1007/s11575-014-0204-9.

Demirbag, M. and Wood, G. (eds.) (2018) *Comparative Capitalism and the Transitional Periphery: Firm Centred Perspectives*. Cheltenham, UK: Edward Elgar Publishing Ltd.

Diario Oficial de la Federación. (2009) *Reglas Generales y Criterios para la Integración y Operación del Sistema Nacional de Competencias*. Available at: http://www.dof.gob.mx/nota_detalle.php?codigo=5121843&fecha=27/11/2009 (Accessed: 30 July 2021).

Dibben, P., et al. (2017) 'Institutional legacies and HRM: similarities and differences in HRM practices in Portugal and Mozambique', *The International Journal of Human Resource Management*, 28(18), pp. 2519–37. https://doi.org/10.1080/09585192.2016.1164225.

Dibben, P., et al. (2020) 'Vanishing value chains, industrial districts and HRM in the Brazilian automotive industry', *International Journal of Human Resource Management*, 31(2), pp. 254–71. https://doi.org/10.1080/09585192.2016.1233446.

Dicken, P., et al. (2001) 'Chains and networks, territories and scales: towards a relational framework for analysing the global economy', *Global Networks*, 1(2), pp. 89–112. https://doi.org/10.1111/1471-0374.00007.

Dicken, P. (2007) *Global Shift: Mapping the Changing Contours of the World Economy*. 5th edn. Thousand Oaks, CA: SAGE Publications Ltd.

Dionisius, R., et al. (2009) 'Costs and benefits of apprenticeship training. A comparison of Germany and Switzerland', *Applied Economics Quarterly*, 55(1), pp. 7–37. https://doi.org/10.3790/aeq.55.1.7.

DİSK-AR (2018) *Asgari Ücret Gerçeği 2019 Raporu*. DİSK. Available at: http://disk.org.tr/wp-content/uploads/2018/12/DISK-AR-2019-Asgari-U%CC%88cret-Raporu-SON-1-Aralik-2018.pdf (Accessed: 15 April 2020).

Dobbins, M. and Busemeyer, M. R. (2015) 'Socio-economic institutions, organized interests and partisan politics: the development of vocational education in Denmark and Sweden', *Socio-Economic Review*, 13(2), pp. 259–84. https://doi.org/10.1093/ser/mwu002.

Dolan, C. S. (2005) 'Benevolent intent? The development encounter in Kenya's horticulture industry', *Journal of Asian and African Studies*, 40(6), pp. 411–37. https://doi.org/10.1177/0021909605059512.

Doner, R. F. and Schneider, B. R. (2016) 'The middle-income trap: more politics than economics', *World Politics*, 68(4), pp. 608–44. https://doi.org/10.1017/S0043887116000095.

Doner, R. and Schneider, B. R. (2020) 'Technical education in the middle income trap: building coalitions for skill formation', *The Journal of Development Studies*, 56(4), pp. 680–97. https://doi.org/10.1080/00220388.2019.1595597.

Dorlach, T. (2015) 'The prospects of egalitarian capitalism in the global South: Turkish social neoliberalism in comparative perspective', *Economy and Society*, 44(4), pp. 519–44. https://doi.org/10.1080/03085147.2015.1090736.

Dube, A., Freeman, E., and Reich, M. (2010) 'Employee replacement costs', *Institute for Research on Labor and Employment*. Available at: http://escholarship.org/uc/item/7kc29981 (Accessed: 28 May 2017).

Dyer, J. and Chu, W. (2011) 'The determinants of trust in supplier—automaker relations in the US, Japan, and Korea: a retrospective', *Journal of International Business Studies*, 42(1), pp. 28–34. https://doi.org/10.1057/jibs.2010.48.

Edwards, T. and Ferner, A. (2002) 'The renewed "American Challenge": a review of employment practice in US multinationals', *Industrial Relations Journal*, 33(2), pp. 94–111. https://doi.org/10.1111/1468-2338.00222.

Edwards, T. and Kuruvilla, S. (2005) 'International HRM: national business systems, organizational politics and the international division of labour in MNCs', *The International Journal of Human Resource Management*, 16(1), pp. 1–21. https://doi.org/10.1080/0958519042000295920.

Elliott, K. A. and Freeman, R. B. (2003) *Can Labor Standards Improve under Globalization?*, *Peterson Institute Press: All Books*. Peterson Institute for International Economics. Available at: https://ideas.repec.org/b/iie/ppress/338.html (Accessed: 24 March 2021).

Erdoğdu, S. (2014) 'Türkiye'de Asgari Ücret Tespit Komisyonu Kararlarında İşçi Ve İşveren Temsilcilerinin Yaklaşımları (1969-2013)', *'İş, Güç' Endüstri İlişkileri ve İnsan Kaynaklari Dergisi*, 16(2), pp. 3–37.

ERG (2012) *Mesleki ve Teknik Eğitimde Kalite ve Strateji Belgesi*. Available at: http://www.egitimreformugirisimi.org/sites/www.egitimreformugirisimi.org/files/pdf/MLMM.StratejiBelgesi_1.pdf (Accessed: 5 August 2016).

ERG (2013) *Eğitim İzleme Raporu 2012*. Available at: http://erg.sabanciuniv.edu/tr/node/978 (Accessed: 5 August 2016).

ERG (2014) *Eğitim İzleme Raporu 2013*. Available at: http://www.egitimreformugirisimi.org/egitim-izleme-rapor-2013/ (Accessed: 11 September 2016).

Esping-Andersen, G. (1990) *The Three Worlds of Welfare Capitalism*. 1st ed. Cambridge: Polity.

Estache, A. and Wren-Lewis, L. (2009) 'Toward a theory of regulation for developing countries: following Jean-Jacques Laffont's lead', *Journal of Economic Literature*, 47(3), pp. 729–70. https://doi.org/10.1257/jel.47.3.729.

Estevez-Abe, M., Iversen, T., and Soskice, D. (2001) 'Social protection and the formation of skills: a reinterpretation of the welfare state', in Hall, P. A. and Soskice, D. (eds.) *Varieties of Capitalism: The Institutional Foundations of Comparative Advantage*. Oxford: Oxford University Press, pp. 145–83.

ETF (2004) *Peer Review. Social Dialogue in Vocational Education and Training and Employment in Turkey*. Available at: http://www.etf.europa.eu/web.nsf/pages/Peer_review._Social_dialogue_in_vocational_education_and_training_and_employment_in_Turkey (Accessed: 7 May 2016).

Eurostat (2020a) *Minimum wage statistics*. Available at: https://ec.europa.eu/eurostat/statistics-explained/index.php?title=Minimum_wage_statistics#General_overview (Accessed: 3 September 2020).

Eurostat (2020b) *Minimum wage statistics*. Available at: https://ec.europa.eu/eurostat/statistics-explained/index.php?title=Minimum_wage_statistics#General_overview (Accessed: 13 March 2020).

Fainshmidt, S., et al. (2018) 'Varieties of institutional systems: a contextual taxonomy of understudied countries', *Journal of World Business*, 53(3), pp. 307–22. https://doi.org/10.1016/j.jwb.2016.05.003.

Farndale, E. and Paauwe, J. (2007) 'Uncovering competitive and institutional drivers of HRM practices in multinational corporations', *Human Resource Management Journal*, 17(4), pp. 355–75. https://doi.org/10.1111/j.1748-8583.2007.00050.x.

Ferner, A. (1997) 'Country of origin effects and HRM in multinational companies', *Human Resource Management Journal*, 7(1), pp. 19–37. https://doi.org/10.1111/j.1748-8583.1997.tb00271.x.

Ferner, A. (2000) 'The underpinnings of "bureaucratic" control systems: HRM in European multinationals', *Journal of Management Studies*, 37(4), pp. 521–40. https://doi.org/10.1111/1467-6486.00192.

Ferner, A., et al. (2004) 'Dynamics of central control and subsidiary autonomy in the management of human resources: case-study evidence from US MNCs in the UK', *Organization Studies*, 25(3), pp. 363–91. https://doi.org/10.1177/0170840604040041.

Ferner, A., Almond, P., and Colling, T. (2005) 'Institutional theory and the cross-national transfer of employment policy: the case of "workforce diversity" in US multinationals', *Journal of International Business Studies*, 36(3), pp. 304–21. https://dx.doi.org/10.1057/palgrave. jibs.8400134.

Ferner, A., Edwards, T., and Tempel, A. (2012) 'Power, institutions and the cross-national transfer of employment practices in multinationals', *Human Relations*, 65(2), pp. 163–87. https://doi.org/10.1177/0018726711429494.

Ferner, A., Quintanilla, J., and Varul, M. Z. (2001) 'Country-of-origin effects, host-country effects, and the management of HR in multinationals: German companies in Britain and Spain', *Journal of World Business*, 36(2), pp. 107–27. https://doi.org/10.1016/S1090-9516(01)00050-5.

Finegold, D. and Soskice, D. (1988) 'The failure of training in Britain: analysis and prescription', *Oxford Review of Economic Policy*, 4(3), pp. 21–53. https://doi.org/10.1093/oxrep/4.3.21.

Fleckenstein, T., Saunders, A. M., and Seeleib-Kaiser, M. (2011) 'The dual transformation of social protection and human capital: comparing Britain and Germany', *Comparative Political Studies*, 44(12), pp. 1622–50. https://doi.org/10.1177/0010414011407473.

Florida, R. and Kenney, M. (1991) 'Transplanted organizations: the transfer of Japanese industrial organization to the U.S.', *American Sociological Review*, 56(3), pp. 381–98. https://doi.org/10.2307/2096111.

Franz, W. and Soskice, D. (1995) 'The German apprenticeship system', in Buttler, F., et al. (eds.) *Institutional Frameworks and Labor Market Performance: Comparative Views on the US and German Economies*. London: Taylor & Francis,pp. 208–34.

Frege, C. and Kelly, J. (2013) 'Theoretical perspectives on comparative employment relations', in Frege, C. and Kelly, J. (eds.) *Comparative Employment Relations in the Global Economy*. London: Routledge, pp. 8–26.

George, A. L. and Bennett, A. (2005) *Case Studies and Theory Development in the Social Sciences*. Cambridge, MA: MIT Press.

Gereffi, G., Humphrey, J., and Sturgeon, T. (2005) 'The governance of global value chains', *Review of International Political Economy*, 12(1), pp. 78–104.

Gereffi, G. and Korzeniewicz, M. (1994) *Commodity Chains and Global Capitalism*. Westport, CN; London: Praeger.

Geringer, J. M. and Hebert, L. (1991) 'Measuring performance of international joint ventures', *Journal of International Business Studies*, 22(2), pp. 249–63.

Giddens, A. (2003) *Runaway World: How Globalization is Reshaping Our Lives*. New York: Routledge.

Greenwood, R., Hinings, C. R., and Whetten, D. (2014) 'Rethinking institutions and organizations', *Journal of Management Studies*, 51(7), pp. 1206–20. https://doi.org/10.1111/joms.12070.

Hall, P. A. (2005) 'Institutional complementarity: causes and effects', *Socio-Economic Review*, 3(2), pp. 373–7. https://doi.org/10.1093/SER/mwi015.

Hall, P. A. and Gingerich, D. W. (2009) 'Varieties of capitalism and institutional complementarities in the political economy: an empirical analysis', *British Journal of Political Science*, 39(3), pp. 449–82. https://doi.org/10.1017/S0007123409000672.

Hall, P. A. and Soskice, D. (eds.) (2001) *Varieties of Capitalism: The Institutional Foundations of Comparative Advantage*. 1st ed. Oxford: Oxford University Press.

Hall, P. A. and Thelen, K. (2009) 'Institutional change in varieties of capitalism', *Socio-Economic Review*, 7(1), pp. 7–34. https://doi.org/10.1093/ser/mwn020.

Hancke, B. (ed.) (2009) *Debating Varieties of Capitalism: A Reader*. Oxford: Oxford University Press.

Hancke, B., Rhodes, M., and Thatcher, M. (eds.) (2007) *Beyond Varieties of Capitalism: Conflict, Contradictions, and Complementarities in the European Economy: Conflict, Contradictions, and Complementarities in the European Economy*. Oxford; New York: Oxford University Press.

Harzing, A.-W. and Sorge, A. (2003) 'The relative impact of country of origin and universal contingencies on internationalization strategies and corporate control in multinational enterprises: worldwide and European perspectives', *Organization Studies*, 24(2), pp. 187–214. https://doi.org/10.1177/0170840603024002343.

Henderson, J., et al. (2002) 'Global production networks and the analysis of economic development', *Review of International Political Economy*, 9(3), pp. 436–64. https://doi.org/10.1080/09692290210150842.

Heper, M. (1991) *Strong State and Economic Interest Groups, The Post-1980 Turkish Experience*. Reprint 2014. Berlin; Boston: De Gruyter. https://doi.org/10.1515/9783110859966.

Herrera, F. and Melgoza, J. (2003) Evolución reciente de la afiliación sindical y la regulación laboral, in de la Garza, E. and Salas, C. (eds.) *La Situación del Trabajo en México*. México, D.F.: Plaza y Valdéz, pp. 323–48.

Herrigel, G. (2013) *Recent Trends in Manufacturing Globalization and Their Effects on the Distribution of R&D, Design, and Production within US, German and Japanese Automobile, Electro-Mechanical, Machinery and related Component MNCs*. Chicago: University of Chicago Press.

Hofstede, G. (1980) *Culture's Consequences: International Differences in Work-Related Values*. Newbury Park, CA: SAGE Publications.

Hollingsworth, J. R. and Boyer, R. (1997) *Contemporary Capitalism: The Embeddedness of Institutions*. Cambridge: Cambridge University Press.

Horwitz, F. and Budhwar, P. S. (2015) 'Human resources management in emerging markets: an introduction', in Horwitz, F. and Budhwar, P. S. (eds.) *Handbook of Human Resource Management in Emerging Markets*. Reprint edition. Cheltenham, UK; Northampton, MA: Edward Elgar Publishing Ltd, pp. 1–18.

Hotho, J. and Saka-Helmhout, A. (2017) 'In and between societies: reconnecting comparative institutionalism and organization theory', *Organization Studies*, 38(5), pp. 647–66. https://doi.org/10.1177/0170840616655832.

House, R. J., et al. (2004) *Culture, Leadership, and Organizations: The GLOBE Study of 62 Societies*. Thousand Oaks, CA: SAGE Publications.

Hualde, A. (1999) Los caminos de la articulación entre el sistema educativo y el sistema productivo, in Taddei, C. and Lara, B. (eds.) *Globalización, Grandes Empresas e Integración Productiva en Sonora*. Sonora, Mexico: Unison, El Colegio Sonora.

Humphrey, J. (2000) 'Assembler-supplier relations in the auto industry: globalisation and national development', *Competition & Change*, 4(3), pp. 245–71. https://doi.org/10.1177/102452940000400301.

Humphrey, J. and Memedovic, O. (2003) *The Global Automotive Industry Value Chain: What Prospects for Upgrading by Developing Countries*. SSRN Scholarly Paper ID 424560. Rochester, NY: Social Science Research Network. Available at: https://papers.ssrn.com/abstract=424560 (Accessed: 25 June 2017).

Humphrey, J. and Schmitz, H. (2002) 'How does insertion in global value chains affect upgrading in industrial clusters?', *Regional Studies*, 36(9), pp. 1017–27. https://doi.org/10.1080/0034340022000022198.

Humphrey, J. and Schmitz, H. (2004) 'Chain governance and upgrading: taking stock', in Schmitz, H. (ed.) *Local Enterprises in the Global Economy: Issues of Governance and Upgrading*. Cheltenham, UK: Edward Elgar, pp. 349–81.

ILO (2014) *Informal Employment in Mexico: Current Situation, Policies and Challenges*. Available at: https://www.ilo.org/wcmsp5/groups/public/—americas/—ro-lima/documents/publication/wcms_245889.pdf (Accessed: 22 March 2021).

ILO (2020a) *ILOSTAT Union Membership database*. Available at: https://ilostat.ilo.org/data/ (Accessed: 4 July 2020).

ILO. (2020b) *ILOSTAT database Informal Employment*. Available at: https://ilostat.ilo.org/topics/informality/ (Accessed: 30 July 2021).

INEGI (2020) *Ocupación: Población ocupada según nivel de ingreso, nacional trimestral (Personas) [data table]*. Available at: https://www.inegi.org.mx/app/tabulados/default.html?nc=602 (Accessed: 22 April 2020).

International Federation of Robotics (2018) *Robot Density Rises Globally*. Available at: https://ifr.org/ifr-press-releases/news/robot-density-rises-globally (Accessed: 1 September 2019).

Iversen, T. and Stephens, J. D. (2008) 'Partisan politics, the welfare state, and three worlds of human capital formation', *Comparative Political Studies*, 41(4–5), pp. 600–37. https://doi.org/10.1177/0010414007313117.

Jackson, G. (2005) 'Modeling complementarity: multiple functions and different levels', *Socio-Economic Review*, 3(2), pp. 378–81. https://doi.org/10.1093/SER/mwi015.

Jackson, G. and Deeg, R. (2019) 'Comparing capitalisms and taking institutional context seriously', *Journal of International Business Studies*, 50(1), pp. 4–19. https://doi.org/10.1057/s41267-018-0206-0.

Jensen, P. D. Ø. (2009) 'A learning perspective on the offshoring of advanced services', *Journal of International Management*, 15(2), pp. 181–93. https://doi.org/10.1016/j.intman.2008.06.004.

Jessop, B. (2011) 'Rethinking the diversity of capitalism: varieties of capitalism, variegated capitalism, and the world market', in Wood, G. and Lane, C. (eds.) *Capitalist Diversity and Diversity within Capitalism*. London: Routledge, pp. 209–237. Available at: https://eprints.lancs.ac.uk/id/eprint/55149/ (Accessed: 25 March 2021).

Jessop, B. (2015) 'Comparative capitalisms and/or variegated capitalism', in Ebenau, M., Bruff, I., and May, C. (eds.) *New Directions in Comparative Capitalisms Research: Critical and Global Perspectives*. London: Palgrave Macmillan UK (International Political Economy Series), pp. 65–82. Available at: https://doi.org/10.1057/9781137444615_5.

Jessop, B. and Sum, N.-L. (2006) *Beyond the Regulation Approach: Putting Capitalist Economies in Their Place*. Cheltenham, UK & Northampton, MA: Edward Elgar Publishing.

Jordaan, J. A. (2011) 'FDI, local sourcing, and supportive linkages with domestic suppliers: the case of Monterrey, Mexico', *World Development*, 39(4), pp. 620–32. https://doi.org/10.1016/j.worlddev.2010.08.012.

Jürgens, U. and Krzywdzinski, M. (2009) 'Changing East–West Division of Labour in the European Automotive Industry', *European Urban and Regional Studies*, 16(1), pp. 27–42. doi: 10.1177/0969776408098931.

Jürgens, U. and Krzywdzinski, M. (2013) 'Breaking off from local bounds : human resource management practices of national players in the BRIC countries', *International Journal of Automotive Technology and Management : IJATM*, 13(2), pp. 114–33.

Jürgens, U. and Krzywdzinski, M. (2015) 'Competence development on the shop floor and industrial upgrading: case studies of auto makers in China', *International Journal of Human Resource Management*, 26(9), pp. 1204–25. https://doi.org/10.1080/09585192.2014.934888.

Jürgens, U. and Krzywdzinski, M. (2016) *New Worlds of Work: Varieties of Work in Car Factories in the BRIC Countries*. Oxford; New York: Oxford University Press.

Jürgens, U., Malsch, T., and Dohse, K. (1993) *Breaking from Taylorism: Changing Forms of Work in the Automobile Industry*. Cambridge: Cambridge University Press.

Kaplinsky, R. (1995) 'Technique and system: the spread of Japanese management techniques to developing countries', *World Development*, 23(1), pp. 57–71. https://doi.org/10.1016/0305-750X(94)00107-A.

Karaca, C. and Kaleli, E. (2019) 'Türkiye'de kayıt dışı istihdama ilişkin çözüm önerileri', *Sosyal Politika Çalışmaları Dergisi*, 19(44), pp. 769–92. https://doi.org/10.21560/spcd.v19i49119.505164.

Katz, H. and Wailes, N. (2014) 'Convergence and divergence in employment relations', in Wilkinson, A., Wood, G., and Deeg, R. (eds.) *The Oxford Handbook of Employment Relations: Comparative Employment Systems*. Oxford; New York: Oxford University Press.

Kenar, N. (2009) *Yaygın Eğitim Kapsamında Mesleki Eğitim Sistemi*. MESS Eğitim Vakfı. Available at: http://www.messegitim.com.tr/ti/579/0/YAYGIN-EGITIM-KAPSAMINDA-MESLEKI-EGITIM-SISTEMI (Accessed: 23 August 2017).

Kenar, N. (2010) *Mesleki ve Teknik Eğitim Sisteminin Genel Değerlendirmesi*. MESS Eğitim Vakfı. Available at: http://www.messegitim.com.tr/ti/577/0/MESLEKI-VE-TEKNIK-EGITIM-SISTEMININ-GENEL-DEGERLENDIRMESI.

Kenney, M. and Florida, R. L. (1993) *Beyond Mass Production: The Japanese System and Its Transfer to the U.S.* Oxford: Oxford University Press.

Kharas, H. and Kohli, H. (2011) 'What is the middle income trap, why do countries fall into it, and how can it be avoided?', *Global Journal of Emerging Market Economies*, 3(3), pp. 281–9. https://doi.org/10.1177/097491011100300302.

Kis, V., Hoeckel, K., and Santiago, P. (2009) *OECD Reviews of Vocational Education and Training: A Learning for Jobs Review of Mexico 2009*. Available at: https://doi.org/10.1787/9789264168688-en (Accessed: 30 July 2021).

Kochan, T. A., Lansbury, R. D., and MacDuffie, J. P. (eds.) (1997) *After Lean Production: Evolving Employment Practices in the World Auto Industry*. Ithaca, NY: Cornell University Press (Cornell International Industrial and Labor Relations Reports).

Kohli, A. (2004) *State-Directed Development: Political Power and Industrialization in the Global Periphery*. Cambridge: Cambridge University Press. https://doi.org/10.1017/CBO9780511754371.

Korkmaz, A. (2004) 'Bir Sosyal Politika Aracı Olarak Türkiye'de Asgari Ücret: 1951–2003', *Kocaeli Üniversitesi Sosyal Bilimler Enstitüsü Dergisi*, 7(1), p. 53–69.

Kristensen, P. H. and Morgan, G. (2012a) 'From institutional change to experimentalist institutions', *Industrial Relations: A Journal of Economy and Society*, 51(s1), pp. 413–37. https://doi.org/10.1111/j.1468-232X.2012.00685.x.

Kristensen, P. H. and Morgan, G. (2012b) 'Theoretical contexts and conceptual frames for the study of twenty-first century capitalisms', in Whitley, R. and Morgan, G. (eds.) *Capitalisms and Capitalism in the Twenty-First Century*. Oxford: Oxford University Press, pp. 11–43.

Krzywdzinski, M. (2017) 'Accounting for cross-country differences in employee involvement practices: comparative case studies in Germany, Brazil and China', *British Journal of Industrial Relations*, 55(2), pp. 321–46. https://doi.org/10.1111/bjir.12230.

Kuş, B. and Özel, I. (2010) 'United we restrain, divided we rule: neoliberal reforms and labor unions in Turkey and Mexico', *European Journal of Turkish Studies. Social Sciences on Contemporary Turkey*, (11), pp. 1–22. Available at: https://ejts.revues.org/4291 (Accessed: 29 May 2017).

Lakhani, T., Kuruvilla, S., and Avgar, A. (2013) 'From the firm to the network: global value chains and employment relations theory', *British Journal of Industrial Relations*, 51(3), pp. 440–72. https://doi.org/10.1111/bjir.12015.

Lane, C. (2008) 'National capitalisms and global production networks: an analysis of their interaction in two global industries', *Socio-Economic Review*, 6(2), pp. 227–60. https://doi.org/10.1093/ser/mwm010.

Lane, C. and Probert, J. (2009) *National Capitalisms, Global Production Networks: Fashioning the Value Chain in the UK, US, and Germany*. Oxford: Oxford University Press.

Lane, C. and Wood, G. (2009) 'Capitalist diversity and diversity within capitalism', *Economy and Society*, 38(4), pp. 531–51. https://doi.org/10.1080/03085140903190300.

Lane, C. and Wood, G. (2011) 'Institutions, change and diversity', in Lane, C. and Wood, G. (eds.) *Capitalist Diversity and Diversity within Capitalism*. London; New York: Routledge, pp. 1–31.

Lanz, R., Miroudot, S. and Nordås, H. K. (2013) 'Offshoring of tasks: Taylorism versus Toyotism', *The World Economy*, 36(2), pp. 194–212. https://doi.org/10.1111/twec.12024.

Lauridsen, C., et al. (2013) 'Mexico central region automotive cluster: microeconomics of competitiveness', *Harvard Business School Student Project*, Spring 2013. Available at: https://www.isc.hbs.edu/Documents/resources/courses/moc-course-at-harvard/pdf/student-projects/Mexico_Automotive_2013.pdf (Accessed: 30 July 2021).

Lawler, J. and Hundley, G. (2008) *Global Diffusion of Human Resource Practices: Institutional and Cultural Limits*. Serial ed. Bingley: JAI Press Inc.

Liker, J. and Choi, T. Y. (2004) 'Building deep supplier relationships', *Harvard Business Review*, 18 (12), pp. 104–13.

Lindley, R. M. (1975) 'The demand for apprentice recruits by the engineering industry, 1951-71', *Scottish Journal of Political Economy*, 22(1), pp. 1–24. https://doi.org/10.1111/j.1467-9485.1975.tb00043.x.

Locke, R. M. (2013) *The Promise and Limits of Private Power: Promoting Labor Standards in a Global Economy*. Cambridge: Cambridge University. https://doi.org/10.1017/CBO9781139381840.

McDuffie, J. P. (1995) 'Human resource bundles and manufacturing performance: organizational logic and flexible production systems in the world auto industry', *Industrial and Labor Relations Review*, 48(2), pp. 197–221. https://doi.org/10.2307/2524483.

MacDuffie, J. P. and Helper, S. (1997) 'Creating lean suppliers: diffusing lean production through the supply chain', *California Management Review*, 39(4), pp. 118–51. https://doi.org/10.2307/41165913.

McDuffie, J. P. and Kochan, T. A. (1995) 'Do U.S. firms invest less in human resources?: training in the world auto industry', *Industrial Relations: A Journal of Economy and Society*, 34(2), pp. 147–68. https://doi.org/10.1111/j.1468-232X.1995.tb00366.x.

MacDuffie, J. P. and Pil, F. K. (1997) 'Changes in auto industry employment practices: an inter-national overview', in Kochan, T. A., Lansbury, R. D., and MacDuffie, J. P. (eds.) *After Lean Production: Evolving Employment Practices in the World Auto Industry*. Ithaca, NY: Cornell University Press.

Mares, I. (2003) *The Politics of Social Risk: Business and Welfare State Development*. New York: Cambridge University Press.

Marois, T. (2012) *States, Banks and Crisis: Emerging Finance Capitalism in Mexico and Turkey*. Cheltenham, UK: Edward Elgar Publishing Ltd.

Mayer, F. W. and Phillips, N. (2017) 'Outsourcing governance: states and the politics of a "global value chain world"', *New Political Economy*, 22(2), pp. 134–52. https://doi.org/10.1080/13563467.2016.1273341.

Mayer, F. W., Phillips, N., and Posthuma, A. C. (2017) 'The political economy of governance in a "global value chain world"', *New Political Economy*, 22(2), pp. 129–33. https://doi.org/10.1080/13563467.2016.1273343.

Mayrhofer, W., Morley, M., and Brewster, C. (2011) 'Convergence, stasis, or divergence?', in Brewster, C., Mayrhofer, W., and Morley, M. (eds.) *Human Resource Management in Europe: Evidence of Convergence?* Routledge/Butterworth-Heinemann, pp. 415–36.

McGrath, S. (2007) 'Transnationals, globalisation and education and training: evidence from the South African automotive sector', *Journal of Vocational Education & Training*, 59(4), pp. 575–589. https://doi.org/10.1080/13636820701651032.

McGrath, S. (2012) 'Vocational education and training for development: a policy in need of a theory?', *International Journal of Educational Development*, 32(5), pp. 623–31. https://doi.org/10.1016/j.ijedudev.2011.12.001.

MEB (2008) *Yüksek Öğretime Geçiş Sisteminin Ticaret Meslek Ve Anadolu Ticaret Meslek Liselerine Etkileri*. Ankara: Eğitimi Araştırma ve Geliştirme Dairesi Başkanlığı (EARGED). Available at: https://www.meb.gov.tr/earged/earged/yukogr_gecis_sist.pdf (Accessed: 30 July 2021).

MEB (2009) *Çıraklık Eğitiminde Güncelliğini Yitiren ve Öğretim Kapsamına Alınacak Yeni Mesleklerin Belirlenmesi*. Ankara: Eğitimi Araştırma ve Geliştirme Dairesi Başkanlığı

(EARGED). Available at: meb.gov.tr/earged/earged/Ciraklik_egitiminde.pdf (Accessed: 30 July 2021)

MEB (2018) *Türkiye'de Meslekî ve Teknik Eğitimin Görünümü. Eğitim Analiz ve Değerlendirme Raporları Serisi*, 1 .Available at: https://mtegm.meb.gov.tr/meb_iys_dosyalar/2018_11/12134429_No1_Turkiyede_Mesleki_ve_Teknik_Egitimin_Gorunumu.pdf (Accessed: 30 July 2021).

MEB (2019) *Organize Sanayi Bölgelerinde Mesleki ve Teknik Eğitim*. Available at: https://www.meb.gov.tr/meb_iys_dosyalar/2019_06/12103640_2019_06_12_Organize_Sanayi_Bolgelerinde_Mesleki_ve_Teknik_Egitim.pdf (Accessed: 3 May 2020).

Merrilees, W. J. (1983) 'Alternative models of apprentice recruitment: with special reference to the British engineering industry', *Applied Economics*, 15(1), pp. 1–21. https://doi.org/10.1080/00036848300000047.

Mert, Z. G. and Akman, G. (2011) *The Profile of the Organized Industrial Zones in Kocaeli/ TURKEY*. ersa11p1137. European Regional Science Association. Available at: https://ideas.repec.org/p/wiw/wiwrsa/ersa11p1137.html (Accessed: 18 May 2018).

Meyer, J. W. (2000) 'Globalization: sources and effects on national states and societies', *International Sociology*, 15(2), pp. 233–48. https://doi.org/10.1177/0268580900015002006.

Milliyet (2017) 'Otomotiv üretim ve ihracatı da 2016'da rekor kırd'. Available at: http://www.milliyet.com.tr/otomotiv-uretim-ve-ihracati-da-ekonomi-2375633/ (Accessed: 20 August 2018).

Mohrenweiser, J. and Zwick, T. (2009) 'Why do firms train apprentices? The net cost puzzle reconsidered', *Labour Economics*, 16(6), pp. 631–37. https://doi.org/10.1016/j.labeco.2009.08.004.

Moody, K. (1997) *Workers in a Lean World: Unions in the International Economy*. London; New York: Verso.

Morgan, G. (2007) 'National business systems research: progress and prospects', *Scandinavian Journal of Management*, 23(2), pp. 127–45. https://doi.org/10.1016/j.scaman.2007.02.008.

Morgan, G., et al. (2010) *The Oxford Handbook of Comparative Institutional Analysis*. Oxford: Oxford University Press.

Morgan, G. and Hull Kristensen, P. (2006) 'The contested space of multinationals: varieties of institutionalism, varieties of capitalism', *Human Relations*, 59(11), pp. 1467–90. https://doi.org/10.1177/0018726706072866.

Muehlemann, S. and Pfeifer, H. (2016) 'The structure of hiring costs in Germany: evidence from firm-level data', *Industrial Relations: A Journal of Economy and Society*, 55(2), pp. 193–218. https://doi.org/10.1111/irel.12139.

Muehlemann, S., Ryan, P., and Wolter, S. C. (2013) 'Monopsony power, pay structure, and training', *ILR Review*, 66(5), pp. 1097–14. https://doi.org/10.1177/001979391306600504.

Muller, F. (1994) 'Societal effect, organizational effect and globalization', *Organization Studies*, 15(3), pp. 407–28. https://doi.org/10.1177/017084069401500305.

Muller, W. and Jacob, M. (2008) 'Qualifications and the returns to training across the life course', in Mayer, K. U. and Solga, H. (eds.) *Skill Formation: Interdisciplinary and Cross-National Perspectives*. 1st ed. New York: Cambridge University Press.

Mülteciler Derneği (2020) *Türkiyedeki Suriyeli Sayısı Mart 2020*. Available at: https://multeciler.org.tr/turkiyedeki-suriyeli-sayisi/ (Accessed: 2 May 2020).

Munyar, V. (2012) 'OİB'de otomotiv eğitimi alan öğrenciye üniversitede öğretecek bir şey kalır mı', *Hürriyet*, 17 September. Available at: https://www.hurriyet.com.tr/oib-de-otomotiv-egitimi-alan-ogrenciye-universitede-ogretecek-bir-sey-kalir-mi-21482689 (Accessed: 3 March 2020).

Murillo, M. V. (2001) *Labor Unions, Partisan Coalitions, and Market Reforms in Latin America*. Cambridge: Cambridge University Press.

MYK (2020) 'Sınav ve belgelendirme ücret tarifesi'. MYK Web Portalı. Available at: https://portal.myk.gov.tr/index.php?option=com_kurulus_ara&view=kurulus_ara&layout=kurulus_tarife&kurId=7060&yetId=0 (Accessed: 3 May 2020).

Nadvi, K. (2004) 'Globalisation and poverty: how can global value chain research inform the policy debate?', *IDS Bulletin*, 35(1), pp. 20–30. https://doi.org/https://doi.org/10.1111/j.1759-5436.2004.tb00105.x.

Nadvi, K. and Wältring, F. (2004) *Making Sense of Global Standards*. Cheltenham, UK: Edward Elgar Publishing. Available at: http://econpapers.repec.org/bookchap/elgeechap/2824_5f3.htm.

Nathan, D. and Kaplana, V. (2007) *Issues in the Analysis of Global Value Chains and Their Impact on Employment and Incomes in India*. ILO Discussion Paper Series 183. Geneva: International Institute for Labor Studies.

Nölke, A. (ed.) (2014) *Multinational Corporations from Emerging Markets: State Capitalism 3.0*. London: Palgrave Macmillan UK (International Political Economy Series). https://doi.org/10.1057/9781137359506.

Nölke, A., et al. (2015) 'Domestic structures, foreign economic policies and global economic order: Implications from the rise of large emerging economies', *European Journal of International Relations*, 21(3), pp. 538–67. https://doi.org/10.1177/1354066114553682.

Nölke, A., et al. (2019) *State-Permeated Capitalism in Large Emerging Economies*. 1st ed. London: Routledge.

Nölke, A. and Vliegenthart, A. (2009) 'Enlarging the varieties of capitalism: the emergence of dependent market economies in East Central Europe', *World Politics*, 61(4), pp. 670–702. https://doi.org/10.1017/S0043887109990098.

Oatey, M. (1970) 'The economics of training with respect to the firm*', *British Journal of Industrial Relations*, 8(1), pp. 1–21. https://doi.org/10.1111/j.1467-8543.1970.tb00568.x.

OECD (2013a) *OECD Employment Protection Database*. Available at: http://www.oecd.org/employment/emp/oecdindicatorsofemploymentprotection.htm (Accessed: 27 October 2016).

OECD (2013b) *Education at a Glance: OECD Indicators*. Available at: https://www.oecd.org/education/eag2013%20(eng)--FINAL%2020%20June%202013.pdf (Accessed: 30 June 2021).

OECD (2015) *In It Together: Why Less Inequality Benefits All*. Paris: OECD Publishing. Available at: http://dx.doi.org/10.1787/9789264235120-en. (Accessed: 30 July 2021).

OECD (2016) *Distribution of Firms in Mexico, 2013: Mexico*. Paris: OECD Publishing. Available at: https://doi.org/10.1787/fin_sme_ent-2016-table214-en. (Accessed: 30 July 2021).

OECD (2017) *Entrepreneurship at a Glance 2017*. Paris: OECD Publishing. Available at: https://doi.org/10.1787/entrepreneur_aag-2017-en. (Accessed: 27 July 2021).

OECD (2018) *OECD Policy Reviews of Vocational Education and Training (VET) and Adult Learning*. Available at: http://www.oecd.org/education/innovation-education/vet.htm (Accessed: 28 May 2018).

OECD (2019) 'GDP per capita and productivity growth (Edition 2019)', in OECD *Productivity Statistics* (database). Available at: https://doi.org/10.1787/5c2aa654-en (Accessed: 24 March 2021).

OECD (2020a) *Strictness of Employment Protection—Individual and Collective Dismissals (Regular Contracts)*. Available at: https://stats.oecd.org/Index.aspx?DataSetCode=EPL_OV (Accessed: 22 March 2021).

OECD (2020b) *Social Expenditure Database (SOCX)*. Available at: https://www.oecd.org/social/expenditure.htm (Accessed: 12 May 2020).

OECD (2020c) *Education at a Glance 2020: OECD Indicators: Educational Finance Indicators*. Paris: OECD Publishing. https://doi.org/10.1787/69096873-en. (Accessed: 30 July 2021).

OECD (2020d) *Earnings: Real Minimum Wages*. Database. Available at: http://dx.doi.org/10.1787/data-00656-en (Accessed: 15 April 2020).

OECD (2020e) *Youth Not in Employment, Education or Training (NEET) (indicator)*. Available at: https://doi.org/10.1787/72d1033a-en (Accessed: 6 April 2020).

OECD (2020f) *Structural Business Statistics ISIC Rev. 4 (database)*. Available at: https://doi.org/10.1787/8e34f7e7-en (Accessed: 21 April 2020).

OECD (2021a) 'Earnings: real minimum wages', in *OECD Employment and Labour Market Statistics (database)*. Available at: https://doi.org/10.1787/data-00656-en (Accessed: 21 March 2021).

OECD (2021b) 'GDP per capita and productivity', in *OECD Compendium of Productivity Indicators*. Available at: https://stats.oecd.org/OECDStat_Metadata/ShowMetadata.ashx?Dataset=PDB_LV&ShowOnWeb=true&Lang=en (Accessed: 24 March 2021).

OECD/CERI (2009) *Systemic Innovation in the Mexican VET System Country Case Study Report*. Available at: http://www.oecd.org/mexico/43139985.pdf (Accessed: 28 May 2018).

Ohmae, K. (1995) *The End of the Nation State: The Rise of Regional Economies*. New York: Free Press.

Okada, A. (2004) 'Skills development and interfirm learning linkages under globalization: lessons from the Indian automobile industry', *World Development*, 32(7), pp. 1265–88. https://doi.org/10.1016/j.worlddev.2004.01.010.

Olson, M. (1965) *The Logic of Collective Action: Public Goods and the Theory of Groups, Second Printing with New Preface and Appendix*. Cambridge, MA: Harvard University Press.

O'Neill, J. (2001) *Building Better Global Economic BRICs*. 66. Goldman Sachs.

Öniş, Z. (2012) 'The triumph of conservative globalism: the political economy of the AKP era', *Turkish Studies*, 13(2), pp. 135–52. https://doi.org/10.1080/14683849.2012.685252.

Örnek-Özden, E. (2016) 'Restructuring the organised industrial zones as the instruments for development', *MEGARON*, 11(1), pp. 106–24. https://doi.org/10.5505/megaron.2016.29200.

Özel, I. (2014) *State–Business Alliances and Economic Development: Turkey, Mexico and North Africa*. London: Routledge.

Özel, I. (2021) 'Market integration and transformation of business politics: diverging trajectories of corporatisms in Mexico and Turkey', *Socio-Economic Review*, 19(1), pp. 219–45. https://doi.org/10.1093/ser/mwy028.

Özkiziltan, D. (2019) 'Authoritarian neoliberalism in AKP's Turkey: an industrial relations perspective', *Industrial Relations Journal*, 50(3), pp. 218–39. https://doi.org/10.1111/irj.12248.

Pavlínek, P., Domański, B., and Guzik, R. (2009) 'Industrial upgrading through foreign direct investment in Central European automotive manufacturing', *European Urban and Regional Studies*, 16(1), pp. 43–63. https://doi.org/10.1177/0969776408098932.

Peters, E. D. (2012) 'The auto parts-automotive chain in Mexico and China: co-operation potential?', *The China Quarterly*, 209, pp. 82–110. https://doi.org/10.1017/S0305741011001494.

Pfeffer, F. T. (2008) 'Persistent inequality in educational attainment and its institutional context', *European Sociological Review*, 24(5), pp. 543–65. https://doi.org/10.1093/esr/jcn026.

Phillips, N. (2013) 'Unfree labour and adverse incorporation in the global economy: comparative perspectives on Brazil and India', *Economy and Society*, 42(2), pp. 171–96. https://doi.org/10.1080/03085147.2012.718630.

Pil, F. K. and McDuffie, J. P. (1996) 'The adoption of high-involvement work practices', *Industrial Relations: A Journal of Economy and Society*, 35(3), pp. 423–55. https://doi.org/10.1111/j.1468-232X.1996.tb00414.x.

Piore, M. and Sabel, C. (1984) *The Second Industrial Divide: Possibilities for Prosperity*. New York: Basic Books.

Plum, O. and Hassink, R. (2011) 'Comparing knowledge networking in different knowledge bases in Germany', *Papers in Regional Science*, 90(2), pp. 355–71. https://doi.org/10.1111/j.1435-5957.2011.00362.x.

Plum, O. and Hassink, R. (2013) 'Analysing the knowledge base configuration that drives southwest Saxony's automotive firms', *European Urban and Regional Studies*, 20(2), pp. 206–26. https://doi.org/10.1177/0969776412454127.

Ponte, S. and Gibbon, P. (2005) 'Quality standards, conventions and the governance of global value chains', *Economy and Society*, 34(1), pp. 1–31. https://doi.org/10.1080/0308514042000329315.

Pontusson, J. (2005) *Inequality and Prosperity: Social Europe vs. Liberal America*. 1st edn. Ithaca, NY: Cornell University Press.

PwC Mexico (2014) *Doing Business in Mexico. Automotive Industry*. Mexico: PwC Mexico. Available at: https://www.pwc.de/de/internationale-maerkte/assets/doing-business-mexico-automotive.pdf (Accessed: 30 July 2021).

Quack, S. (2016) 'Legal professionals and transnational law-making: a case of distributed agency', *Organization*, 14(5), pp. 643–66. https://doi.org/10.1177/1350508407080313.

Quintanilla, J. and Ferner, A. (2003) 'Multinationals and human resource management: between global convergence and national identity', *The International Journal of Human Resource Management*, 14(3), pp. 363–8. https://doi.org/10.1080/0958519022000031799.

Raiser, M. and Azevedo, J. P. (2013) *Inclusive Growth in Turkey—Can it Be? Future Development*. Available at: http://blogs.worldbank.org/futuredevelopment/inclusive-growth-turkey-can-it-be (Accessed: 15 May 2018).

Ramirez, P. and Rainbird, H. (2010) 'Making the connections: bringing skill formation into global value chain analysis', *Work, Employment and Society*, 24(4), pp. 699–710. https://doi.org/10.1177/0950017010380641.

Reforma (2016) *Industrial Real Estate Development in Mexico*. Mexico: Periódico Reforma Suplementos Especiales.

Ricart, C., Morán, T. and Kappaz, C. (2014) *Toward a National Framework of Lifelong Learning in Mexico*. Inter-American Development Bank (IADB). Available at: https://publications.iadb.org/handle/11319/6756 (Accessed: 28 May 2017).

Riisgaard, L. and Hammer, N. (2011) 'Prospects for labour in global value chains: labour standards in the cut flower and banana industries', *British Journal of Industrial Relations*, 49(1), pp. 168–90. https://doi.org/https://doi.org/10.1111/j.1467-8543.2009.00744.x.

Robertson, P. L. (2003) 'The role of training and skilled labour in the success of SMEs in developing economies', *Education + Training*, 45(8/9), pp. 461–73. https://doi.org/10.1108/00400910310508856.

Robinson, N. (2011) 'Russian patrimonial capitalism and the international financial crisis', *Journal of Communist Studies and Transition Politics*, 27(3–4), pp. 434–55. https://doi.org/10.1080/13523279.2011.595155.

Rosenberg, N. (1992) 'Economic experiments', *Industrial and Corporate Change*, 1(1), pp. 181–203. https://doi.org/10.1093/icc/1.1.181.

Rothstein, J. S. (2005) 'Economic development policymaking down the global commodity chain: attracting an auto industry to Silao, Mexico', *Social Forces*, 84(1), pp. 49–69.

Roxborough, I. (1983) El sindicalismo en el sector automotriz. *Estudios Sociológicos*, 1(1), 59–92.

Rubery, J. (2015) 'Change at work: feminisation, flexibilisation, fragmentation and financialisation', *Employee Relations*. Edited by P. Ralph Darlington, 37(6), pp. 633–44. https://doi.org/10.1108/ER-04-2015-0067.

Rudra, N. (2008) *Globalization and the Race to the Bottom in Developing Countries: Who Really Gets Hurt?* Cambridge: Cambridge University Press. https://doi.org/10.1017/CBO9780511491870.

Rueda, D. and Pontusson, J. (2000) 'Wage inequality and varieties of capitalism', *World Politics*, 52(3), pp. 350–83. https://doi.org/10.1017/S0043887100016579.

Ryan, P. (1998) 'Is apprenticeship better? A review of the economic evidence', *Journal of Vocational Education and Training: The Vocational Aspect of Education*, 50(2), pp. 289–325.

Ryan, P. (2000) 'The institutional requirements of apprenticeship: evidence from smaller EU countries', *International Journal of Training and Development*, 4(1), pp. 42–65. https://doi.org/10.1111/1468-2419.00095.

Sallai, D. and Schnyder, G. (2021) 'What is "Authoritarian" about Authoritarian Capitalism? The Dual Erosion of the Private–Public Divide in State-Dominated Business Systems', *Business & Society*, 60(6), pp. 1312–48. https://doi.org/10.1177/0007650319898475.

Sancak, M. (2011) *Social Security Reforms in Clientelistic Social Policy Regimes: A Comparison Between the Turkish and Greek Cases.* MSc Thesis. University of Oxford.

Sancak, M. (2020) 'Partisan politics of skills in middle-income countries: insiders, outsiders and the vocational education system of Turkey', *Competition & Change*, 24(3–4), pp. 291–314. https://doi.org/10.1177/1024529419888430.

Sancak, M. (forthcoming-a) 'The political economy of skill formation in middle income countries: The persisting role of the state in Mexico and Turkey'.

Sancak, M. (forthcoming-b) 'Varieties of digitalisation in global value chains: Online platforms in automotive supply chains and learning prospects of Mexican and Turkish auto parts suppliers'.

Sancak, M. and Özel, I. (2018) 'When politics gets in the way: domestic coalitions and the making of skill systems', *Review of International Political Economy*, 25(3), pp. 340–63. https://doi.org/10.1080/09692290.2018.1455062.

Sánchez-Ancochea, D. (2009) 'State, firms and the process of industrial upgrading: Latin America's variety of capitalism and the Costa Rican experience', *Economy and Society*, 38(1), pp. 62–86. https://doi.org/10.1080/03085140802560520.

Sayan, S. and Yavçan, B. (2013) *Mapping of VET Policies and Practices for Social Inclusion and Social Cohesion in the Western Balkans, Turkey and Israel Country Report: Turkey.* European Training Foundation. Available at: http://www.etf.europa.eu/web.nsf/pages/EV_2013_Mapping_of_VET_policies_and_practices_for_social_inclusion_and_social_cohesion_in_the_Western_Balkans_Turkey_and_Israel_____?opendocument (Accessed: 9 June 2018).

Schedelik, M., et al. (2021) 'Comparative capitalism, growth models and emerging markets: the development of the field', *New Political Economy*, 26(4), pp. 514–26. https://doi.org/10.1080/13563467.2020.1807487.

Schlumberger, O. (2008) 'Structural reform, economic order, and development: patrimonial capitalism', *Review of International Political Economy*, 15(4), pp. 622–49. https://doi.org/10.1080/09692290802260670.

Schmidt, V. (2003) 'French capitalism transformed, yet still a third variety of capitalism', *Economy and Society*, 32(4), pp. 526–54. https://doi.org/10.1080/0308514032000141693.

Schmidt, V. (2009) 'Putting the political back into political economy by bringing the state back in yet again', *World Politics*, 61(3), pp. 516–46. https://doi.org/10.1017/S0043887109000173.

Schneider, B. R. (2009a) 'A comparative political economy of diversified business groups, or how states organize big business', *Review of International Political Economy*, 16(2), pp. 178–201.

Schneider, B. R. (2009b) 'Hierarchical market economies and varieties of capitalism in Latin America', *Journal of Latin American Studies*, 41(3), pp. 553–75. https://doi.org/10.1017/S0022216X09990186.

Schneider, B. R. (2013a) *Hierarchical Capitalism in Latin America: Business, Labor, and the Challenges of Equitable Development.* New York: Cambridge University Press.

Schneider, B. R. (2013b) *Institutions for Effective Business-Government Collaboration: Micro Mechanisms and Macro Politics in Latin America.* No. IDB-WP-418. IDB. Available at: https://publications.iadb.org/handle/11319/4674 (Accessed: 15 May 2018).

Schneider, B. R. and Karcher, S. (2010) 'Complementarities and continuities in the political economy of labour markets in Latin America', *Socio-Economic Review*, 8(4), pp. 623–51. https://doi.org/10.1093/ser/mwq022.

Schneider, B. R. and Soskice, D. (2009) 'Inequality in developed countries and Latin America: coordinated, liberal and hierarchical systems', *Economy and Society*, 38(1), pp. 17–52. https://doi.org/10.1080/03085140802560496.

Schneider, C. Q. and Makszin, K. (2014) 'Forms of welfare capitalism and education-based participatory inequality', *Socio-Economic Review*, 12(2), pp. 437–62. https://doi.org/10.1093/ser/mwu010.

Schneider, M. R. and Paunescu, M. (2012) 'Changing varieties of capitalism and revealed comparative advantages from 1990 to 2005: a test of the Hall and Soskice claims', *Socio-Economic Review*, 10(4), pp. 731–53. https://doi.org/10.1093/ser/mwr038.

Schuler, R. and Jackson, S. (2014) 'Human resource management and organizational effectiveness: yesterday and today', *Journal of Organizational Effectiveness: People and Performance*, 1(1), pp. 35–55. https://doi.org/10.1108/JOEPP-01-2014-0003.

Schuler, R. S. and Jackson, S. E. (eds.) (2008) *Strategic Human Resource Management: Global Perspectives*. 2nd ed. London: Wiley-Blackwell.

Selwyn, B., Musiolek, B., and Ijarja, A. (2020) 'Making a global poverty chain: export footwear production and gendered labor exploitation in Eastern and Central Europe', *Review of International Political Economy*, 27(2), pp. 377–403. https://doi.org/10.1080/09692290.2019.1640124.

Sengenberger, W. and Pyke, F. (1992) 'Industrial districts and local economic regeneration: research and policy issues', in Sengenberger, W. and Pyke, F. (eds.) *Industrial districts and local economic regeneration*. Geneva: ILO, pp. 3–30. Available at: http://www.ilo.org/global/publications/ilo-bookstore/order-online/books/WCMS_PUBL_9290144718_EN/lang—en/index.htm (Accessed: 15 May 2018).

Shadlen, K. C. (2002) 'Orphaned by democracy: small industry in contemporary Mexico', *Comparative Politics*, 35(1), pp. 43–62. https://doi.org/10.2307/4146927.

Shadlen, K. C. (2004) *Democratization Without Representation: The Politics of Small Industry in Mexico*. New edition. University Park: Penn State University Press.

Shapiro, H., Souto-Otero, M., Bilbao-Osorio, B., Shadoian, V., and Pedro, F. (2009) *Systemic Innovation in the Mexican VET system. Country Case Study Report*. OECD/CERI. http://www.oecd.org/dataoecd/51/55/43139985.pdf (Accessed: 30 July 2021).

SHCP (2013) *Cuenta Pública de la Hacienda Pública Federal 2012, Apartado Educación Pública*. SHCP.

SHCP (2014) *Presupuesto de Egresos de La Federación, Apartado Educación Pública*. SHCP.

Simoes, A. J. G. and Hidalgo, C. A. (2011) 'The economic complexity observatory: an analytical tool for understanding the dynamics of economic development', in *Workshops at the Twenty-Fifth AAAI Conference on Artificial Intelligence*, Cambridge, MA.

Singh, S., et al. (2017) 'Institutions, complementarity, human resource management and performance in a South-East Asian Petrostate: the case of Brunei', *The International Journal of Human Resource Management*, 28(18), pp. 2538–69. https://doi.org/10.1080/09585192.2016.1170713.

Sorge, A. (2014) 'Cross-national Differences in human resources and organisation', in Harzing, A.-W. and Pinnington, A. (eds.) *International Human Resource Management*. Fourth edition. London: SAGE Publications, pp. 117–40.

Sorge, A. and Streeck, W. (2018) 'Diversified quality production revisited: its contribution to German socio-economic performance over time', *Socio-Economic Review*, 16(3), pp. 587–612. https://doi.org/10.1093/ser/mwy022.

Steier, L. P. (2009) 'Familial capitalism in global institutional contexts: implications for corporate governance and entrepreneurship in East Asia', *Asia Pacific Journal of Management*, 26(3), p. 513. https://doi.org/10.1007/s10490-008-9117-0.

Stevens, M. (1994) 'An investment model for the supply of training by employers', *Economic Journal*, 104(424), pp. 556–70.

Stevens, M. (1999) 'Human capital theory and UK vocational training policy', *Oxford Review of Economic Policy*, 15(1), pp. 16–32. https://doi.org/10.1093/oxrep/15.1.16.

Streeck, W. (1989) 'Skills and the limits of neo-liberalism: the enterprise of the future as a place of learning', *Work, Employment and Society*, 3(1), pp. 89–104. https://doi.org/10.1177/0950017089003001006.

Streeck, W. (1991) 'On the institutional conditions of diversified quality production', in Matzner, E. and Streeck, W. (eds.) *Beyond Keynesianism: The Socio-Economics of Production and Full Employment.* Aldershot, England:Edward Elgar, pp. 21–61. Available at: http://scholar.google.com/scholar?cluster=15391416275166567003&hl=en&oi=scholarr.

Streeck, W. (1992a) *Social Institutions and Economic Performance: Studies of Industrial Relations in Advanced Capitalist Economies.* London: SAGE Publications.

Streeck, W. (1992b) 'The logics of associative action and the territorial organization of interests: the case of German handwerk', in Streeck, W. (ed.) *Social Institutions and Economic Performance: Industrial Relations in Advanced Capitalist Economies.* London: SAGE Publications.

Streeck, W. (1997) 'Beneficial constraints: on the economic limits of rational voluntarism', in Hollingsworth, J. R. and Boyer, R. (eds.) *Contemporary Capitalism: The Embeddedness of Institutions.* Revised ed. Cambridge: Cambridge University Press, pp. 197–219.

Streeck, W. (2012) 'Skills and politics: general and specific', in Busemeyer, M. R. and Trampusch, C. (eds.) *The Political Economy of Collective Skill Formation.* Oxford: Oxford University Press, pp. 317–52.

Streeck, W. and Thelen, K. (eds.) (2005) *Beyond Continuity: Institutional Change in Advanced Political Economies.* Oxford: Oxford University Press.

Sturgeon, T. J. (2007) 'How globalization drives institutional diversity: the Japanese electronics industry's response to value chain modularity', *Journal of East Asian Studies*, 7(1), pp. 1–34.

Sturgeon, T. J., et al. (2009) 'Globalisation of the automotive industry: main features and trends', *International Journal Technological Learning, Innovation and Development*, 2, pp. 7–24.

Sturgeon, T. J. and Biesebroeck, J. (2011) 'Global value chains in the automotive industry: an enhanced role for developing countries?', *International Journal of Technological Learning, Innovation and Development*, 4(1–3), pp. 181–205. https://doi.org/10.1504/IJTLID.2011.041904.

Sturgeon, T. J., Biesebroeck, J., and Gereffi, G. (2008) 'Value chains, networks and clusters: reframing the global automotive industry', *Journal of Economic Geography*, 8(3), pp. 297–321.

Székely, M. (2013) *Evaluación final del componente 2 del Programa Multifase de Formación de Recursos Humanos Basada en Competencias (PROFORHCOM), Fase II.* IDB.

Taylor, P., Newsome, K., and Rainnie, A. (2013) '"Putting labour in its place": global value chains and labour process analysis', *Competition & Change*, 17(1), pp. 1–5. https://doi.org/10.1179/1024529412Z.00000000028.

Tempel, A. and Walgenbach, P. (2007) 'Global standardization of organizational forms and management practices? What new institutionalism and the business-systems approach can learn from each other*', *Journal of Management Studies*, 44(1), pp. 1–24. https://doi.org/https://doi.org/10.1111/j.1467-6486.2006.00644.x.

Thelen, K. (2004) *How Institutions Evolve: The Political Economy of Skills in Germany, Britain, the United States, and Japan.* Cambridge: Cambridge University Press.

Thelen, K. (2014) *Varieties of Liberalization and the New Politics of Social Solidarity.* Cambridge: Cambridge University Press.

Thelen, K. and Kume, I. (2006) 'Coordination as a political problem in coordinated market economies', *Governance*, 19(1), pp. 11–42. https://doi.org/10.1111/j.1468-0491.2006.00302.x.

Tipton, F. B. (2009) 'Southeast Asian capitalism: history, institutions, states, and firms', *Asia Pacific Journal of Management*, 26(3), pp. 401–34. https://doi.org/10.1007/s10490-008-9118-z.

Tripney, J. S. and Hombrados, J. G. (2013) 'Technical and vocational education and training (TVET) for young people in low- and middle-income countries: a systematic review and meta-analysis', *Empirical Research in Vocational Education and Training*, 5(1), p. 3. https://doi.org/10.1186/1877-6345-5-3.

Türk-İş (2018) *Dört Kişilik Ailenin Aylık Zorunlu Harcaması (Yoksulluk Sınırı)*. Available at: http://www.turkis.org.tr/dosya/6TF2I64A2pl2.pdf (Accessed: 3 February 2020).

TurkStat (2015) *Yaygın Eğitim Faaliyetleri Araştırması*.Türkiye İstatistik Kurumu. Available at: http://hbogm.meb.gov.tr/www/tuik-yaygin-egitim-faaliyetleri-arastirmalari/icerik/803 (Accessed: 30 July 2021).

Turnbull, P., Oliver, N., and Wilkinson, B. (1992) 'Buyer-supplier relations in the UK - automotive industry: strategic implications of the Japanese manufacturing model', *Strategic Management Journal*, 13(2), pp. 159–68. https://doi.org/10.1002/smj.4250130207.

UNCTAD (2017) *UNCTAD- Trade Structure by Partner, Product or Service Category*. Available at: http://unctadstat.unctad.org/wds/ReportFolders/reportFolders.aspx (Accessed: 30 May 2018).

UNDP IICPSD (2018) *Skills Development*. Available at: http://www.iicpsd.undp.org/content/istanbul/en/home/our-work/private-sector-role-skills-development/overview.html (Accessed: 28 May 2018).

Valiente, O. (2014) 'The OECD skills strategy and the education agenda for development', *International Journal of Educational Development*, 39, pp. 40–8. https://doi.org/10.1016/j.ijedudev.2014.08.008.

Vega, C. A. (2005) 'Las Relaciones entre los Empresarios y el Estado a finales del Siglo XX', in Bizberg, I. and Meyer, L. (eds.) *Tiempo de Mexico, Una Historia Contemporanea de Mexico: Transformaciones y Permanencias*. Mexico City: Oceana.

Vincent, S. and Thompson, P. (2010) 'Realism, beyond the boundary? Labour process theory and critical', in Thompson, P. and Smith, C. (eds.) *Working Life: Renewing Labour Process Analysis*. Basingstoke: Palgrave Press, pp. 47–69.

Wad, P. (2006) 'The automotive supplier industry between localizing and globalizing forces in Malaysia, India, and South Africa', in Hansen, M. W. and Schaumburg-Muller, H. (eds.) *Transnational Corporations and Local Firms in Developing Countries: Linkages and Upgrading*. Copenhagen: Copenhagen Business School Press, pp. 233–62.

Wad, P. (2009) 'The automobile industry of Southeast Asia: Malaysia and Thailand', *Journal of the Asia Pacific Economy*, 14(2), pp. 172–93. https://doi.org/10.1080/13547860902786029.

Wade, R. (1990) *Governing the Market: Economic Theory and the Role of Government in East Asian Industrialization*. Princeton, NJ: Princeton University Press. https://doi.org/10.2307/j.ctv346sp7.

Walter, A. and Zhang, X. (2012) *East Asian Capitalism: Diversity, Continuity, and Change*. Oxford: Oxford University Press. https://doi.org/10.1093/acprof:oso/9780199643097.001.0001.

Webster, E. and Wood, G. (2005) 'Human resource management practice and institutional constraints: the case of Mozambique', *Employee Relations*, 27(4), pp. 369–85. https://doi.org/10.1108/01425450510605705.

Wenzelmann, F., Jansen, A. Pfeifer, H., and Schönfeld, G. (2015) 'Apprenticeship training in Germany remains investment-focused – results of BIBB Cost-Benefit Survey 2012/13', *BIBB*, 9(1). Available at: https://www.bibb.de/en/25852.php (Accessed: 30 July 2021).

Whitley, R. (1999) *Divergent Capitalisms: The Social Structuring and Change of Business Systems*. Oxford: Oxford University Press.

Whitley, R. (2000) *Divergent Capitalisms: The Social Structuring and Change of Business Systems*. Oxford: Oxford University Press.

Whitley, R. (2005) 'How national are business systems? The role of states and complementary institutions in standardizing systems of economic coordination and control at the national level', in Morgan, G., Whitley, R., and Moen, E. (eds.) *Changing Capitalisms?: Internationalization, Institutional Change, and Systems of Economic Organization*. Oxford; New York: Oxford University Press.

Whitley, R. (2007) *Business Systems and Organizational Capabilities: The Institutional Structuring of Competitive Competences*. Oxford; New York: Oxford University Press.

Wilkinson, A. and Wood, G. (2017) 'Global trends and crises, comparative capitalism and HRM', *The International Journal of Human Resource Management*, 28(18), pp. 2503–18. https://doi.org/10.1080/09585192.2017.1331624.

Wilkinson, A., Wood, G., and Deeg, R. (2014a) 'Comparative employment systems', in Wilkinson, A., Wood, G., and Deeg, R. (eds.) *The Oxford Handbook of Employment Relations: Comparative Employment Systems*. Oxford; New York: Oxford University Press (Oxford Handbooks), pp. 1–22.

Wilkinson, A., Wood, G., and Deeg, R. (eds.) (2014b) *The Oxford Handbook of Employment Relations: Comparative Employment Systems*. Oxford; New York: Oxford University Press.

Wilkinson, B., et al. (2001) 'The new international division of labour in Asian electronics: work organization and human resources in Japan and Malaysia', *Journal of Management Studies*, 38(5), pp. 675–95. https://doi.org/10.1111/1467-6486.00254.

Witt, M. A., et al. (2018) 'Mapping the business systems of 61 major economies: a taxonomy and implications for varieties of capitalism and business systems research', *Socio-Economic Review*, 16(1), pp. 5–38. https://doi.org/10.1093/ser/mwx012.

Witt, M. A. and Jackson, G. (2016) 'Varieties of capitalism and institutional comparative advantage: a test and reinterpretation', *Journal of International Business Studies*, 47(7), pp. 778–806. https://doi.org/10.1057/s41267-016-0001-8.

Witt, M. A. and Redding, G. (eds.) (2014) *Oxford Handbook of Asian Business Systems*. Illustrated edn. Oxford: Oxford University Press.

Womack, J. P., Jones, D. T., and Roos, D. (1990) *The Machine That Changed the World: The Story of Lean Production*. New York: Rawson Associates.

Woo-Cumings, M. (2019) *The Developmental State*. Ithaca, NY: Cornell University Press.

Wood, G., Brewster, C., and Brookes, M. (eds.) (2014) *Human Resource Management and the Institutional Perspective*. 1st edn. New York: Routledge.

Wood, G., Dibben, P., and Meira, J. (2016) 'Knowledge transfer within strategic partnerships: the case of HRM in the Brazilian motor industry supply chain', *International Journal of Human Resource Management*, 27(20), pp. 2398–414. https://doi.org/10.1080/0958519 2.2016.1221841.

Wood, G., Dibben, P., and Ogden, S. (2013) 'Comparative capitalism without capitalism, and production without workers: the limits and possibilities of contemporary institutional analysis', *International Journal of Management Reviews*, 16, pp. 384–96. https://doi.org/ 10.1111/ijmr.12025.

Wood, G. and Frynas, J. G. (2006) 'The institutional basis of economic failure: anatomy of the segmented business system', *Socio-Economic Review*, 4(2), pp. 239–77. https://doi.org/10.1093/ SER/mwj034.

Wood, G. and Schnyder, G. (2021) 'Intro: comparative capitalism research in emerging markets – a new generation', *New Political Economy*, 26(4), pp. 509–13. https://doi.org/10.108 0/13563467.2020.1807488.

Wood, S. (1996) 'How different are human resource practices in Japanese "transplants" in the United Kingdom?', *Industrial Relations: A Journal of Economy and Society*, 35(4), pp. 511–25. https://doi.org/10.1111/j.1468-232X.1996.tb00419.x.

World Bank (2008) *Investing in Turkey's Next Generation: The School-to-Work Transition and Turkey's Development*. Washington, DC: World Bank. Available at: http://documents. worldbank.org/curated/en/375001468338988799/Investing-in-Turkeys-next-generation-the-school-to-work-transition-and-Turkeys-development (Accessed: 8 January 2016).

World Bank (2010) *Enterprise Surveys Mexico (dataset)*. World Bank. Available at: http://www. enterprisesurveys.org/data/survey-datasets (Accessed: 28 August 2018).

World Bank (2013) *Analysis of the Skills Development Sector in Mexico*. Available at: http://databank.worldbank.org/data/download/WDI-2013-ebook.pdf (Accessed: 2 January 2018).

World Bank (2020a) *TCdata 360 Revealed Comparative Advantage*. Available at: https://tcdata360.worldbank.org/indicators/h62a3e8cc?country=BRA&indicator=40085&viz=line_chart&years=1988,2016#comparison-link (Accessed: 22 March 2021).

World Bank (2020b) *Labor Force Participation Rate, Female (% of Female Population Ages 15+) (National Estimate) (data)*.World Development Indicators. Available at: https://data.worldbank.org/indicator/SL.TLF.CACT.FE.ZS (Accessed: 30 July 2021).

World Bank (2021a) *World Bank Country and Lending Groups*. Available at: https://datahelpdesk.worldbank.org/knowledgebase/articles/906519-world-bank-country-and-lending-groups (Accessed: 22 March 2021).

World Bank (2021b) *World Development Indicators Foreign Direct Investment, Net Inflows (% of GDP)*. Available at: https://data.worldbank.org/indicator/BX.KLT.DINV.WD.GD.ZS (Accessed: 22 March 2021).

World Bank (2021c) *World Development Indicators Exports of Goods and Services (% of GDP)*. Available at: https://data.worldbank.org/indicator/NE.EXP.GNFS.ZS (Accessed: 22 March 2021).

World Inequality Database (2020) *Income Inequality*. Available at: https://wid.world/data/ (Accessed: 12 September 2019).

Wright, C. F. and Kaine, S. (2015) 'Supply chains, production networks and the employment relationship', *Journal of Industrial Relations*, 57(4), pp. 483–501. https://doi.org/10.1177/0022185615589447.

Wright, P. M. and McMahan, G. C. (1992) 'Theoretical perspectives for strategic human resource management', *Journal of Management*, 18(2), pp. 295–320. https://doi.org/10.1177/014920639201800205.

Zhu, J. and Morgan, G. (2018) 'Global supply chains, institutional constraints and firm level adaptations: A comparative study of Chinese service outsourcing firms', *Human Relations*, 71(4), pp. 510–35. https://doi.org/10.1177/0018726717713830.

Index